Decision Making
for Leaders

Decision Making for Leaders

THE ANALYTICAL HIERARCHY PROCESS FOR DECISIONS IN A COMPLEX WORLD

Thomas L. Saaty

LIFETIME LEARNING PUBLICATIONS
A division of Wadsworth, Inc.
BELMONT, CALIFORNIA

London, Singapore, Sydney
Toronto, Mexico City

Designer: Rick Chafian

Copy Editor: Don Yoder

Illustrator: John Foster

Printed in the United States of America

1 2 3 4 5 6 7 8 9 10—85 84 83 82

Library of Congress Cataloging in Publication Data

Saaty, Thomas L.
    Decision making for leaders.

    Includes bibliographical references and index.
    1. Decision-making.   I. Title.
HD30.23.S192   658.4′03   81-13668
ISBN 0-534-97959-9   AACR2

Contents

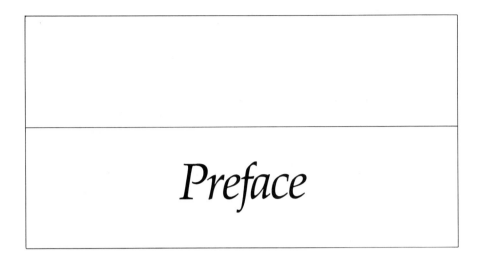

Preface

PURPOSE AND SCOPE

My primary purpose in writing this book is to introduce the reader to a new way of making decisions in a complex environment. The method is based on the user's experience and judgments supported by explanations that ensure a sense of realism and a broad perspective.

Because of the interaction among the multitude of factors affecting a complex decision, it is essential to identify the important ones and to determine the degree to which they affect each other before a clear decision can be made. This is the only book of its kind that addresses the issue of how to structure a complex situation, identify its criteria and other factors whether intangible or concrete, measure the interactions among them in a simple way, and synthesize all the information to obtain priorities. The priorities can then be used in a benefit/cost setting to develop portfolios of activities, one of the major concerns of corporations today. They can also be used in government and other organizations with different goals and purposes. Moreover, the method offers practitioners a simple test of the consistency of their judgments. It can also help them test the compatibility of projected policies with established ones.

AUDIENCE

This book is for those who must set priorities and make decisions. Perhaps their many activities, both daily and long range, do not permit them to analyze situations at a microscopic level, but they must be able to assess the overall situation in which they have to make the decision together with its consequences. Thus the book is for those with a certain level of expertise in their field, for the method represented here can give faithful answers primarily when the information itself is faithful.

USING THE BOOK

The book makes no demands on the reader. It simply explains the philosophy and general approach to defining the problem and setting priorities. The book is best used by reading it through once and then going back to Chapters 4, 5, and 6 to work out simple examples of how to buy a car, choose a job, or, as one admiral did, buy a yacht. For quick estimates, a simple numerical method for calculating the priorities is given that readers can work out by hand. The most important applications of the method are in planning, resource allocation, and making benefit/cost decisions. However, the reader can first concentrate on how to structure problems hierarchically and how to set priorities (Chapters 4, 5, and 6).

UNIQUE FEATURES

The unique features of the book are the simplicity of the approach (it involves only simple arithmetic), the variety and structure of many examples, computer applications, and a new philosophy for dealing with complex problems. This approach should not be regarded simply as a technique; it is a general method for coping with unstructured problems.

FORMAT

The book presents concepts, illustrations, and practical examples on setting priorities, planning, resolving conflict, making benefit/cost decisions, allocating resources, and making group decisions. The first three chapters explain the philosophy behind this method of formulating and solving unstructured problems. Chapters 5 and 6, in a step-by-step fashion, show the reader how to set priorities. Chapter 7 describes the approach to planning and Chapter 13 explains how to plan by means of group decisions. The remaining chapters deal with specific applications of these themes of setting priorities, planning, and group participation. A variety of computer and small calculator programs are included in the appendix. The underlying technical theory is presented in a mathematical supplement.

ACKNOWLEDGMENTS

I wish to express my gratitude to Mrs. Jacqueline Dormitzer, who read the entire original manuscript with care, reorganized it, and rewrote parts in an attractive style. Also, my appreciation goes to several colleagues and students for their assistance: Joyce Alexander, Omar Ashur, Nilardri Bagchi, Robert D. Baron, J. P. Bennett, Luis Calingo, Richard Fox, Hamid Gholamnezhad, Paul Rogers, Luis Vargas, Leonard Davis Research Institute—The Wharton School. I also owe thanks to Rodney E. Anderson, Steven L. Hart, Theodore P. Gerwing, and Hao-Che-Pu for their computer programs, to my associates on the Sudan Project, and many others.

THOMAS L. SAATY

*To S. Lester Landau—one
of the finest leaders I know.*

Introduction

Our present complex environment calls for a new logic—a new way to cope with the myriad factors that affect the achievement of goals and the consistency of the judgments we use to draw valid conclusions. This approach should be justifiable and appeal to our wisdom and good sense. It should not be so complex that only the educated can use it, but should serve as a unifying tool for thought in general.

That we are all very much creatures of the moment needs little debate. Try to reconstruct what was said two minutes before in a conversation and you will soon discover that, even for a short duration, your recollection is fuzzy. Even when you remember, the precision of your recollection is usually less than exacting. Our understanding of the world not only needs repetition to improve our recollection and precision, but it also depends very much on the *intensity* of our participation. It is an exaggeration to conclude that humans are logical creatures. It is more accurate to say that our judgment depends on the totality of our impressions, even if they cannot be logically and rigorously justified. For better understanding we need to deal with experience as an ongoing process. We need concentration, repetition, diversity, debate, and, when necessary, consensus.

Several good lessons have been learned in recent years from political leadership. Having a clearly defined goal has again been demonstrated to be the core of successful statecraft. Being consistent is another vital ingredient. Persuasion and support for one's view are still considered two of the main attributes of a great leader. What ensues is largely designed to help leaders get their points across.

More and more people are finding it hard to put all their trust in the unspoken, unjustified, and intuitive thinking of their leaders' decisions on complex matters. Whatever internal mechanism leaders have needs to be

1

articulated and understood. Just as language itself and the rules of thought had to be organized in a formal manner long ago, so must we now organize our thought processes so they lead us to good decisions. We should be able to say that, given the information, we agree on the method of making the decision (but not necessarily on the quality of that decision). The matter will then become a common concern rather than a mystical phenomenon.

The following pages offer the reader a method for organizing the information and judgments used in making decisions. This method reflects the strength of feelings and logic bearing on the issues and then synthesizes these diverse judgments into an outcome that agrees with our intuitive expectations as represented in all the judgments we give.

The process contributes to solving complex problems by structuring a hierarchy of criteria, stakeholders, and outcomes and by eliciting judgments to develop priorities. It also leads to prediction of likely outcomes according to these judgments.

The outcome can be used to rank alternatives, allocate resources, conduct benefit/cost comparisons, exercise control in the system by evaluating the sensitivity of the outcome to changes in judgment, and carry out planning of projected and desired futures. A useful by-product is the measurement of how well the leader understands the relations among factors. Although people generally are not consistent, the main concern here is the strength of their inconsistency. Is their understanding close to capturing the interactions observed? Or is it a random understanding that only hits the target now and then?

The process described in this book has had many applications so far—to energy rationing, the Middle East conflict (1972), Sudan transport planning (1973–1975), mineral exploration in Mauritania (1976), planning for higher education in the United States (1976), the presidential election (1976), the conflict in Northern Ireland (1977), planning for a research institute (1977), terrorism (1978), predicting the outcome of a world chess championship match (1978), product portfolio selection (1979), the stock market (1980), the presidential election (1980), oil prices in 1990 (1980), the conflict in South Africa (1981), and several specific corporate applications. All the applications have contributed to refinement of the principles set forth in the following pages. They have also been instrumental in showing us how to deal with larger and more complex decision problems. The theory has been enriched and immensely bettered by the scope and variety of these applications.

1

Making Decisions in a Complex World

This chapter deals with the following questions:

- How can we understand complex problems involving a great many factors?

- What are the basic processes of thought and behavior involved in making decisions?

- What role should ethics play in the decision-making process?

- Why do we need a *new* way of thinking about complex problems?

- How might a group of people holding varying opinions debate an issue in search of an acceptable compromise?

- What can they do about their differences?

COPING WITH COMPLEXITY

To the best of our understanding, the world is a complex system of interacting elements. The economy, for example, depends on energy and other resources; the availability of energy depends on geography and politics; politics depends on military strength; military strength depends on technology; technology depends on ideas and resources; ideas depend on politics for their acceptance and support; and so on. In such an intricate network of factors, first causes and final effects cannot be identified easily. Our minds have not yet evolved to the point where we can clearly see these ultimate relationships and readily resolve important issues like nuclear energy, world trade, and environmental regulations.

In our complex world system, we are forced to cope with more problems than we have the resources to handle. To deal with unstructured social, economic, and political issues, we need to order our priorities, to agree that one objective outweighs another in the short term, and to make tradeoffs to serve the greatest common interest.

But it is often difficult to agree on which objective outweighs another—particularly in complex issues where a wide margin of error is possible in making tradeoffs. Leaders may be confused by the diverse information provided by their assistants; they may need help in identifying differences of opinion and seeing positions where compromise can be reached. They may need to know which important issues must be researched in depth to obtain better information and how sensitive the outcome is to slight or drastic changes in opinion and judgments. Intuitive thought processes that serve us well in the familiar routine of daily life can mislead us on complicated matters where sources of information and opinions are varied. Increasingly we need to articulate and map out the issues to see whether what we think and what we feel lead us to the same kind of answers.

Most of us believe life is so complicated that in order to solve problems we need more complicated ways of thinking. Yet thinking even in simple ways can be taxing. If we struggle to examine collections of only a few ideas at a time, how can we understand complex problems involving a great many factors? Simple thinking about such problems leads to combinations of ideas whose structure is not unlike a dish of spaghetti in which all strands are separate—but tangled.

RATIONALE FOR A NEW FRAMEWORK

What we need is not a more complicated way of thinking, since it is difficult enough to do simple thinking. Rather, we need to view our problems in an organized but complex framework that allows for interaction and interdependence among factors and still enables us to think about them in a simple way. This new way of thinking should be accessible to all without straining our innate capabilities.

The analytic hierarchy process (AHP) described in this book provides such a framework. It enables us to make effective decisions on complex issues by simplifying and expediting our natural decision-making processes. Basically the AHP is a method of breaking down a complex, unstructured situation into its component parts; arranging these parts, or variables, into a hierarchic order; assigning numerical values to subjective judgments on the relative importance of each variable; and synthesizing the judgments to determine which variables have the highest priority and should be acted upon to influence the outcome of the situation.

The AHP also provides an effective structure for group decision making by imposing a discipline on the group's thought processes. The necessity of assigning a numerical value to each variable of the problem helps decision makers to maintain cohesive thought patterns and to reach a conclusion. In addition, the consensual nature of group decision making improves the consistency of the judgments and enhances the reliability of the AHP as a decision-making tool.

In this chapter we consider the human behavioral and thought processes involved in decision making. These natural processes form the basis for the analytic hierarchy process, which is described in Chapter 2 and explained in greater detail in Chapters 3, 4, and 5. The rest of the book shows how the AHP can be applied to a variety of decision-making situations and problems.

ORGANIZING KNOWLEDGE FOR DECISIONS

The AHP can best be appreciated by first looking into how the human mind organizes knowledge for decisions. The two fundamental approaches humans have developed so far for analysis are the deductive approach and the inductive or systems approach.

The Deductive Approach and the Systems Approach

We can analyze a system logically by representing it as a network and structuring it into chains and cycles. In analyzing natural systems, for example, biologists break down networks into food chains, hydrologic cycles, and so on. After structuring the network, we look for explanations for the functioning of its parts. Then, by an act of imagination, as no rules of logic exist for combining these piecemeal explanations, we synthesize an explanation for the whole network. But this scientific, deductive approach ignores the feedback mechanisms among the parts and between the parts and the environment that affect the whole system.

Systems theorists have pointed out that we can better understand an entire system by examining it from a general, holistic perspective that does not give as much attention to the function of the parts. For example, a car is better understood by observing how it functions in the environment than by studying the operation of its mechanical parts. In this way we see it as a whole; we can simultaneously perceive how the car runs and how it interacts with other cars, road conditions, traffic signals, and so on.

Clearly both the deductive and the systems approach contribute to our understanding of complex systems. We can benefit by combining the two within an integrated, logical framework: the analytic hierarchy process. The AHP enables us to structure a system and its environment into mutually interacting parts and then to synthesize them by measuring and ranking the impact of these parts on the entire system. We will see how this process works with systems as diverse as a transport network in the Sudan and the steel industry in the United States. By providing a new logic for synthesis, this structured approach to decision making eliminates much of the guesswork and confusion of our ordinary method of synthesizing an overall explanation for a system from piecemeal explanations arrived at through deduction.

The Role of Logic, Intuition, and Experience

The everyday way we proceed to understand and solve problems is to use logical deduction to argue through familiar matters. For example, it is easy to reason that to increase capital one must obtain a good return on it by investing it or by obtaining a good interest rate. In this case we know that in order for capital to increase from size A to size B, money has to be added to A somehow. That much we can say with bold certainty. But we tend to treat larger, imprecise perceptions of a problem by relying on feeling, experience, emotion, appeal to other people's understanding, and sometimes even force. Many political problems in advanced as well as less developed countries are handled in such a fashion. In unstructured situations people often act on their "gut feelings" rather than strictly on rational grounds. Logic plays a role mostly in arranging words and ideas after the conclusions have been reached.

People in the public and private sectors tend to cooperate in defining and structuring their problems broadly and richly so that all their ideas can be included. But when they need to explain which factors have the greatest impact on the outcome of a decision, not even experts with the clearest logic can hold fast to their positions in the face of objections. As a result they are willing to compromise. Thus decisions are based not so much on the clarity of ideas or amount of information exchanged as on the persistence of some participant in the decision-making process and on that person's ability to persuade others to accept his or her ideas, like a politician selling himself in a campaign.

People, then, not only have different feelings about the same situation, but their feelings change or can be changed by discussion, new evidence, and interaction with other experienced people. Usually the outcome is a compromise of many viewpoints involving substantial change in individual attitudes. The fact is that when we make decisions, personal preference and persuasion usually prevail over clear and straight logic. Our actual decision-making processes have been illuminated by recent studies conducted by behaviorists, other psychologists, and brain researchers. Let us examine their findings.

Behaviorist Theories

Those who study and explain ways, reasons, and consequences of human and animal behavior are finding it difficult to uphold the idea that humans are rational animals. Their theories are helping to create an atmosphere in which people are accepted as they really are rather than as they were idealistically portrayed during the Renaissance and the Age of Rationalism. Human behavior is enormously complex; the many theories explaining human action are deep and multilayered, and probably all contribute to our understanding of human behavior.

Instinct-Drive Theory. Some theorists consider rational thinking to be but a thin veneer over human behavior. Much of our action is driven by instinct—patterns woven into the mind, bone, and muscle. Just as wasps have an instinct for nest building and birds have their characteristic songs, humans also follow certain unlearned patterns of behavior, such as seeking food, mating, avoiding pain, caring for young, and so on. Although instinct-drive theory describes such patterns, it does not explain them. It is inadequate to account for most adult behavior, including sentiment, value, ambition, attitude, taste, and inclination.

Reason-Impulse Theory. We tend to regard ourselves as rational animals capable of making choices based on objective, or real, criteria. We feel that most of our decisions flow from logical necessity, not from whim and caprice. Although we may acknowledge that needs and personal motives are the driving forces behind human behavior, we contend that we use reason to attain our goals efficiently and without harm or injury. Through reason we get what we want within the limits of available resources. And many of us ultimately do learn to apply rational techniques to decision making, regardless of what our personal wishes may dictate.

But critics of this view say that our so-called reason is an abyss of unconscious or barely conscious urges and habits that overwhelm the intellect. They argue that human relationships are essentially governed by irrational, emotional forces; rational appeal in most cases plays only a minor role. These reason-impulse theorists hold that our actions are based on imitation, habit, suggestion, or other subrational forms of thinking and are rarely due to pure logic. Planned actions are the result of analysis based on preferences as to which objectives are served best—and preferences are strongly influenced by habit and training rather than by rational thinking.

Dynamic Field Theory.   Other behaviorists point to the influence of environmental factors on human behavior. We act in response to a "dynamic field" of stresses and tensions when we perceive the environment to deny or fulfill the satisfaction of our wants and needs. The hierarchy of human needs that motivate behavior has been examined by Abraham H. Maslow and others; these needs range from the most basic physiological and safety and security needs to sophisticated self-actualization and esthetic needs.

Learning Theories

Most people tend to assume that the way we think and the logic we use to develop our thinking are innately human and that the basics of human knowledge have come down to us as a package from heaven. But recent learning theories argue that we learn mainly by trial and error and through feeling rather than through logic. Stimulus-response theory, for example, maintains that we gravitate somewhat randomly in certain directions to satisfy our needs and desires; acts that bring satisfaction are reinforced. Gestalt theory tells us that even what we consider to be "insight"—perceiving the necessary relationships in a situation—results from feeling.

Generally we have vague feelings and inklings about what we think we have experienced, but we are not attentive enough to register ideas and feelings sharply. We have no systematic way of reconstructing from memory that which we did not learn, understand, or memorize consciously. Most of our daily experience goes before our senses and passes through our feelings like a hazy cloud that slightly moistens the environment but makes little difference to the growth of our understanding.

Our understanding does grow when a particular experience connects well with our earlier experiences, not merely with our knowledge, or when it shocks us, capturing our attention involuntarily as it intrudes into our being (sometimes unconsciously) either pleasantly or forcefully. Learning can be defined as the ability to recognize a specific act in the light of previous experience. It is an iterative, or repeated, process of adding knowledge that elaborates on or expands existing knowledge. Learning can be conscious and intentional, as in memorizing facts, or it can be unconscious and unintentional, as in discovering physically from experience that eating green apples results in a stomachache. We generally agree that people who experience a phenomenon firsthand are the ones who can best shed light on our understanding of it; indeed, knowledge derived from experience is basic to all understanding.

Brain Research Findings

The importance of intuition, feeling, and experience in human behavior and decision making is further underscored by the findings of brain researchers. In particular, they have discovered a distinction in the functions of the two halves of the neocortex of the brain—the left is the logical, rational, and calculating member; the right is the intuitive, creative, and verbally inarticulate half. The verbal half's job is to interpret for ourselves and the world the decisions of its mute brother. Note that the decisions are actually made by the intuitive, not the logical, half. The right hemisphere merely arranges and puts into words the insights of the left.

Studies of human perception show that our senses both condition and limit whatever enters our consciousness. Older people who have experienced life longer often recognize that illusion is primary experience. (Perhaps this awareness results from the aging of the senses, but more likely it is due to the wisdom of age.) Our senses shape our world; thus we can never interpret the universe with absolute accuracy. The qualities we study are simply those we can perceive, and the laws we develop are concoctions of our sense-limited brains.

Another life form could have many more senses than we have; for example, it could have a magnetic eye, could perceive the colors of the spectrum in white light, or could see through objects. As a result, its consciousness would be different from ours. Of course, our senses have expanded through human inventions such as the microscope, telescope, and X ray. We can perceive many qualities not directly accessible to our senses, and these are only a small portion of the potential total.

If we had more senses acting at once, we would probably have difficulty sorting out our perceptions and understanding their relations, given the present stage of the evolution of our brains. Although sense data can be organized in chronological sequence, brain events are not rigidly bound by time. Ideas can occur before or after other ideas. Because the way we think is fluid, we are freer to arrange our ideas in the manner we desire— for good or evil purposes.

ETHICAL CONSIDERATIONS

When complexity makes normal life appear difficult and even hopeless to many, a strong individual may emerge to take over leadership charismatically by declaring that all the pain and confusion are simply due to a single problem that must be solved; Hitler is an infamous example. Such leaders draw attention to one problem and persuade or force others to believe in them. By oversimplifying the situation, they banish all other problems to narrow the perspective and make themselves appear logical in their explanations; they linearize the workings of a system in a deductive fashion.

We accept new ideas as truths on the basis of the manner in which they cohere with knowledge we already possess. A system of beliefs could be perfectly consistent, and yet each belief could be false. Several examples come to mind. The Gregorian calendar (1582) was based on a set of consistent assumptions that the earth is the center of the universe. Yet it was so accurate that the accumulated error was one day every 3323 years. Our calendar is in error every 20,000 years. This is an example of a consistent prevailing view that was in error according to modern astronomy but produced good results. An example of a consistent theory of our time that produced bad results until recently involves the humble golf ball. People used to believe that it is the perfectly spherical golf ball that travels farthest when hit—until it was discovered that the more a ball is used, the more dents and dimples it develops, which serve as wings countering drag and sustaining it longer in the air. Now golf balls are made according to precisely dimpled patterns.

Consistent thinking with no real validity is frequently espoused by lunatics and other mental cases (sometimes of a seemingly respectable genre). Beliefs can be deduced from one another in perfect consistency depending solely on the observance of formal, linear relationships between them. Thus one may develop a consistent deductive system with no real validity in this world.

Because it is possible in complex, unstructured situations to present convincing arguments that have little correspondence to reality and may harm society, one must apply certain ethical standards to the decision-making process. The philosopher Alasdair MacIntyre of Boston University has identified four qualities that should characterize a decision maker's approach to dealing with social issues:

- *Truthfulness by not oversimplifying complexity.* Our political and legislative processes demonstrate that it is easier to consider issues such as environmental protection or health care in a narrow, piecemeal way than to look at all the critical variables, fit them together, and determine their priorities and implications. In the short run a simplistic approach may satisfy local contending parties, but it is no way to get at the answers to complex problems.

- *Justice by evaluating costs and benefits and assigning costs to those who get the benefits.* Everyone involved in a decision-making situation—family members deciding whether to purchase a home computer or corporate executives deciding which companies to invest in—should have a chance to weigh costs and benefits. Those who receive the benefits should be the ones who pay the costs, and vice versa. Justice demands not only that everyone have a voice and a vote but also that those who will bear the risks and dangers have more of a voice and vote than others. (People should also be informed about where and how they are paying for benefits, particularly for commodities whose prices are controlled or subsidized.)

- *Ability to plan for the unknown by calculating changes, determining where they are likely to occur, and deciding which priorities should dictate action.* Leaders must be able to plan and deal both with projected futures, such as higher energy prices in 1985, and with desired and less predictable futures, such as energy independence by the year 2000.

- *Flexibility in adapting to change by planning, implementing, and, in response to new conditions, replanning and reimplementing.* This iterative approach is essentially a learning process; it tempers our tendency to let immediate needs dictate short-term solutions. For example, flexibility is necessary in planning strategies for the use of alternative resources in dealing with the energy situation.

As we will see, the analytic hierarchy process encourages socially responsible decision making by helping leaders to avoid oversimplification, to identify and evaluate costs and benefits, to plan for the future, and to adapt to change.

PERSPECTIVE

Most of us have trouble coping with ordinary problems of society that cannot be understood by a deductive, linear, cause-and-effect explanation. Our respect for the scientific method, which relies on deduction, has led us to try to solve all our problems through logical debate. As a result of our scientific education and because science usually deals with things we can observe through our physical senses, we are made to feel that there is precision in what we do. Our senses are trained to be consistent in focusing on their objects; thus our minds have a sense of consistency in synthesizing and interpreting sense data. But when we deal directly with ideas rather than with sense perceptions, things lose their precision. The reason is that we use words whose meanings are imprecise. Philosophers have long recognized that primary language does not express thoughts or ideas but feelings and affections. Moreover, we cannot be exact in describing abstract relationships, and our understanding is conditioned by our states of mind, feeling, and imagination at the moment we are thinking. Thought without language is impossible. Abelard says that "language is generated by intellect and generates intellect." According to the Chandogya Upanishad, "The essence of man is speech."

We are very much creatures of the moment. At any given time our attention is captured by whatever our senses perceive. We cannot remember the past clearly, not even what the tomorrow of our personal lives will be like, despite the fact that some of us may have lived more than ten thousand days on this earth, repeating the same pattern that many times. With all this experience we are still unable to see the immediate future with adequate clarity. But some would try to venture predictions on serious issues of politics or economics in which they have had little experience.

To understand and deal with what is going on in the world, we need to improve our recollection of events and the precision of our knowledge by reviewing the facts and organizing them in a logical framework. If we are to make decisions that are rational and effective, we must participate intensely in the act of understanding the world around us. It is an exaggeration to say that humans are logical creatures. More accurately, our understanding is filtered through our senses, and our judgment relies on often hazy impressions of reality. With experience and through the perceptions and opinions of other people, our views of reality may change and become more precise. For a better understanding of the world, we need to persevere in thinking matters through carefully and to debate with others who hold different views.

But the complexity of social systems cannot await a full, logical analysis of situations on which our health, safety, and even survival depend. We need to rethink the traditional use of logic to derive knowledge. We also need to expand our analytic procedures to improve our understanding of situations in which not only time and space but also human behavior plays a fundamental role in determining the outcome.

The analytic hierarchy process enables decision makers to represent the simultaneous interaction of many factors in complex, unstructured situations. It helps them to identify and set priorities on the basis of their objectives and their knowledge and experience of each problem. As we have seen, our feelings and intuitive judgments are probably more representative of our thinking and behavior than are our verbalizations of them. The new framework organizes feelings and intuitive judgments as well as logic so that we can map out complex situations as we perceive them. It reflects the simple, intuitive way we actually deal with problems, but it improves and streamlines the process by providing a structured approach to decision making.

KEY CONCEPTS

☐ In our complex world system, we are forced to cope with more problems than we have the resources to handle.

☐ What we need is not a more complicated way of thinking but a framework that will enable us to think of complex problems in a simple way.

☐ There are two fundamental approaches to solving problems: the deductive approach and the systems approach. Basically, the deductive approach focuses on the parts whereas the systems approach concentrates on the workings of the whole. The analytic hierarchy process, the approach proposed in this book, combines these two approaches into one integrated, logical framework.

☐ Humans are not often logical creatures. Most of the time we base our judgments on hazy impressions of reality and then use logic to defend our conclusions.

☐ The analytic hierarchy process organizes feelings and intuition and logic in a structured approach to decision making.

2

The Analytic Hierarchy Process

This chapter deals with the following questions:

- What are the three basic principles of logical analysis?

- How do these three principles relate to a new approach to decision making—the analytic hierarchy process?

- What can we do when the usual scales of measurement—dollars, time, tons, and so forth—fail to measure intangible qualities?

- Why is the analytic hierarchy process such a powerful method for tackling complex political and socioeconomic problems?

- What can you expect to gain by using the analytic hierarchy process?

WHAT IT IS AND HOW IT WORKS

To introduce the analytic hierarchy process, consider the following example of a decision problem. The Brandywine River Region in Pennsylvania faces possible urbanization and its environmental effects. What actions should the people of the region take to maintain environmental quality? Should they allow development and invest money to prevent environmental deterioration or should they limit development?

Planners who used the AHP to study this problem first defined the situation carefully, including as many relevant details as possible. Then they structured it into a hierarchy of levels of detail (Figure 2-1). The highest level was the overall objective of protecting environmental quality. The lowest included the final actions, or alternative plans, that would contribute positively or negatively to the main objective through their impact on the intermediate criteria. The alternatives were (A) to leave the area nonurbanized, (B) to allow partial urbanization, and (C) to allow total urbanization. The intermediate levels of the hierarchy comprised the two basic criteria for evaluating environmental quality: (1) esthetic criteria, which were further structured into properties of vividness, intactness, and

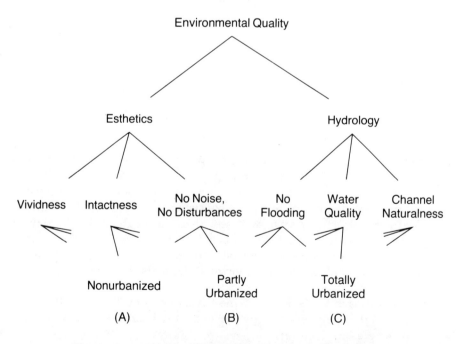

Figure 2-1   Hierarchy for Brandywine River Region

no noise or disturbances; and (2) hydrologic criteria, subdivided into no flooding, water quality, and channel naturalness. This hierarchy graphically depicts the interdependence of elements in the problem; it both isolates the relevant factors and displays them in the larger context of their relationship to each other and to the system as a whole.

After developing the hierarchy, the planners judged the relative importance of all the elements. They quantified these judgments by assigning them numbers from 1 to 9—and sometimes they disagreed. On many major issues where an impasse in the judgment of different people occurs, careful assessment of the differences in the intensity with which these people defend their preferences and opinions is necessary. Often words alone or logical argument cannot express the subtleties of deeply felt differences. But these differences can be measured by numbers, as we will see later on. After debate and compromise, the planners determined priorities for the elements of the hierarchy. Through a sequential process the judgments were synthesized and the desirability of each of the three alternative plans was estimated mathematically. The plan with the highest numerical value, and therefore priority (in this case, plan B), was the obvious best choice.

Judgments on the relative importance of each element in the hierarchy were made by people who were knowledgeable about the Brandywine River Region and about problems of urbanization and environmental quality. Yet even experts can make mistakes in setting up a hierarchy or discriminating between pairs of elements to judge priorities. The AHP also tests the consistency of judgments; too great a departure from the perfectly consistent value indicates a need to improve the judgments or to restructure the hierarchy. Suppose we take a closer look at the question of consistency.

The consistency is perfect if all the judgments relate to each other in a perfect way. If you say that you prefer spring to summer three times more and that you prefer summer to winter twice more, then when you give the judgment comparing your preference of spring to winter it should be 6 and not anything else. The greater your deviation from 6, the greater your inconsistency. This observation applies to relations among all the judgments given. We would have perfect consistency, then, if all the relations checked out correctly. As we will see, there is a rather simple way of verifying inconsistency and how much it deviates from perfect consistency. There is also a good way for interpreting what inconsistency means in practical terms. When we are revising judgments, this method is useful and necessary.

This approach to the Brandywine River problem illustrates the basic principles of the analytic hierarchy process. Now let us take a closer look at these principles.

PRINCIPLES OF ANALYTIC THINKING

In solving problems by explicit logical analysis, three principles can be distinguished: the principle of constructing hierarchies, the principle of establishing priorities, and the principle of logical consistency. As suggested in the Brandywine River example, these natural principles of analytic thought underlie the AHP.

Structuring Hierarchies

Humans have the ability to perceive things and ideas, to identify them, and to communicate what they observe. For detailed knowledge our minds structure complex reality into its constituent parts, and these in turn into their parts, and so on hierarchically. The number of parts usually ranges between five and nine. In the Brandywine River Region study, the idea of environmental quality was structured into six elements: vividness, intactness, no noise or disturbance, no flooding, water quality, and channel naturalness. By breaking down reality into homogeneous clusters and subdividing these clusters into smaller ones, we can integrate large amounts of information into the structure of a problem and form a more complete picture of the whole system. (This process is explored further in the next chapter.)

Setting Priorities

Humans also have the ability to perceive relationships among the things they observe, to compare pairs of similar things against certain criteria, and to discriminate between both members of a pair by judging the intensity of their preference for one over the other. Then they synthesize their judgments—through imagination or, with the AHP, through a new logical process—and gain a better understanding of the whole system.

In the Brandywine River Region study, the planners established relationships between the elements of each level of the hierarchy by comparing the elements in pairs. These relationships represent the relative impact of the elements of a given level on each element of the next higher level. In this context the latter element serves as a criterion and is called a *property*. The result of this discrimination process is a *vector of priority*, or of relative importance, of the elements with respect to each property. This pairwise comparison is repeated for all the elements in each level. The final step is to come down the hierarchy by weighing each vector by the priority of its property. This synthesis results in a set of net priority weights for the bottom level. The element with the highest weight—plan B (partial urbanization) in our example—is the one that merits the most serious consideration for action, although the others are not ruled out entirely. This principle and the next are fully explained in Chapter 5.

Logical Consistency

The third principle of analytic thought is logical consistency. Humans have the ability to establish relationships among objects or ideas in such a way that they are coherent—that is, they relate well to each other and their relations exhibit consistency. Consistency means two things. The first is that similar ideas or objects are grouped according to homogeneity and relevance. For example, a grape and a marble can be grouped into a homogeneous set if roundness is the relevant criterion but not if flavor is the criterion. The second meaning of consistency is that the intensities of relations among ideas or objects based on a particular criterion justify each other in some logical way. Thus if sweetness is the criterion and honey is judged to be five times sweeter than sugar, and sugar twice as sweet as molasses, then honey should be taken to be ten times sweeter than molasses. If honey is judged to be only four times sweeter than molasses, then the judgments are inconsistent and the process may have to be repeated if more accurate judgments could be obtained.

In utilizing these principles, the analytic hierarchy process incorporates both the qualitative and the quantitative aspects of human thought: the qualitative to define the problem and its hierarchy and the quantitative to express judgments and preferences concisely. The process itself is designed to integrate these dual properties. It clearly shows that for better decision making the quantitative is basic to making sound decisions in complex situations where it is necessary to determine priorities and make tradeoffs. To calculate priorities, we need a practical method of generating scales for measurement.

MEASUREMENT

People are generally wary, if not distrustful, when numbers are introduced into the traditional process of decision making. But appropriately chosen numbers can represent variations in feelings more faithfully than can words or rhetoric. In the face of complexity, we run out of words to express adequately our full awareness of what we sense to be taking place. Words limit the perspectives of our feelings.

Numbers are used in many different ways in our civilization to measure all kinds of physical experience. We find this application acceptable. The question is whether we can extend and justify the use of numbers in some reasonable, easily understood way to reflect our feelings on various social, economic, and political matters. We need to look into whether numbers are simply artifacts that give us the illusion of greater precision than we are capable of feeling, or whether we are missing a great deal by not realizing that numbers are a creation of our minds to reflect feelings and distinctions. Perhaps we have not yet recognized and appreciated their value in solving complex, unstructured problems.

In a moment we will briefly consider how numbers have come to be used in our lives to measure our perceptions of physical stimuli. Later we will see that numbers can also be used to reflect accurately our subjective judgments and their intensity; they can be used to distinguish among intangible as well as physical stimuli. Chapter 5 describes a simple way to use numbers to synthesize outcomes that faithfully represent our intuitive feeling and understanding of what we perceive the outcomes to be. The advantage is that finer shades of differences in judgment can be identified for their effect on the outcome and that we can accommodate different opinions in the decision-making framework.

Evolution of Scales

Our highly organized civilization depends on scales to measure such qualities as time, length, temperature, and money. Such measures were not handed down through the burning bush but evolved historically.

Time.   Time is a fundamental quality of nature; its measurement is at the foundation of science. The Sumerians were the first to divide the year and the day into units. Their year contained twelve months; and each month, thirty days. Egyptian priests divided the year into 365 days. The full sunlight period of a day was divided into ten hours, corresponding to ten fingers; dawn and dusk were each allotted one hour, bringing the total to twelve. The night was also allotted twelve hours, making twenty-four hours in a day. The daylight hours were marked by shadow clocks, precursors of sundials, and the night hours were marked by the appearance of stars. Thus neither daylight nor night hours were uniform in length; they depended on the seasonal transit of the sun and the rising of the stars.

The real beginning of time measurement was the clepsydra, a water clock that measured time by the emptying and filling of a vessel. As the clepsydra became more common, so too did the notion of time as a thing in itself, a flowing reality measured independently of the heavens. In the tenth century Arab scientists developed an improved sundial that marked off the hours accurately year round and was the first use of fixed time units. In the thirteenth century mechanical clocks measured time by uniform periodic motions. Europeans developed precision in measuring time during the seventeenth and eighteenth centuries. In October 1960 the Eleventh General Conference on Weights and Measures, meeting in Paris, refined chronological precision by defining the second as the duration of 9,192,631,770 cycles of the radiation associated with a specified transition, or change in energy level, of the cesium atom.

Length.   The Babylonians, Egyptians, Greeks, and Chinese all had their own units and subunits of length and other physical qualities such as area, weight, and liquid volume. In the thirteenth century the English introduced a standard yard and divided it into three feet of twelve inches each. They also defined a rod as five and a half yards and a furlong as one-eighth of a mile. In 1878 the yard was redefined as "the straight line or distance between the centers of two gold plugs or pins in the bronze bar . . . measured when the bar is at the temperature of sixty-two degrees of Fahrenheit's thermometer, and when it is supported by bronze rollers placed under it in such a manner as best to avoid flexure of the bar."

The French Revolution contributed the metric system. In 1792 Louis XVI issued a proclamation directing two engineers to determine the length of the meter. They set out to measure the distance on the meridian from Barcelona, Spain, to Dunkirk, France, but civil war intervened and the task took years to complete. A provisional meter was established in 1795 and was adopted by the French Assembly four years later: The meter was "one ten-millionth part of a meridional quadrant of the earth." Again in October 1960 the meter was redefined as 1,650,753.73 wavelengths in a vacuum of the orange-red line of the spectrum of krypton-86.

Temperature.   The mercury thermometer was invented by the German physicist Gabriel Daniel Fahrenheit in the eighteenth century. He considered body temperature to be 100° on his scale (later found to be 98.6°, as he erred in determining his fixed points) and the temperature of the coldest thing he could produce in his laboratory—a mixture of salt and ice—to be 0°. The freezing and boiling points of pure water at sea level had to be 32° and 212°, respectively. Although the thermometer has been improved, Fahrenheit's scale survives unchanged. It is sometimes preferred to the Celsius scale, devised by the Swedish astronomer Anders Celsius in 1742, because it has smaller subdivisions. For highly accurate temperature readings, Lord Kelvin (William Thompson) first suggested the use of the gas thermometer in the nineteenth century. Absolute zero is equal to −273° Celsius, the temperature at which all atomic activity stops.

Money.   Monetary standards differ from the other units of measure in that they are neither uniform nor consistent. The monetary value we attribute to goods and services fluctuates according to supply and demand and perceived desirability or utility. The evolution of money is closely interwoven with that of civilization. In some cases, as in ancient Egypt, the prevailing monetary system evolved from the political, social, and economic systems, whereas in ancient Lydia these institutions followed the progress of monetary evolution. Although goods and services can be exchanged directly, the adoption of a monetary system simplifies trade and promotes higher productivity.

The Need for a New Scale

Just as we can distinguish and measure physical relationships—meters for length, for example, and seconds for time—we are capable of doing the same with abstract relationships. We have the capacity for a range of feeling and discrimination that permits us to develop relationships among the elements of a problem and to determine which elements have the greatest impact on the desired solution. In dealing with concrete matters, such as repairing a car, we perceive the varying intensity of impact through our senses, by hearing a faulty motor or seeing a leak, or through their refinement by scientific instruments such as a voltmeter or pressure gauge. We carry out this process of measuring the priorities of impacts in order to solve problems.

So to determine the intensity of impact of the various components of a system, we must perform some type of measurement on a scale with units such as pounds, seconds, miles, and dollars. But these scales limit the nature of ideas we can deal with. Social, political, and other qualitative factors can in no reasonable way be assessed in terms of physical or economic measurement. What then can we do?

We can devise a scale that enables us to measure intangible qualities, just as scales evolved for measuring physical qualities. Chapter 5 presents such a scale to measure priority impacts in unstructured systems. This new way of assessing intangible qualities should hold up in areas where we already know the unit of measurement, which can then be used to validate the method. And in fact examples show that this approach to measuring priorities can be used to generate results conforming to classic ratio scale measurement in physics, economics, and other fields where standard measures already exist.

To measure priorities, we compare one element with another. The old adage that one cannot compare apples and oranges is false. Apples and oranges have many properties in common: size, shape, taste, aroma, color, seediness, juiciness, and so on. We may prefer an orange for some properties and an apple for others; moreover, the strength of our preference may vary. We may be indifferent to size and color, but have a strong preference for taste, which again may change with the time of day. It is my thesis that this sort of complicated comparison occurs in real life over and over again, and some kind of mathematical approach is required to help us determine priorities and make tradeoffs. This approach is the analytic hierarchy process.

AHP: A FLEXIBLE MODEL FOR DECISION MAKING

These basic observations on human nature, analytic thinking, and measurement have led to the development of a useful model for solving problems quantitatively. The analytic hierarchy process is a flexible model that allows individuals or groups to shape ideas and define problems by making their own assumptions and deriving the desired solution from them. It also enables people to test the sensitivity of the solution, or outcome, to changes in information. Designed to accommodate our human nature rather than force us into a mode of thinking that may violate our better judgment, the AHP is a powerful process for tackling complex political and socioeconomic problems.

The AHP incorporates judgments and personal values in a logical way. It depends on imagination, experience, and knowledge to structure the hierarchy of a problem and on logic, intuition, and experience to provide judgments. Once accepted and followed, the AHP shows us how to connect elements of one part of the problem with those of another to obtain the combined outcome. It is a process for identifying, understanding, and assessing the interactions of a system as a whole.

To define a complex problem and to develop sound judgments, the AHP must be progressively repeated, or iterated, over time; one can hardly expect instant solutions to complicated problems with which one has wrestled for a long time. The AHP is flexible enough to allow revision—decision makers can both expand the elements of a problem hierarchy and change their judgments. It also permits them to investigate the sensitivity of the outcome to whatever kinds of change may be anticipated. Each iteration of the AHP is like hypothesis making and testing; the progressive refinement of hypotheses leads to a better understanding of the system. The many practical applications of the AHP have generated sample hierarchies, some of which are presented in Chapter 4. With minor modification, some of these paradigms can be used to structure new problems.

Another feature of the AHP is that it provides a framework for group participation in decision making or problem solving. We have seen that ideas and judgments can be questioned and strengthened or weakened by evidence that other people present. The way to shape unstructured reality is through participation, bargaining, and compromise. Indeed, the conceptualization of any problem by the analytic hierarchy process requires one to consider ideas, judgments, and facts accepted by others as essential aspects of the problem. Group participation can contribute to the overall validity of the outcome, although perhaps not to the ease of implementation if the views diverge widely. Thus one could include in the process any information derived scientifically or intuitively.

The process can be applied to real problems and is particularly useful for allocating resources, planning, analyzing the impact of policy, and

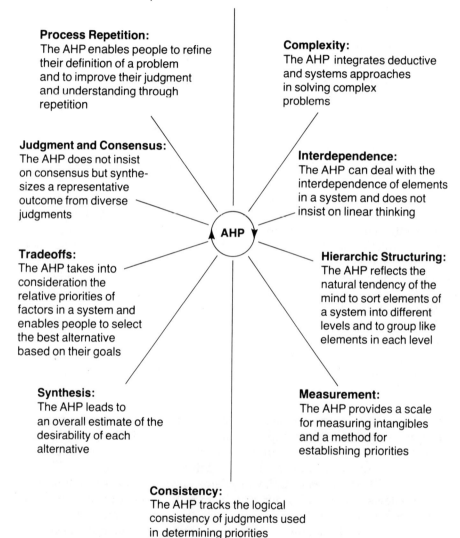

Unity:
The AHP provides a single, easily understood, flexible model for a wide range of unstructured problems

Process Repetition:
The AHP enables people to refine their definition of a problem and to improve their judgment and understanding through repetition

Complexity:
The AHP integrates deductive and systems approaches in solving complex problems

Judgment and Consensus:
The AHP does not insist on consensus but synthesizes a representative outcome from diverse judgments

Interdependence:
The AHP can deal with the interdependence of elements in a system and does not insist on linear thinking

AHP

Tradeoffs:
The AHP takes into consideration the relative priorities of factors in a system and enables people to select the best alternative based on their goals

Hierarchic Structuring:
The AHP reflects the natural tendency of the mind to sort elements of a system into different levels and to group like elements in each level

Synthesis:
The AHP leads to an overall estimate of the desirability of each alternative

Measurement:
The AHP provides a scale for measuring intangibles and a method for establishing priorities

Consistency:
The AHP tracks the logical consistency of judgments used in determining priorities

Figure 2-2   Advantages of the Analytic Hierarchy Process

resolving conflicts. Social and physical scientists, engineers, policymakers, and even laypersons can use the method without intervention by so-called experts; those who have a problem are ordinarily best informed about that particular problem. Currently the AHP is being widely used in corporate planning, portfolio selection, and benefit/cost analysis by government agencies for resource allocation purposes. And it is being used more widely on an international scale for planning infrastructure in developing countries and for evaluating natural resources for investment. Figure 2-2 summarizes the advantages of using the AHP as a new approach to problem solving and decision making.

PERSPECTIVE

The analytic hierarchy process reflects the way we naturally behave and think. But it improves upon nature by accelerating our thought processes and broadening our consciousness to include more factors than we would ordinarily consider. The AHP is a process of "systemic rationality": It enables us to consider a problem as a whole and to study the simultaneous interaction of its components within a hierarchy. This process is rather sophisticated. If we observed an individual, such as a child, who does not have to deal with complex issues or do several tasks at the same time, we most likely would not note a talent for hierarchic organization. Over long periods of time, however, the mind learns shortcuts and groups activities into clusters. This mental process gradually develops into a style for looking at the world and organizing it in such a way that we can deal with it efficiently.

Some people have gone so far as to point out that nature itself organizes matter and life hierarchically. But it is difficult to separate this observation from the fact that to understand the complexity of nature, it is we who have to sort and arrange what we perceive and see hierarchically. Moreover, the interactions among elements of a hierarchy do not always have an inherent structure apart from what we can observe. We must identify and synthesize these interactions based on our objectives and the knowledge and experience we have of each problem.

The AHP addresses complex problems on their own terms of interaction. It allows people to lay out a problem as they see it in its complexity and to refine its definition and structure through iteration. To identify critical problems, to define their structure, and to locate and resolve conflicts, the AHP calls for information and judgments from several participants in the process. Through a mathematical sequence it synthesizes their judgments into an overall estimate of the relative priorities of alternative courses of action. The priorities yielded by the AHP are the basic units used in all types of analysis; for example, they can serve as guidelines for allocating resources or as probabilities in making predictions.

The AHP can be used to stimulate ideas for creative courses of action and to evaluate their effectiveness. It helps leaders determine what information is worth acquiring to evaluate the impact of relevant factors in complex situations. And it tracks inconsistencies in the participants' judgments and preferences, thereby enabling leaders to assess the quality of their assistants' knowledge and the stability of the solution.

The next three chapters elaborate on this new approach to decision making. Here is what one can expect to gain by using it:

1. A practical way to deal quantitatively with different kinds of functional relations in a complex network.

2. A powerful tool for integrating forward (projected) and backward (desired) planning in an interactive manner that reflects the judgments of all relevant managerial personnel. The output of this process is explicit rules for allocating resources among current and new strategy offerings—or to satisfy a specific set of corporate objectives—or under alternative environmental scenarios.

3. A new way to:
   - Integrate hard data with subjective judgments about intangible factors.
   - Incorporate judgments of several people and resolve conflicts among them.
   - Perform sensitivity analysis and revision at low cost.
   - Use marginal as well as average priorities to guide allocation.
   - Enhance the capacity of management to make tradeoffs explicitly.

4. A technique complementing other ones (benefit/cost, priority, risk minimization) for selecting projects or activities.

5. A single replacement for a variety of schemes for projecting the future and protecting against risk and uncertainty.

6. A vehicle for monitoring and guiding organizational performance toward a dynamic set of goals.

KEY CONCEPTS

☐   There are three basic principles of the analytic hierarchy process:

1. Hierarchic representation and decomposition, which we call hierarchic structuring—that is, breaking down the problem into separate elements.

2. Priority discrimination and synthesis, which we call priority setting—that is, ranking the elements by relative importance.

3. Logical consistency—that is, ensuring that elements are grouped logically and ranked consistently according to a logical criterion.

☐ We cannot measure without a scale, but traditional scales such as time and money limit the nature of ideas we can deal with. Thus we need a new scale for measuring intangible qualities.

☐ The analytic hierarchy process is a flexible model that allows us to make decisions by combining judgment and personal values in a logical way.

3

Analyzing and Structuring Hierarchies

This chapter deals with the following questions:

- Why are hierarchies fundamental to human thinking?

- How can they be used to understand complex systems?

- What is the difference between a structural hierarchy and a functional hierarchy?

- How do we go about constructing a hierarchy?

HIERARCHIES: A TOOL OF THE MIND

Complex systems can best be understood by breaking them down into their constituent elements, structuring the elements hierarchically, and then composing, or synthesizing, judgments on the relative importance of the elements at each level of the hierarchy into a set of overall priorities. This chapter explains how to structure problems hierarchically.

Hierarchies are a fundamental tool of the human mind. They involve identifying the elements of a problem, grouping the elements into homogeneous sets, and arranging these sets in different levels. The simplest hierarchies are linear, rising or descending from one level to another, such as physics hierarchies that rise from atoms to molecules to compounds and so on; the most complex are networks with interacting elements, such as systems representing the learning process of a child.

CLASSIFYING HIERARCHIES

Hierarchies can be divided into two kinds: structural and functional. In structural hierarchies, complex systems are structured into their constituent parts in descending order according to structural properties such as size, shape, color, or age. A structural hierarchy of the universe would descend from galaxies to constellations to solar systems to planets, and so on, down to atoms, nucleii, protons, and neutrons. Structural hierarchies relate closely to the way our brains analyze complexity by breaking down the objects perceived by our senses into clusters, subclusters, and still smaller clusters.

In contrast, functional hierarchies decompose complex systems into their constituent parts according to their essential relationships. A conflict over school busing to achieve integration can be structured into a cluster of major stakeholders (majority and minority communities, city officials, board of education, federal government); a cluster of stakeholders' objectives (education for children, retention of power, and the like); and alternative outcomes (complete, partial, or no busing). Such functional hierarchies help people to steer a system toward a desired goal—like conflict resolution, efficient performance, or overall happiness. For the purposes of this book, functional hierarchies are the only kind that need be considered.

Each set of elements in a functional hierarchy occupies a level of the hierarchy. The top level, called the *focus,* consists of only one element: the broad, overall objective. Subsequent levels may each have several elements, although their number is usually small—between five and nine. Because the elements in one level are to be compared with one another against a criterion in the next higher level, the elements in each level must be of the same order of magnitude. If the disparity between them is great, they should belong to different levels. For example, we cannot make a precise comparison between two jobs whose performances differ in difficulty by a factor of 100 because our judgment would be subject to significant error. Instead, we first group simple jobs into a cluster and compare the cluster with a job one order of magnitude more difficult to perform than a simple job. We then compare the jobs in the cluster among themselves according to difficulty of performance. When we compare the results of the two comparison processes, we obtain a net comparison of a simple job with the more difficult one. To avoid making large errors, we must carry out this process of clustering. By forming hierarchically arranged clusters of like elements—simple jobs in this case—we can efficiently complete the process of comparing the simple with the very complex. Similarly, to compare small stones with boulders or atoms with stars, we must intervene between them several levels of objects of slightly different magnitude to make the transition and comparison possible.

Because a hierarchy represents a model of how the brain analyzes complexity, the hierarchy must be flexible enough to deal with that complexity. The levels of a hierarchy interconnect like layers of cell tissue to form an organic whole that serves a certain function. A spiraling effect is noticeable when we move from the focus expanding the hierarchy to the level of simple elements. The expansion may be continued to the level of elements of minutest concern. The next chapter illustrates the flexibility of hierarchies with a variety of examples. All are functional hierarchies, but some are *complete*—that is, all the elements in one level share every property in the next higher level—and some are *incomplete* in that some elements in a level do not share properties.

CONSTRUCTING HIERARCHIES

No inviolable rule exists for constructing hierarchies. The sample hierarchies offered throughout the book are presented not to prescribe certain frameworks but to stimulate thinking about what types of hierarchical levels to choose and what kinds of elements to include in the levels. The numbers of levels and elements may be more or less than those in the examples.

The great variety of examples that lend themselves to hierarchies suggests that the subjects that can be approached with the analytic hierarchy process are infinite. In all these areas we are limited only by our experiences and feelings as represented by words from the dictionary. Languages that are limited in vocabulary may pose problems of ambiguity or may not represent human experience adequately. Recognizing these limitations, we may be encouraged to innovate by creating the needed vocabulary and other symbols, such as computer languages, to represent feelings and ideas that we may become aware of in the process of identification and structuring.

One's approach to constructing a hierarchy depends on the kind of decision to be made. If it is a matter of choosing among alternatives, we could start from the bottom level by listing the alternatives. The next level would consist of the criteria for judging the alternatives. And the top level would be a single element, the focus or overall purpose, in terms of which the criteria can be compared according to the importance of their contribution.

Suppose we wanted to decide whether to buy one of five sports cars (Figure 3-1). These alternatives form the bottom level of the hierarchy. The criteria in terms of which the alternatives will be judged form another level and might include adequacy of salary, prestige, basic necessities, comfort, satisfaction of other needs, large savings account, and freedom from worry. The priorities of these criteria will be judged in terms of their contribution to the focus of the hierarchy: our overall happiness.

Note that once we construct this hierarchy, it is not necessarily cast in bronze. We can always alter parts of it later to accommodate new criteria that we may think of or that we did not consider to be important when we first designed it. The computer programs that assist us in the task are constructed with this flexibility in mind. After we rank the criteria and arrive at overall priorities for the alternatives, we might still have some doubts about the final decision. In that case we would simply go through the process again and perhaps change some of our judgments on the relative importance of the criteria. If the same alternative is still significantly ahead of the others in overall priority, we know that it is the right choice for us.

Sometimes the criteria themselves must be examined in detail, so a level of subcriteria should be inserted between those of the criteria and the alternatives. To select a school from three possible choices, for example, several criteria might be used—such as educational, cultural, and social

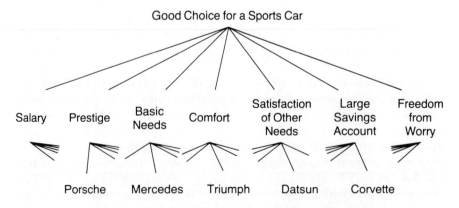

Figure 3-1 Hierarchy for Choosing a Sports Car

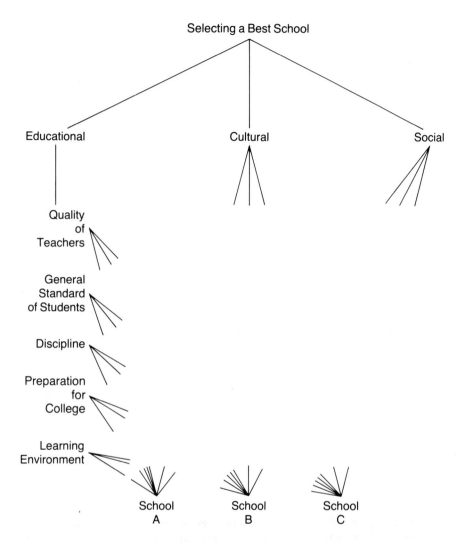

Figure 3-2   Hierarchy for Selecting a School

(Figure 3-2). The educational criterion might be broken down into subcriteria of (1) quality of teachers, (2) general standard of students, (3) discipline, (4) preparation for college, and (5) learning environment; the other criteria could similarly be broken down as well. In this case the subcriteria would be compared in terms of the criterion to which they belonged and not to the other criteria. Such a hierarchy would then be called incomplete because the subcriteria are not all compared in terms of all the criteria of the next higher level.

There is no limit to the number of levels in a hierarchy. If one is unable to compare the elements of a level in terms of the elements of the next higher level, one must ask in what terms they *can* be compared and then seek an intermediate level that should amount to a breakdown of the elements of the next higher level. Thus a new level has been introduced to facilitate the analysis for comparisons and to increase the precision of the judgments. Now we can answer the main question: How much more does one element contribute than another to satisfying a criterion in the next higher level of the hierarchy?

Hierarchies may be more complicated than the ones described above. Those related to projected planning and repeated later, for example, include the following levels:

- Uncontrollable environmental constraints
- Risk scenarios
- Controllable systemic constraints
- Overall objectives of the system
- Stakeholders
- Stakeholders' objectives (separate ones for each stakeholder)
- Stakeholders' policies (separate ones for each stakeholder)
- Exploratory scenarios (outcomes)
- Composite or logical scenario (outcome)

But decision makers do not have to pursue a problem to the full level of detail indicated here. The depth of detail depends on how much knowledge one has about the problem and how much can be gained by using that knowledge without unnecessarily tiring the mind.

PERSPECTIVE

Although hierarchies have been known for a very long time, the analytic hierarchy process makes it possible to generate new levels and arrange them in a logical fashion so they relate to each other naturally. By making paired comparisons of the elements in a level in terms of the elements of the next higher level, it is possible to decide on an appropriate choice of that upper level. Moreover, when the elements of a level cannot be compared except in terms of finer criteria than identified so far, a new level must be created for this purpose. Thus the analytic aspects of the AHP serve as a stimulus to create new dimensions for the hierarchy. It is a process for inducing cognitive awareness. A logically constructed hierarchy is a by-product of the entire AHP approach. Indeed, experience indicates that there are a few patterns that all decision hierarchies seem to follow. In the next chapter we will see how this concept of hierarchies can be applied to a broad range of real situations.

KEY CONCEPTS

☐ In a functional hierarchy, complex systems are broken down into their constituent parts according to their essential relationships.

☐ The top level of the hierarchy—the focus—consists of only one element: the overall objective. The other levels contain several elements (usually between five and nine).

☐ There is no limit to the number of levels in a hierarchy.

☐ When the elements of a level cannot be compared readily, a new level with finer distinctions must be created.

☐ Hierarchies are flexible. We can always alter them to accommodate new criteria.

4

Practical Examples of Hierarchies

This chapter deals with the following questions:

- What is the main purpose of arranging goals, attributes, issues, and stakeholders in a hierarchy?

- How can hierarchies be applied to business decisions—choosing equipment, deciding whether to buy or lease, making financial decisions, and so on?

- How can hierarchies be applied to personal and domestic decisions—choosing a car, choosing a career, purchasing a house, and so on?

- How can hierarchies be applied to public policy decisions—choosing areas for R&D programs, allocating resources in a juvenile

correction program, analyzing a school busing
conflict, and so on?

- How can hierarchies be applied to planning
  economic policies—for example, planning
  economic strategy for an underdeveloped
  country?

- How can hierarchies be used for estimating
  and predicting—predicting the presidential
  election, estimating the popularity of a rock
  group, and so on?

- How can hierarchies be used for measuring
  influences—for example, parental influence on a
  child's psychological well-being?

- How can hierarchies be used to represent
  systems networks—the network of a child's
  learning system, the network of a volleyball
  team, and so on?

AN APPROACH TO HIERARCHIES

In later chapters we will discuss in detail specific applications of the
AHP to planning, conflict resolution, benefit/cost analysis, and resource
allocation. This chapter offers examples of different kinds of hierarchies to
suggest ways of approaching problems and structuring them into their
constituent parts with enough detail to make reasonable decisions.

Most problems arise because we do not know the internal dynamics of
a system in enough detail to identify cause-and-effect relationships. If we
were able to do so, the problem could be reduced to one of social engineering, as we would know at what points in the system intervention is necessary to bring about the desired objective. The crucial contribution of the
analytic hierarchy process is that it enables us to make practical decisions
based on a "precausal" understanding—namely, on our feelings and
judgments about the relative impact of one variable on another.

In sum, when constructing hierarchies one must include enough relevant detail to depict the problem as thoroughly as possible. Consider the
environment surrounding the problem. Identify the issues or attributes

that you feel contribute to the solution. Identify the participants associated with the problem. Arranging the goals, attributes, issues, and stakeholders in a hierarchy serves two purposes: It provides an overall view of the complex relationships inherent in the situation, and it permits the decision maker to assess whether he or she is comparing issues of the same order of magnitude in weight or impact on the solution.

The elements should be clustered into homogeneous groups of five to nine so they can be meaningfully compared to elements in the next higher level. The only restriction on the hierarchic arrangement of elements is that any element in one level must be capable of being related to some elements in the next higher level, which serves as a criterion for assessing the relative impact of elements in the level below.

The hierarchy does not need to be complete; that is, an element in a given level does not have to function as a criterion for *all* the elements in the level below. Thus a hierarchy can be divided into subhierarchies sharing only a common topmost element. Further, a decision maker can insert or eliminate levels and elements as necessary to clarify the task of setting priorities or to sharpen the focus on one or more parts of the system. Elements that are of less immediate interest can be represented in general terms at the higher levels of the hierarchy and elements critical to the problem at hand can be developed in greater depth and specificity.

In addition to identifying within a hierarchic structure the major factors that influence the outcome of a decision, we need a way to decide whether these factors have equal effects on the outcome or whether some of them are dominant and others so insignificant they can be ignored. This is accomplished through the process of priority setting. The task of setting priorities requires that the criteria, the subcriteria, the properties or features of the alternatives being compared, and the alternatives themselves are gradually layered in the hierarchy so that the elements in each level are comparable among themselves in relation to the elements of the next higher level. Now the priorities are set for the elements in each level several times—once with respect to each criterion of the upper level. These in turn are prioritized with respect to the elements of the next higher level and so on. Finally a weighting process is used to obtain overall priorities. This is done by coming down the hierarchy and weighting the priorities measured in a level with respect to a criterion in the next higher level with the weight of that criterion. The weighted priorities can then be added for each element in the level to obtain its overall priority.

Finally, after judgments have been made on the impact of all the elements, and priorities have been computed for the hierarchy as a whole, the less important elements can be dropped from further consideration because of their relatively small impact on the overall objective. Now let us examine some of the real-world applications of the hierarchy.

BUSINESS DECISIONS

Hierarchy for Choosing Urethane Equipment

To decide on the purchase of urethane manufacturing equipment (Figure 4-1), three principal considerations are price, technical features, and service. "Technical features" is really a cluster of several specific desired qualities to which it is further decomposed. The overall priorities obtained through successive priority setting represent the relative importance of the considerations bearing upon the purchase decision.

The three products under consideration are then ranked with respect to each criterion or subcriterion. The overall priority gives the relative superiority of the brands.

Hierarchy for Choosing Word Processing Equipment

For the selection of word processing equipment for an office (Figure 4-2), the benefit and cost hierarchies are considered separately and benefit/cost ratios are obtained. The qualities desired of a word processing machine form the second level in the benefit hierarchy, and their priorities represent the relative weights assigned by the user. The equipment charac-

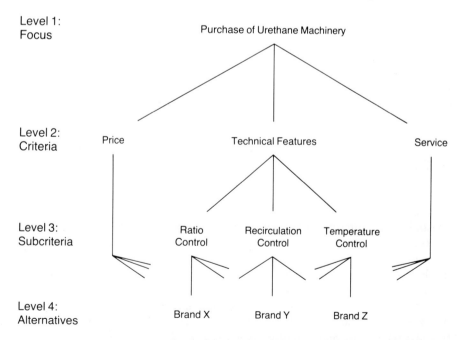

Level 1:
Focus

Purchase of Urethane Machinery

Level 2:
Criteria

Price   Technical Features   Service

Level 3:
Subcriteria

Ratio   Recirculation   Temperature
Control   Control   Control

Level 4:
Alternatives

Brand X   Brand Y   Brand Z

Figure 4-1   Hierarchy for Choosing Urethane Equipment

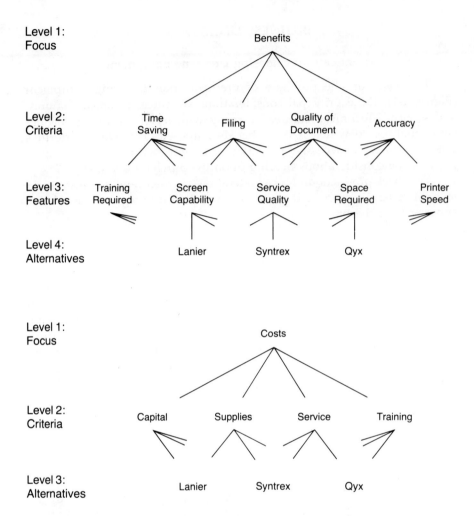

Figure 4-2   Hierarchies for Choosing Word Processing Equipment

teristics that contribute to these qualities fall in the third level. They are ranked with respect to each desired quality, and the overall priority represents the relative importance of each characteristic. The overall priorities of the brands under consideration represent the relative superiority regarding benefits expected from each.

In the cost hierarchy, likewise, the overall priorities represent the relative weights of the costs. The benefit/cost ratio for each indicates the relative superiority of one machine over the others.

Hierarchy for Deciding on Buying or Leasing

The decision regarding company ownership or leasing of a piece of capital equipment (Figure 4-3) depends on its contribution to the company's profitability. This profitability has two dimensions: economic and intangible. The benefits depend on a number of factors that, in turn, depend on certain characteristics of the company. Buying or leasing would promote these characteristics to a varying extent.

By setting priorities for the factors at a certain level with respect to the relevant factors at the previous level and finding the composite priorities, we can find to what extent, relatively speaking, the factors in the same level contribute to the firm's overall profitability. Extending this logic to the question of company ownership or leasing, we can say, in the judgment of the decision maker, which alternative is preferable.

In this example we take the intangible benefits explicitly into consideration for a decision, so the subjective judgments of the decision maker

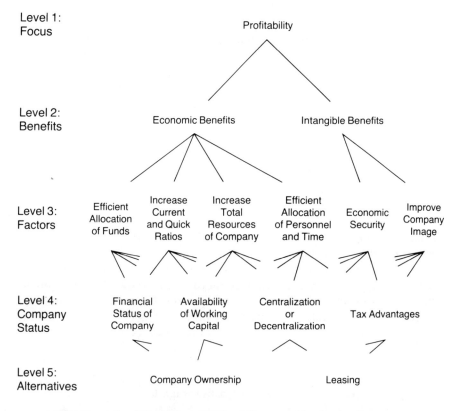

Figure 4-3   Hierarchy for Deciding on Buying or Leasing

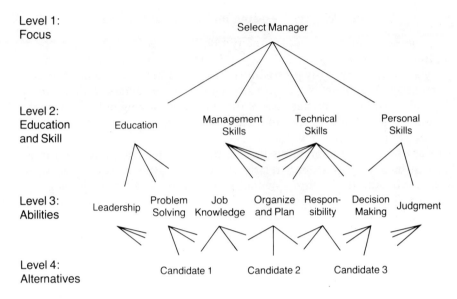

Figure 4-4   Hierarchy for Choosing a Management Candidate

are also considered. This is unlike a conventional exercise where only the hard economic data are considered and then managerial judgment is used in a qualifying manner at the end.

Hierarchy for Choosing a Candidate for Management

To select the proper person to fill a management position, we first identify the four areas of evaluation and then the specific traits to which these areas contribute (Figure 4-4). Successive stages of priority setting give the overall priorities for the relevant traits in level 3, which represent the relative weights believed to be associated with them for a person to function effectively in that position.

Once all the candidates have been reviewed and the choice has been narrowed down to a few seemingly equal candidates, they may be ranked with respect to each trait. The composite priority for each candidate then represents his or her relative superiority on the basis of overall judgment and is useful in comparing candidates and ranking them in order of preference.

Hierarchy for Choosing a Beverage Container

To evaluate the desirability of different containers to be used by the soft drink beverage industry (Figure 4-5), we first consider the criteria for evaluation and then rank them according to their relative importance on the final outcome. Next we judge the alternative containers with respect to each criterion per unit of beverage delivered. This prioritization shows the desirability from the point of view of each criterion, and the composite priorities show the overall superiority of the containers in relative terms.

Hierarchy for Staggering Industry Hours for Energy Conservation

To decide how to stagger industry work hours, we first examine the relevant consequences of staggered work hours and judge how important they are with respect to one another. This is done by ranking the relevant criteria with respect to the focus (Figure 4-6).

Next the various shift patterns under consideration are ranked with respect to each of the criteria above to see how much they would affect it in relative terms. The composite priorities indicate the overall desirability of the considerations in relative terms. The highest-priority shift is the most desirable decision.

Hierarchy for Choosing a Site for Combustion Turbines

The problem of site selection for an electric utility company was narrowed to four alternatives after preliminary screening (Figure 4-7). The company identified nine relevant factors they would have to consider in the selection process. Since many of the considerations were in conflict, they were first ranked to find their relative importance bearing upon the

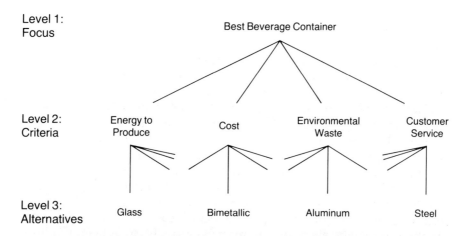

Figure 4-5   Hierarchy for Choosing a Beverage Container

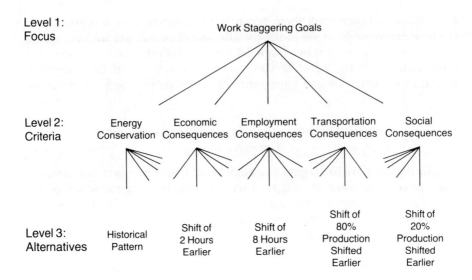

Figure 4-6   Hierarchy for Staggering Work Hours

decision. Next the sites were ranked with respect to each factor and composite priorities were found. These overall priorities indicate the relative merits of selecting the sites in question when all the factors are taken into consideration.

Hierarchy for Allocating Resources Among R&D Projects in a Bank

This decision regarding resource allocation is done as a benefit/cost exercise involving the benefits expected to accrue from the projects and the costs expected to be increased thereby (Figure 4-8).

In the benefits hierarchy, the benefits are ranked according to their impact on the bank's performance. The projects are ranked according to how far they can generate that benefit. The composite priorities represent their overall benefit contributions on a ratio scale. In the costs hierarchy, likewise, the various costs are ranked by their severity and the projects are ranked with respect to their contribution to that cost. The resulting composite priorities represent their overall costs. The benefit/cost ratios measure the superiority of benefit for cost incurred and also each R&D project's expected attractiveness. Ratios comparing the greatest marginal benefits to costs are often more useful than simple benefit/cost ratios. Sometimes discounting of benefits and costs is more realistically done before forming such ratios.

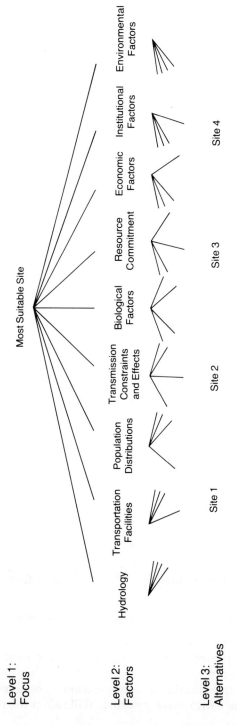

Figure 4-7 Hierarchy for Choosing a Turbine Site

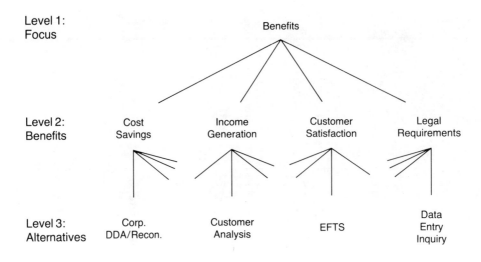

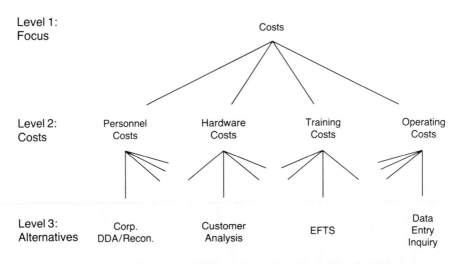

Figure 4-8   Hierarchies for Allocating R&D Resources

Hierarchy for Making Financial Decisions

To select one from a number of financial projects, we may consider the benefits and costs separately (Figure 4-9). In the benefits hierarchy, three possible scenarios are considered for the future. The company would like to base its decision on a number of considerations whose impact depends on the scenario. Hence the overall priorities will reflect the relative impor-

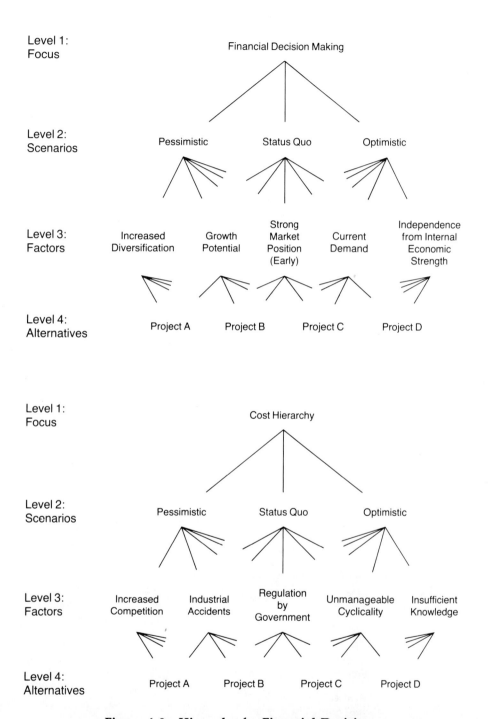

Level 1:
Focus — Financial Decision Making

Level 2:
Scenarios — Pessimistic   Status Quo   Optimistic

Level 3:
Factors — Increased Diversification   Growth Potential   Strong Market Position (Early)   Current Demand   Independence from Internal Economic Strength

Level 4:
Alternatives — Project A   Project B   Project C   Project D

Level 1:
Focus — Cost Hierarchy

Level 2:
Scenarios — Pessimistic   Status Quo   Optimistic

Level 3:
Factors — Increased Competition   Industrial Accidents   Regulation by Government   Unmanageable Cyclicality   Insufficient Knowledge

Level 4:
Alternatives — Project A   Project B   Project C   Project D

Figure 4-9   Hierarchy for Financial Decisions

tance of these factors. The projects are ranked according to their contribution to each factor. The composite priorities give relative measures of the benefits accruing from them.

In the costs hierarchy, in a similar way, we find the relative importance of a number of factors the company would like to avoid or minimize. The overall priorities of the projects in this hierarchy, then, give the relative measure of the negative contribution of these projects. The benefit/cost ratios give the superiority of the benefits over costs on a ratio scale. The project with the highest marginal benefit/cost ratio is the best selection.

Hierarchy for Choosing a Marketing Strategy

The decision regarding a company's product/market posture depends on a number of external factors that determine how far the company can strive to maintain the status quo or expect an optimistic or a pessimistic environment. The company's objective regarding economic growth and

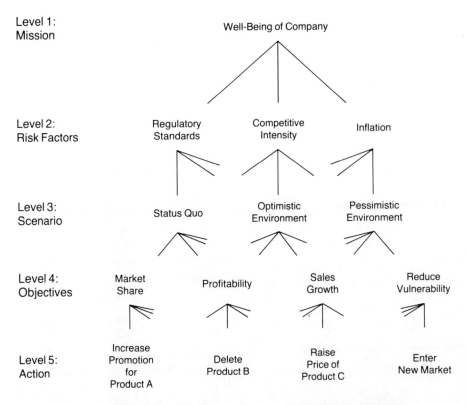

Figure 4-10   Hierarchy for Choosing a Marketing Strategy

risk depends on the scenarios envisioned and will be achieved in varying degrees by following different alternatives of product and market. The decision model is thus represented in the form of a complete hierarchy (Figure 4-10).

By prioritizing the factors in one level with respect to each factor in the preceding level and finding the overall priorities, we can find the relative influence, feasibility, importance, or contribution, as the case may be, of the factors in a level with respect to the focus: the company's well-being. The priority of each course of action is therefore a relative measure of how far that product/market posture would achieve the desired well-being.

Hierarchy for Evaluating a Division's Performance

There are several dimensions of the performance of a division in a corporation. The principal dimensions to be considered in this evaluation are government dealings, management, imports, and customers (Figure 4-11). There are several factors for each dimension. Level 3 of the hierarchy shows those pertaining to management alone; other factors can be similarly included for the other dimensions.

The overall priorities of the factors at level 3 are the relative weights by which the evaluators would view performance in that area. Composite priorities of the various divisions with respect to all the factors at this level show the relative performance rating of the division on an overall basis.

PERSONAL AND DOMESTIC DECISIONS

Hierarchy for Choosing a Car

The problem of choosing from a number of cars, both new and old, is structured into a hierarchy of three levels (Figure 4-12). In the second level, the various factors—costs as well as benefits—going into the decision maker's judgment are prioritized. Next the specific alternatives are compared with respect to each factor in level 2. The overall priority of each alternative indicates its ranking and strength of preference as far as the buyer is concerned. (This is an example of a complete hierarchy because all the factors at any level relate to all the factors in the next higher level.)

Hierarchy for Choosing a Home Computer

There are both benefits and costs in having a home computer. Three choices are prioritized in two separate hierarchies for benefits and costs (Figure 4-13). In each hierarchy, the priorities are determined through

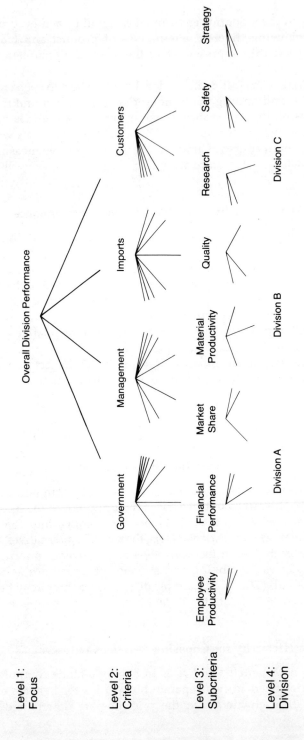

Figure 4-11 Hierarchy for Evaluating Division Performance

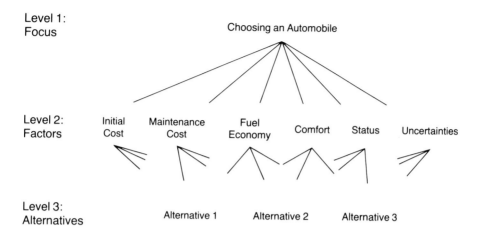

Figure 4-12   Hierarchy for Choosing a Car

intermediate levels of factors and subfactors contributing to the benefit or cost of home computers. Finally, the benefit/cost ratio for each alternative is calculated to find out where the benefits stand relative to the costs. The alternative with the highest marginal benefit/cost ratio is the preferred choice for the decision maker.

Hierarchy for Choosing a Career

In choosing a career, a person desires satisfaction in several dimensions: intellectual, financial, social, and personal. However, one's sources of satisfaction are from expectations of learning, growth, leisure, friends, and prestige. Each source of satisfaction may derive fulfillment from several dimensions, which therefore occupy a superior level (Figure 4-14). The priority of each career with respect to any criterion of satisfaction reflects its desirability with respect to that criterion only. The overall priority of the career shows the overall preference for that career; the highest-priority career is the one preferred. (This is an example of an incomplete hierarchy, as factors in level 3 do not relate to all the factors in level 2.)

Hierarchy for Choosing an Ideal Investment

The different criteria affecting an investment are prioritized to find out how important they are in relative terms to the investor in question (Figure 4-15). In the next step, the different investment alternatives are ranked with respect to each criterion to examine how well they satisfy the criterion in question. The overall priority will show the relative superiority of an

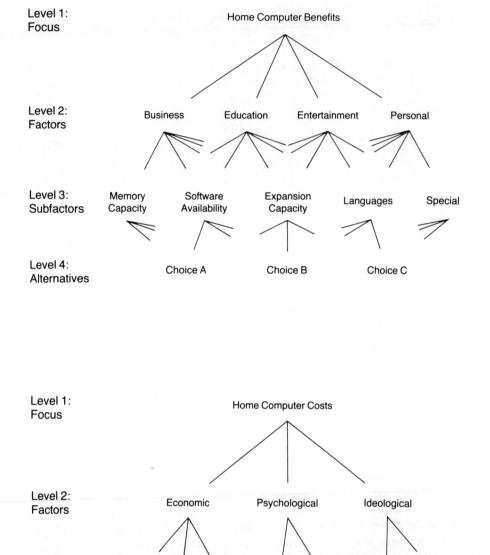

Figure 4-13 Hierarchy for Choosing a Home Computer

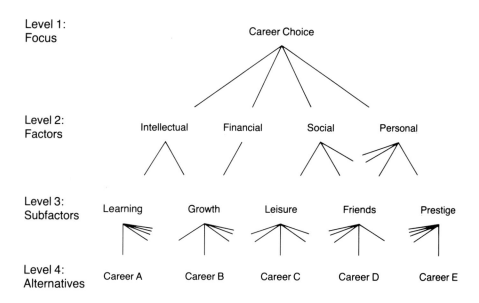

Figure 4-14   Hierarchy for Choosing a Career

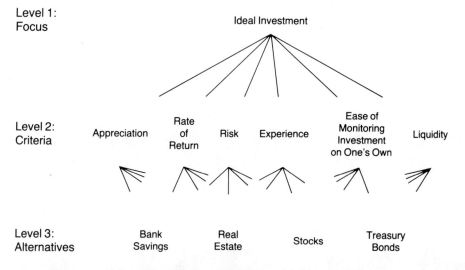

Figure 4-15   Hierarchy for Choosing an Ideal Investment

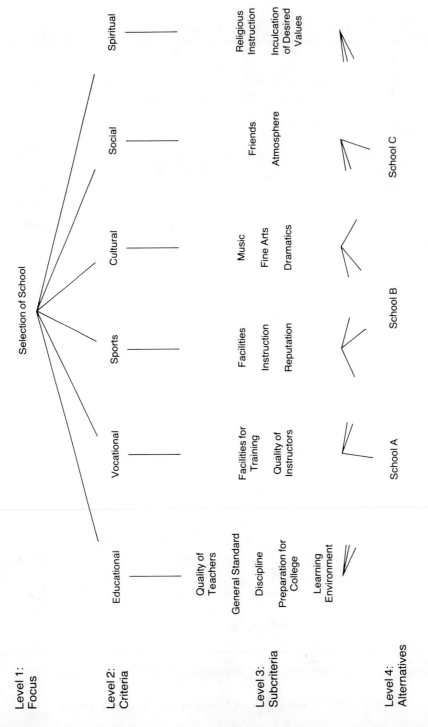

Figure 4-16   Hierarchy for Choosing a School

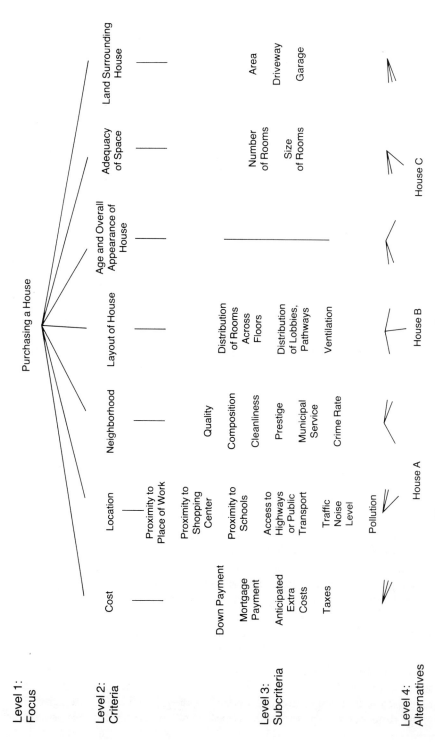

Figure 4-17 Hierarchy for Purchasing a House

Level 1: Focus

Purchasing a House

Level 2: Criteria

Cost | Location | Neighborhood | Layout of House | Age and Overall Appearance of House | Adequacy of Space | Land Surrounding House

Level 3: Subcriteria

Down Payment
Mortgage Payment
Anticipated Extra Costs
Taxes

Proximity to Place of Work
Proximity to Shopping Center
Proximity to Schools
Access to Highways or Public Transport
Traffic Noise Level
Pollution

Quality
Composition
Cleanliness
Prestige
Municipal Service
Crime Rate

Distribution of Rooms Across Floors
Distribution of Lobbies, Pathways
Ventilation

Number of Rooms
Size of Rooms

Area
Driveway
Garage

Level 4: Alternatives

House A   House B   House C

alternative as viewed by the investor. For a large investor, the priorities also indicate the proportions in which the total investment could be distributed among the various alternatives available—that is, a representation of the investor's portfolio.

Hierarchy for Choosing a School

First we establish priorities for the criteria of the student and the parents to establish their relative importance (Figure 4-16). In the next level, we resolve the criteria in greater detail and prioritize the subcriteria. Each of the schools under consideration is then prioritized with respect to the subcriteria. The overall priorities show how strongly a school is rated by student and parents in relation to the others.

Hierarchy for Purchasing a House

Considerations that apply to purchasing a house are the criteria, which are prioritized to find their relative importance (Figure 4-17). In the next level, these criteria are decomposed into further subcriteria, which are similarly prioritized. In the next stage, the alternative houses under consideration are prioritized with respect to each criterion or subcriterion, and their overall priorities indicate the buyer's preferences for the houses in question. This is a comprehensive model in which the criteria pertaining to the neighborhood and those pertaining to the qualities of the house are dealt with simultaneously.

PUBLIC POLICY DECISIONS

Hierarchy for Choosing a Mode for Crossing a River

To decide which mode to use for crossing a river would be beneficial to the community as a whole. We consider the nature of benefits envisaged and enlist under each the details (Figure 4-18). Setting priorities for the benefits gives an idea which ones the community regards as important. We can also establish priorities for the costs.

Hierarchy for Choosing Areas for R&D Programs

This hierarchy (Figure 4-19) is concerned with the selection of areas for research and development to ensure adequate power and electricity in the future. At the first stage, the focus is on the range of planning by prioritizing the time horizon of the plan. Next we set priorities for the potential

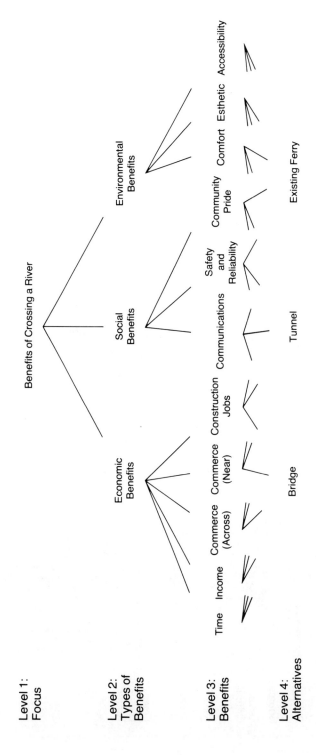

Figure 4-18 Hierarchy for Means of Crossing a River

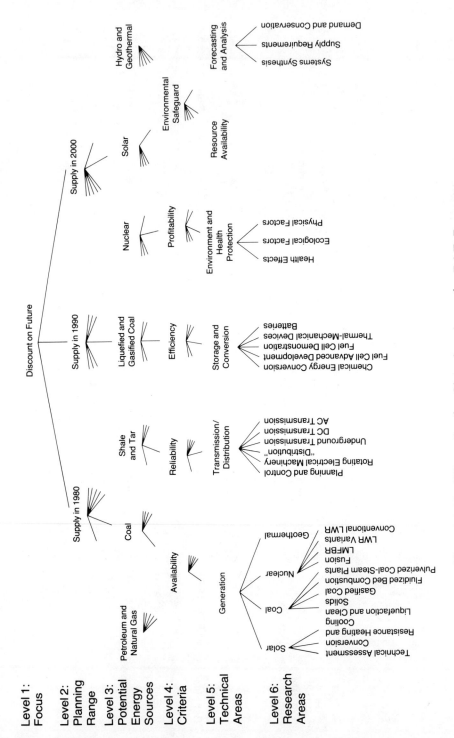

Figure 4-19 Hierarchy for Choosing Areas for R&D Programs

areas of energy resources to determine which one holds the most promise. With respect to each energy source, several criteria are considered that require attention; these criteria are prioritized according to the importance they command for the energy resource.

For each criterion, several technical aspects are identified and then prioritized for relative importance. The overall priority at this level shows the share of effort and resources that should be devoted to the technical field concerned. As a continuation of the process, each technical field is further subdivided into research areas and subareas that need attention. The overall priorities at each level again represent the extent to which resources should be devoted to those areas according to the best overall judgment of the decision makers.

Hierarchy for Choosing a Program to Increase Harbor Capacity

Deciding on means to improve harbor capacity in a small country with three harbors is viewed as a joint political process. The three principal stakeholders are the evaluation group of specialists, the transportation committee of legislators, and the harbor bureau (Figure 4-20). Their priorities represent their influence in the matter.

The objectives and considerations to be followed by each stakeholder are identified and prioritized. At the next stage, the three existing harbors are prioritized with respect to each objective to find out how much they contribute to the objectives. The overall priority at this level shows the extent to which resources and attention should be devoted to each harbor development.

The specific programs to increase harbor capacity are next identified and prioritized with respect to each harbor. In the context of each harbor, these priorities show the effectiveness of each action in achieving the goal. The overall priorities, obtained by weighting the harbor priorities, reflect the effectiveness for the whole country. The actual policy that is adopted will consist of several individual programs pursued with varying degrees of emphasis as represented by these priorities.

Hierarchy for Evaluating Energy Storage Systems

To evaluate four advanced energy storage systems, six feasibility criteria are set (Figure 4-21). They are then prioritized to see which would be dominant over others in relative terms.

Next we prioritize the energy storage systems with respect to each criterion regarding their suitability. The overall priorities, obtained by weighting them with criteria priorities, show how they are expected to

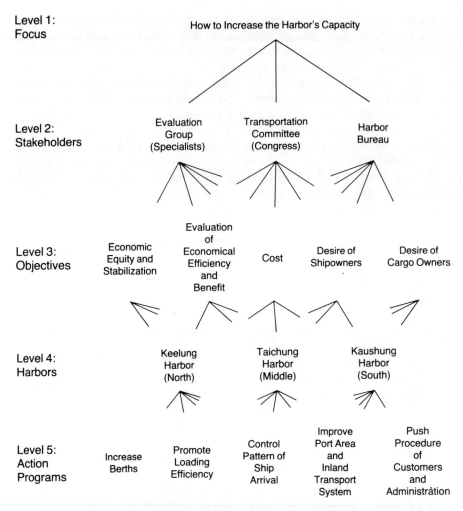

Figure 4-20   Hierarchy for Increasing Harbor Capacity

satisfy the criteria. The highest-priority storage system is the one preferred.

Hierarchy for Allocating Resources in Juvenile Correction Programs

A group of public officials were interested in juvenile law enforcement and wanted to allocate resources in five programs the staff had suggested. To start with, they considered three principal areas of correction and

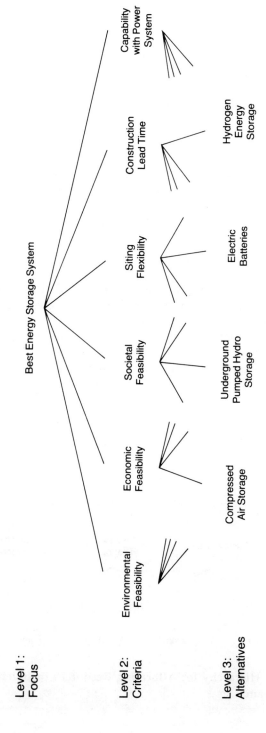

Figure 4-21 Hierarchy for Evaluating Energy Storage Systems

prioritized them to find out how much attention they should receive (Figure 4-22).

Each principal area could be associated with the programs identified, so the programs were prioritized regarding their effectiveness with respect to each area. The overall priorities obtained after weighting by the area priorities show how much relative importance each program commands for the optimum juvenile correction system.

Hierarchy for Analyzing School Busing Conflict

The introduction of busing due to the 1954 Supreme Court ruling has been a source of friction in a certain school district. The minority community wants to introduce complete busing for racial integration at school; the majority community wants segregation to protect the privileged position they now enjoy. To analyze the situation and judge the potential outcome, we rank the stakeholders according to their relative influence on the political scene (Figure 4-23). Then we prioritize the objectives of each stakeholder to see which objectives weigh more and should thus be pursued in preference to others. The overall priorities give a picture of the relative strengths of the forces at work on the scene.

The outcomes under consideration here are three scenarios spanning the complete spectrum of possibilities. They are prioritized with respect to each stakeholder objective to find out which outcome is favored by that objective. The overall priorities indicate the relative likelihood that each possible outcome will occur. This exercise shows the interaction of various

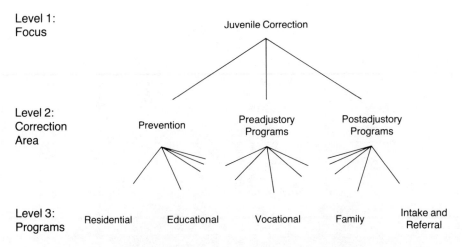

Figure 4-22   Hierarchy for Allocating Resources in Juvenile Correction Programs

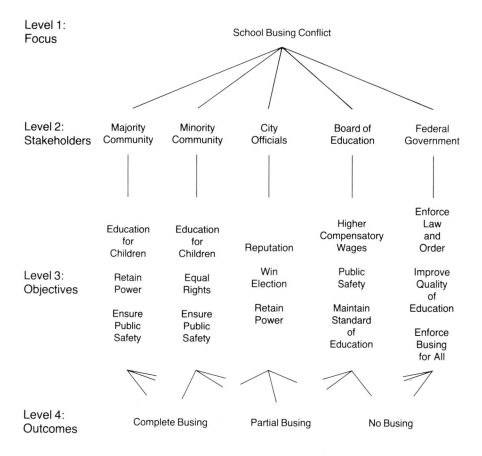

Figure 4-23   Hierarchy for Analyzing School Busing Conflict

factors and forces at work, so that if one stakeholder wanted to influence the outcome, he or she could decide accordingly on a course of action such as coalition or persuading others to change their objectives.

Hierarchy for Analyzing Health Administration Conflict

This hierarchy for resolving conflict in health administration finds the likelihood of various health plans being adopted as national policy (Figure 4-24). First we prioritize the principal actors regarding their relative influence on the issue. Next their objectives are identified and prioritized to indicate the relative extent to which the actors are motivated by various considerations.

At the next stage, we establish which policies of the actors would satisfy the objectives. The policies that relate to the same objective are

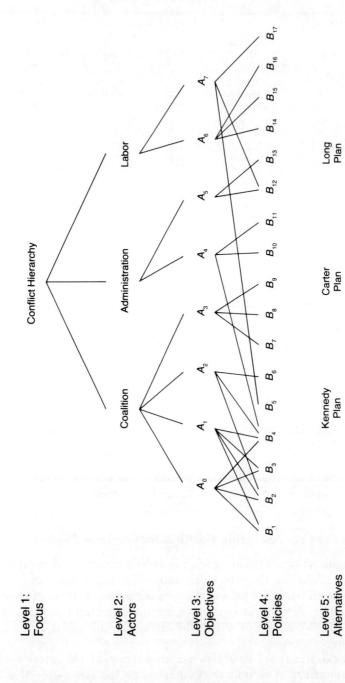

Figure 4-24 Hierarchy for Analyzing Health Plan Conflict

prioritized to find the importance of the policies to serve the objective in question. The composite priorities show the overall influence of the policies in national health administration.

There are three main health plans being debated nationally. By prioritizing the plans with respect to each policy, we find to what extent a plan satisfies the policy in question. Thus the overall priorities of the plans show the relative extent of support for the plans from various interested quarters. The overall priorities are also the likelihoods of the plans being adopted nationally.

The elements of that hierarchy are defined as follows:

A_0: comprehensive health insurance
A_1: mixed private-public financing
A_2: containment of health care costs
A_3: minimum government involvement
A_4: expanded health coverage
A_5: control of health care costs
A_6: comprehensive health services
A_7: containment of the total costs of health care
B_1: employer-employee contribution
B_2: limited public funding
B_3: tax subsidy
B_4: deductibles/coinsurance
B_5: planning/integration
B_6: utilization control
B_7: advisory federal agency
B_8: state regulation of NHI
B_9: no provider's charge control
B_{10}: increased spending of public funds
B_{11}: employer only paid premium
B_{12}: control of provider's charges
B_{13}: administrative reorganization of Medicare and Medicaid
B_{14}: wage-related premiums
B_{15}: non-wage-related premium
B_{16}: premium paid from public funds
B_{17}: competition between providers and insurers

PLANNING ECONOMIC POLICIES

Hierarchy for Planning Economic Strategy for an Underdeveloped Country

To map the strategy of economic development in an underdeveloped country where oil is the chief source of revenue, we draw up a planning

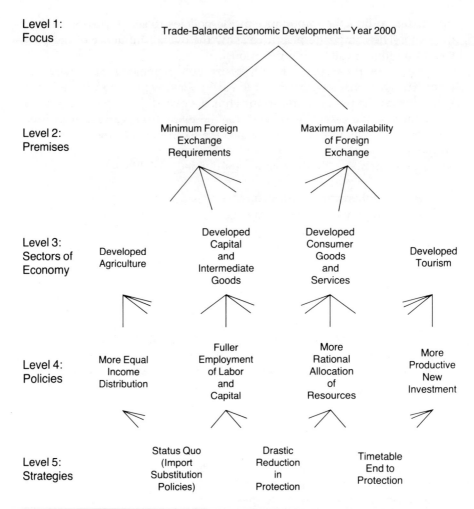

Figure 4-25 Hierarchy for Planning Economic Strategy

hierarchy (Figure 4-25). Although oil plays a very important role in the economy now, it is expected to be depleted by the year 2000. The country's planners must develop a strategy with that eventuality in view.

First, two principal underlying premises for a future oil-free economy are identified and then prioritized to indicate which one will have a more dominant influence. Next the important sectors of the future economy are prioritized to indicate the degree to which they will become important according to the premises. Specific rational policies are then prioritized with respect to each sector of the economy to determine which would be more effective. Finally, the strategies in question are prioritized with re-spect to the policies regarding their beneficial role on each.

The overall priorities for the policies as well as strategies show the national planners which ones will be more effective and hence should be actively promoted in an overall context.

ESTIMATING AND PREDICTING

Hierarchy for Estimating Popularity of Rock Groups

To estimate the popularity of various rock groups, we structure the overall performance of a music group into three main components by which they are judged (Figure 4-26). These components are then prioritized regarding their relative influence.

Each component is further judged in light of several characteristics of performance, and the characteristics are prioritized regarding their relative influence. Finally, we prioritize the rock groups with respect to the charac-teristics to give their relative standing. The composite priority we obtain gives a relative measure of overall superiority and hence an index of their popularity.

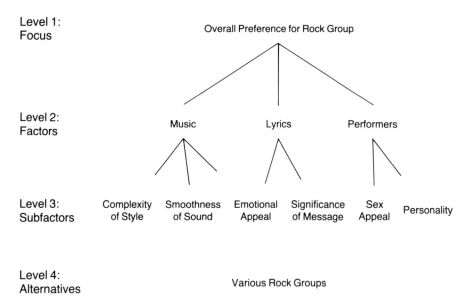

Figure 4-26   Hierarchy for Estimating Popularity of Rock Groups

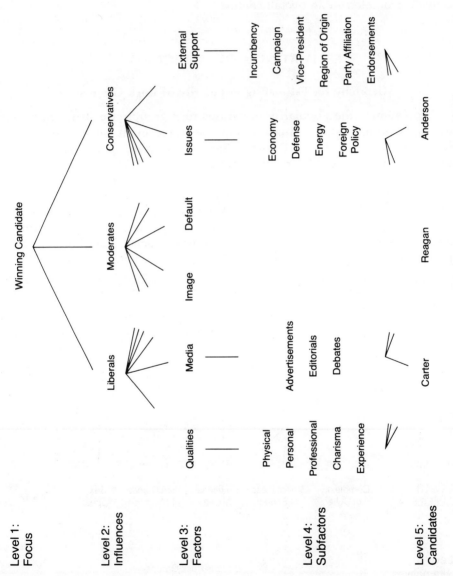

Figure 4-27 Hierarchy for Predicting the Presidential Election

Hierarchy for Predicting the Presidential Election

To predict a presidential election, we begin by identifying the principal political strains influencing all coalitions and allies—liberals, moderates, and conservatives—and prioritize them regarding their influence on the contemporary political scene (Figure 4-27). Next we consider the characteristics of the candidates and prioritize them to find to what extent they are decisive. These factors are subdivided into more detailed elements and then prioritized. The overall priorities we obtain assess how far these individual elements influence popular choice.

Finally, the three principal candidates are prioritized with respect to each subfactor to estimate their relative superiority. The overall priority we obtain is an index of the predictability of the candidate's winning the election.

Hierarchy for Predicting Likelihood of Technical Innovation

We can investigate the likelihood of technical innovation associated with corporate planning with respect to three forms of corporate control: traditional public ownership, employee ownership, and government ownership. We study the relationship in three representative industries (Figure 4-28).

For each industry, the related corporate factors are prioritized with respect to each form. Next the actors are prioritized with respect to each corporate factor to obtain their relative impact on the factor in question. The objectives of each actor are prioritized to find their relative strengths in influencing decisions, and, finally, the three forms of corporate control are prioritized to indicate how far each would facilitate the objectives in question. Therefore, the overall priorities at this level show the relative likelihood that technical innovation will be fostered by the different forms of corporate control.

Hierarchy for Predicting Number of Children in an Average Family

This exercise is carried out to anticipate the number of children an average family is likely to have. Several criteria are considered to influence the number of children in a family: the availability of birth control measures, working mother, older age at motherhood, education of mother, cost of raising children, and social pressure (Figure 4-29). These criteria are prioritized to show the relative degrees of influence they exert.

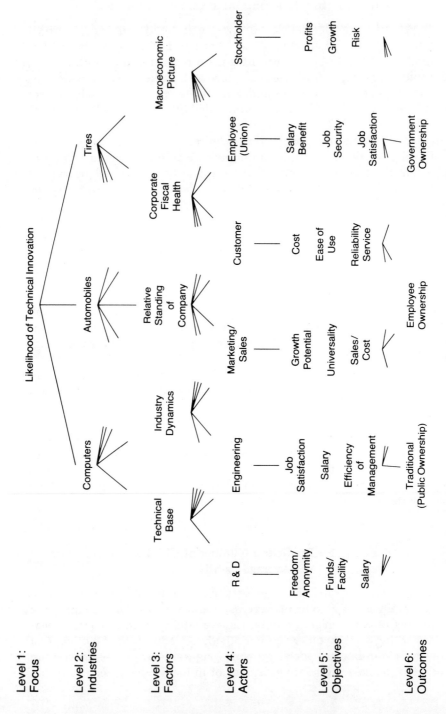

Figure 4-28 Hierarchy for Predicting Likelihood of Technical Innovation

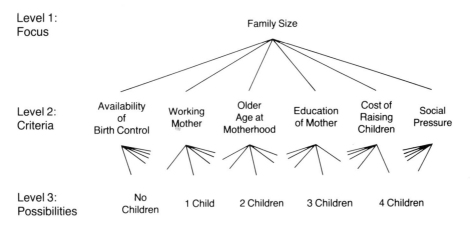

Figure 4-29   Hierarchy for Predicting Average Number of Children

The number of children considered here runs from zero to four. (We assume that the number of families having more children is very small.) With respect to each criterion, the priority of the number of children is found by ranking on the basis of best judgment. The overall priorities obtained after weighting by the priorities of the criteria reflect the distribution of the number of children in an average family. The expected value of this distribution is the average number of children a family is likely to have.

MEASURING INFLUENCES

Hierarchy for Measuring Parental Influence on Psychological Well-Being

A study of an individual's psychological well-being traces the extent to which it is influenced by the mother and the father separately and by both jointly. Psychological well-being depends on self-respect, a sense of security, and the ability to adapt to others (Figure 4-30). The factors that contribute to these qualities in one's developing years are in the third level; all are influenced by the parents separately and jointly.

The overall priorities of the factors at any level show their relative contribution to the person's well-being. The overall priorities at the lowest level represent the influences that the parents brought to bear separately and jointly in the person's formative years.

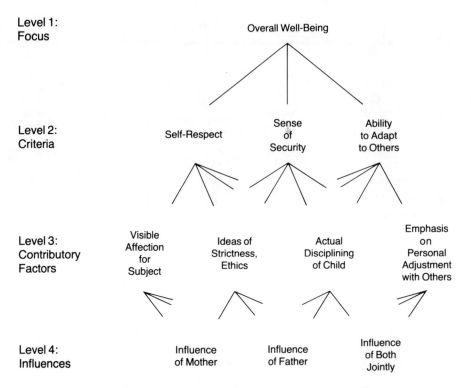

Figure 4-30   Hierarchy for Measuring Parental Influence

REPRESENTING SYSTEMS NETWORKS

Network of a Child's Learning System

A child's learning process in the formative years is influenced by many factors. These factors may be classified into certain groups. What is significant, however, is that the various factors interact with and influence one another. Hence we represent them in the form of a system consisting of subsystems and further divisions interacting with one another (Figure 4-31).

By prioritizing the factors in a group with respect to each factor in each group separately, weighting them by the relative importance of the groups themselves, and finding how they influence one another, we can come to a conclusion regarding the intrinsic importance of the various factors bearing upon the child's upbringing.

The system depicted here consists of five subsystems, which all impact on the child's learning elements (CHL) (motivation, M; creativity, C;

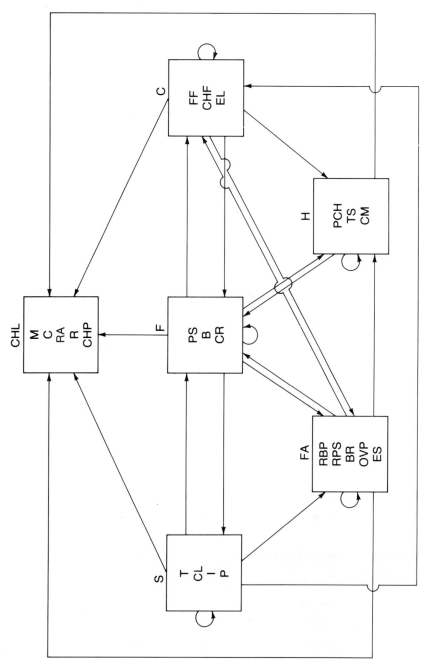

Figure 4-31 Network of a Child's Learning System

reflection ability, RA; retention and assimilation, R; character and personality, CHP)

1. The school (S)
2. The family (F)
3. The community (C)
4. The family atmosphere (FA)
5. The home (H)

The most important components associated with the school subsystem (S) are:

1. Teachers (T)
2. Classmates (CL)
3. Installations (I)
4. Study programs (P)

Those for the family (F) are:

1. Parents (PS)
2. Brothers and sisters (B)
3. Close relatives (those who interact directly with the family) (CR)

Those for the community (C) are:

1. Family friends (FF)
2. The child's friends (CHF)
3. The environmental living characteristics (EL)

Those for the family atmosphere (FA) are:

1. The relation between the parents (RBP)
2. The relation between the parents and the child (RPS)
3. The relation between the child and brothers and sisters (BR)
4. The overprotection of people older than the child (OVP)
5. The family's economic status (ES)

And those for the home (H) are:

1. Physical characteristics (PCH)
2. The child's toys (TS)
3. The communication media (radio and television) (CM)

   This model has been evaluated for a certain community, at an average socioeconomic level, in a democratic regime, and for children eight years old with normal psychological characteristics.

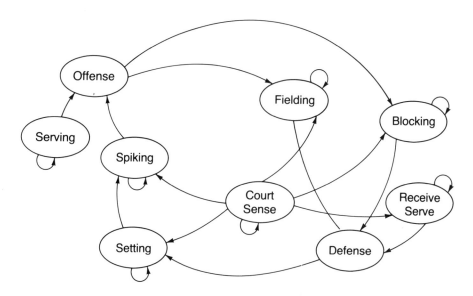

Figure 4-32   Network of a Volleyball Team

Network of a Volleyball Team

Volleyball is a game of teamwork and simple skills, but the players are required to change positions and possess *all* the skills. Since few players have all the skills to the same extent, the coach has to use players with the proper mix of skills. Thus the coach has to know the relative importance of skills and play the proper combination of players. Since the various skills depend upon one another, we use systems analysis and not hierarchical representation (Figure 4-32).

By prioritizing the skills for a good game of volleyball and prioritizing the players with respect to one another's skills, we get the relative standings of the players and skills in the ultimate analysis. This information helps the coach to select players with basic skills.

PERSPECTIVE

The hierarchies just presented are only a few of those that have actually been used to make decisions with the AHP. But they suggest the wide range of problems to which the AHP can be applied—from choosing a car to crossing a river. Specifically, the AHP can be used for the following kinds of decision problems:

· Setting priorities
· Generating a set of alternatives

- Choosing the best policy alternative
- Determining requirements
- Allocating resources
- Predicting outcomes and assessing risks
- Measuring performance
- Designing a system
- Ensuring system stability
- Optimizing
- Planning
- Resolving conflicts

The sample hierarchies in this chapter should give some insight into the need for various levels in different kinds of hierarchies. Different people may have their own idea about how to deal with a problem, and that is how they should carry it out. Only when a group must act together, as in a corporation, do people need to agree on the structure of their problem.

In forming a hierarchy, one should include as much detail as seems to be needed to understand the problem; the prioritization process will eliminate elements that are unimportant. A new level should be added to the hierarchy if it facilitates the comparison and evaluation of the elements in the level immediately below and contributes to improving precision in the judgments. One contribution of a good hierarchy is that it enables people to make better guesses about the effects of the unknown by laying out its components and studying each separately instead of lumping everything together and making one big guess at the consequences of decisions made in the face of that unknown. The hierarchy can provide an effective buffer between reason and worry.

Clearly the design of an analytic hierarchy—like the structuring of a problem by any other method—is more art than science. There is no precise formula for identification or stratification of elements. But structuring a hierarchy does require substantial knowledge about the system or problem in question. A strong aspect of the AHP is that the experienced decision makers who specify the hierarchy also supply judgments on the relative importance of the elements—which brings us to the next topic: establishing priorities.

5

Establishing Priorities

This chapter deals with the following questions:

- How do we establish priorities in a decision problem?

- Why is the matrix useful in setting priorities?

- How do we synthesize our judgments to get a set of overall priorities?

- How can we check the consistency of our judgments? And how important *is* consistency?

- What do we do when the elements we are ranking overlap?

THE NEED FOR PRIORITIES

In this chapter we complete the analytic hierarchy process by establishing priorities among the elements of the hierarchy, synthesizing our judgments to yield a set of overall priorities, checking the consistency of these judgments, and coming to a final decision based on the results of this process.

Systems theorists point out that complex relationships can always be analyzed by taking pairs of elements and relating them through their attributes. The object is to find from many things those that have a necessary connection. This causal approach to understanding complexity is complemented by the systems approach, whose object is to find the subsystems or dimensions in which the parts are connected.

We have seen that the analytic hierarchy process deals with both approaches simultaneously. Systems thinking is addressed by structuring ideas hierarchically, and causal thinking, or explanation, is developed through paired comparison of the elements in the hierarchy and through synthesis.

The judgments we apply in making paired comparisons combine logical thinking with feeling developed from informed experience. The mathematical sequence described in this chapter is a more efficient method of arriving at a solution than the intuitive means we usually employ, but the end result is not necessarily more accurate. If the solution reached through the AHP does not feel right to an experienced, well-informed decision maker, then he or she would do well to repeat the process and restructure the hierarchy or improve the judgments. On the other hand, the AHP provides its own check on the consistency of judgments, and experience has shown that the results of the AHP closely approximate decisions reached more laboriously in the business world.

It is important to note that the calculations described here can be carried out by computer. My aim is not to dwell on the mathematics of the process—a mathematical supplement is available for those interested—but to explain how subjective judgments can be quantified and converted into a set of priorities on which decisions can be based.

SETTING PRIORITIES

The first step in establishing the priorities of elements in a decision problem is to make pairwise comparisons—that is, to compare the elements in pairs against a given criterion. For pairwise comparisons, a matrix is the preferred form. The matrix is a simple, well-established tool that offers a framework for testing consistency, obtaining additional information through making all possible comparisons, and analyzing the sensitivity of overall priorities to changes in judgment. The matrix approach uniquely reflects the dual aspects of priorities: dominating and dominated.

To begin the pairwise comparison process, start at the top of the hierarchy to select the criterion C, or property, that will be used for making the first comparison. Then, from the level immediately below, take the elements to be compared: A_1, A_2, A_3, and so on. Let us say there are seven elements. Arrange these elements in a matrix as in Figure 5-1.

C	A_1	A_2	$\cdots$	A_7
A_1	1			
A_2		1		
.				
.				
.				
A_7				1

Figure 5-1   Sample Matrix for Pairwise Comparison

In this matrix compare the element A_1 in the column on the left with the elements A_1, A_2, A_3, and so on in the row on top with respect to property C in the upper left-hand corner. Then repeat with column element A_2 and so on. To compare elements, ask: How much more strongly does this element (or activity) possess—or contribute to, dominate, influence, satisfy, or benefit—the property than does the element with which it is being compared?

The phrasing of the question is important. It must reflect the proper relationship between the elements in one level with the property in the next higher level. If time or another probabilistic criterion is used, then ask: How much more probable or likely is one element than another? If the elements are dominated by the property rather than vice versa, ask how much more strongly the element is possessed, dominated, affected by, and so on, this property. In projecting an outcome, ask which element is more likely to be decisive or to result in the outcome.

To fill in the matrix of pairwise comparisons, we use numbers to represent the relative importance of one element over another with respect to the property. Table 5-1 contains the scale for pairwise comparisons. It defines and explains the values 1 through 9 assigned to judgments in comparing pairs of like elements in each level of a hierarchy against a criterion in the next higher level. Experience has confirmed that a scale of nine units is reasonable and reflects the degree to which we can discriminate the intensity of relationships between elements. When using the scale in a social, psychological, or political context, express the verbal judgments first and then translate them to numerical values. The numerically translated judg-

Table 5-1   The Pairwise Comparison Scale

Intensity of Importance	Definition	Explanation
1	Equal importance of both elements	Two elements contribute equally to the property
3	Weak importance of one element over another	Experience and judgment slightly favor one element over another
5	Essential or strong importance of one element over another	Experience and judgment strongly favor one element over another
7	Demonstrated importance of one element over another	An element is strongly favored and its dominance is demonstrated in practice
9	Absolute importance of one element over another	The evidence favoring one element over another is of the highest possible order of affirmation
2, 4, 6, 8	Intermediate values between two adjacent judgments	Compromise is needed between two judgments
Reciprocals	If activity i has one of the preceding numbers assigned to it when compared with activity j, then j has the reciprocal value when compared with i	

ments are approximations; their validity can be evaluated by a test of consistency, which will be described later, and by real-life applications for which the answers are already known.

When comparing one element in a matrix with itself—for example, A_1 with A_1 in Figure 5-1—the comparison must give unity (1), so fill in the diagonal of the matrix with 1s. Always compare the first element of a pair (the element in the left-hand column of the matrix) with the second (the element in the row on top) and estimate the numerical value from the scale in Table 5-1. The reciprocal value is then used for the comparison of the second element with the first. For example, if the two elements are stones and the first is five times heavier than the second, then the second is one-fifth as heavy as the first.

Why not simply use arbitrary numbers for ranking the elements according to their impact on a criterion? If the problem concerns simple ranking, and the degree to which the elements being ranked reflect the criterion is obvious, then one can simply assign numbers. To discriminate the relative strength with which each element possesses or contributes to the criterion (property), numbers can be used directly by starting with the smallest element and perhaps using it as a unit. This procedure may be useful in organizing one's thinking, but the logic is not clear and, moreover, feeling is not integrated into the process. For fine distinctions, the pairwise comparison matrix and scale provide a more satisfactory framework.

When tradeoffs must be made among several criteria, the problem of ranking becomes complex. It is no longer sufficient simply to assign arbitrary numbers. We must select with care the numbers used to express the strength with which each element possesses or contributes to the property in question. Such care ensures that in the end we obtain the correct overall priorities for the elements by considering all tradeoffs. (These priorities can also then be used to allocate resources.)

SYNTHESIS

To obtain the set of overall priorities for a decision problem, we have to pull together or synthesize the judgments made in the pairwise comparisons—that is, we have to do some weighting and adding to give us a single number to indicate the priority of each element. The following example explains how to synthesize.

Suppose we want to decide which of three new cars—a Chevrolet, a Thunderbird, and a Lincoln—to buy on the basis of comfort. We draw a matrix with the criterion "comfort" listed in the upper left-hand corner and the cars listed in the column on the left and in a row on top (Figure 5-2). We

Comfort	C	T	L
Chevrolet (C)	1	1/2	1/4
Thunderbird (T)	2	1	1/2
Lincoln (L)	4	2	1

Figure 5-2   Simple Matrix Comparing Three Cars for Comfort

then put 1s in the diagonal positions as indicated. This matrix has nine entries to fill. Three are already committed to 1s. Three of the remaining six are reciprocals. This leaves three judgments to make. In general, if the matrix deals with, say, seven elements, the number of judgments needed to fill the entries is $7 \times 7 - 7 \div 2 = 21$. We subtract the seven unit entries down the diagonal and divide by 2 because half the judgments are reciprocals that are entered automatically.

We then ask: How much more comfortable is an average new Chevrolet than an average new Thunderbird and an average new Lincoln? Based on our experience and personal preference, our judgment is that a Chevrolet is one-half as comfortable as a Thunderbird and one-fourth as comfortable as a Lincoln. To state these judgments in terms of the quantifiers in the scale (Table 5-1), a Thunderbird is slightly more comfortable than a Chevrolet, and a Lincoln is between slightly and strongly more comfortable than a Chevrolet. Thus we enter the values 2 for the Thunderbird over the Chevrolet and 4 for the Lincoln over the Chevrolet. These numbers are the reciprocals of the two judgments comparing the Chevrolet with the other cars.

Remember that the element that appears in the left-hand column is always compared with the element appearing in the top row, and the value is given to the element in the column as it is compared with the element in the row. If it is regarded less favorably, the judgment is a fraction. The reciprocal value is entered in the position where the second element, when it appears in the column, is compared with the first element when it appears in the row.

In this example, because the Chevrolet is regarded less favorably when compared with the other two cars, we enter 1/2 and 1/4 in the second and third positions of the first row and enter 2 and 4 in what are known as the *transpose positions* in the first column. We then compare the Thunderbird with the Lincoln and enter a value of 1/2 in the second row, third column position, and its reciprocal 2 in the second column, third row position. We now have the three judgments needed to complete the pairwise comparison matrix (Figure 5-2).

Next we want to synthesize our judgments to get an overall estimate of the relative priorities of these cars with respect to comfort. To do so, we first add the values in each column (Figure 5-3). Then we divide each entry

Comfort	C	T	L
C	1	1/2	1/4
T	2	1	1/2
L	4	2	1
Column total	7	3.5	1.75

Figure 5-3   Synthesizing the Judgments

in each column by the total of that column to obtain the *normalized matrix*, which permits meaningful comparison among elements (Figure 5-4). Fi-

Comfort	C	T	L
C	1/7	1/7	1/7
T	2/7	2/7	2/7
L	4/7	4/7	4/7

Figure 5-4   Normalized Matrix

nally, we average over the rows by adding the values in each row of the normalized matrix and dividing the rows by the number of entries in each:

$$\frac{1/7 + 1/7 + 1/7}{3} = 1/7 = 0.14$$

$$\frac{2/7 + 2/7 + 2/7}{3} = 2/7 = 0.29$$

$$\frac{4/7 + 4/7 + 4/7}{3} = 4/7 = 0.57$$

This synthesis yields the percentages of overall relative priorities, or preferences, for the Chevrolet, the Thunderbird, and the Lincoln: 14, 29, and 57 percent, respectively. As far as comfort is concerned, the Thunderbird and the Lincoln are thus about twice and four times more preferable than the Chevrolet.

The answer in this case was very simple, because all the columns in the normalized matrix were the same. They turned out to be the same because the pairwise comparison matrix (Figure 5-2) was consistent. That is, from the relationship of the Chevrolet to the Thunderbird in the first row of the matrix,

$$C = (1/2)T$$

and from its relationship with the Lincoln,

$$C = (1/4)L$$

we can deduce that

$$(1/2)T = (1/4)L$$

and that

$$T = (1/2)L$$

which is precisely what we have in the second row, third column entry. In other words, if the Chevrolet is preferred half as much as the Thunderbird and one-fourth as much as the Lincoln, then the Thunderbird must be preferred half as much as the Lincoln. The information in the first row is used to force judgmental consistency.

CONSISTENCY

In decision-making problems it may be important to know how good our consistency is, because we may not want the decision to be based on judgments that have such low consistency that they appear to be random. On the other hand, perfect consistency is hard to live up to. Our judgments on the relative comfort of the three cars were consistent, but in real life specific circumstances often influence preferences, and circumstances change.

If apples are preferred to oranges, for example, and oranges are preferred to bananas, then in a perfectly consistent relationship apples must be preferred to bananas. But the same individual may sometimes like bananas better than apples, depending on the time of day, the season, and other circumstances. In the example of the cars, we identified a couple of relationships that showed the strength of our preference for a Thunderbird over a Chevrolet and for a Lincoln over a Chevrolet and forced these relationships on the comparison between a Thunderbird and a Lincoln—the Thunderbird was preferred half as much as the Lincoln. But often such a relationship does not hold true. Violating it, which we do all the time, leads to inconsistency.

How damaging is inconsistency? Usually we cannot be so certain of our judgments that we would insist on forcing consistency in the pairwise comparison matrix. Rather, we guess our feelings or judgments in all the positions except the diagonal ones (which are always 1), force the reciprocals in the transpose positions, and look for an answer. We may not be perfectly consistent, but that is the way we tend to work. (It is also the way we grow. When we integrate new experiences into our consciousness, previous relationships may change and some consistency is lost. As long as there is enough consistency to maintain coherence among the objects of our experience, the consistency need not be perfect.) It is useful to remember that most new ideas that affect our lives tend to cause us to rearrange some of our preferences, thus making us inconsistent with our previous commitments. If we were to program ourselves never to change our minds, we would be afraid to accept new ideas. All knowledge has to be admitted into our narrow corridor between tolerable inconsistency and perfect consistency.

Of course, a certain degree of consistency in setting priorities for elements or activities with respect to some criterion is necessary to get valid results in the real world. The AHP measures the overall consistency of judgments by means of a *consistency ratio*. The value of the consistency ratio should be 10 percent or less. If it is more than 10 percent, the judgments may be somewhat random and should perhaps be revised. Let us continue with the example of the cars and see how the AHP measures consistency.

Suppose that we keep the first row of our pairwise comparison matrix in Figure 5-2 but do not pay much attention to consistency with our previous judgments. In comparing the Thunderbird with the Lincoln, we enter the value 1/4 in the second row, third column, and enter its reciprocal 4 in the third row, second column (Figure 5-5). Following the steps described

Comfort	C	T	L
C	1	1/2	1/4
T	2	1	1/4
L	4	4	1
Column total	7	5.5	1.5

Figure 5-5 Inconsistent Matrix

earlier, we obtain the normalized matrix, its row sums, and the percentages of relative overall priorities (Figure 5-6). The percentages, 13, 21, and 66 percent, constitute the *priority vector* of the three cars with respect to comfort. The value of the priority vector is approximate. (We can find the

Comfort	C	T	L	Row Sums	Average Row Sum
C	1/7	1/1̄1̄	1/6	0.40	0.40/3 = 0.13
T	2/7	2/11	1/6	0.63	0.63/3 = 0.21
L	4/7	8/11	4/6	1.97	1.97/3 = 0.66

Figure 5-6 Normalized Matrix, Row Sums, and Overall Priorities

exact value, but the solution is complicated. Besides, when the judgments are perfectly consistent, the two values are identical; nearly consistent, the values are close.) Although the standing of the Chevrolet has not been changed by much, the other two have changed by our reducing the value for the Thunderbird and raising it for the Lincoln.

With inconsistency all the values are changed. The question is: How significant is this change? Presumably we want to compare our inconsistency with the value it would have if the judgments were random. To do this, multiply the first column of the inconsistent matrix (Figure 5-5), changed to decimal form, by the relative priority of the Chevrolet (0.13), the second column by that of the Thunderbird (0.21), and the third column by that of the Lincoln (0.66). Then total the entries in the rows (Figure 5-7).

Comfort	C (0.13)	T (0.21)	L (0.66)	Comfort	C	T	L	Row Total
C	1	0.5	0.25	C	0.13	0.11	0.17	0.41
T	2	1	0.25	T	0.26	0.21	0.17	0.64
L	4	4	1	L	0.52	0.84	0.66	2.02

Figure 5-7   Totaling the Entries

Now take the column of row totals and divide each of its entries by the corresponding entry from the priority vector (Figure 5-8). We can now find the average of the three entries in the last column of Figure 5-8:

$$\frac{3.15 + 3.05 + 3.06}{3} = \frac{9.26}{3} \approx 3.09$$

By convention, the symbol for this number is λ_{max} (lambda max). The consistency index (CI) is

$$\frac{3.09 - 3}{2} = \frac{0.09}{2} = 0.045$$

The random value of the CI for $n = 3$ is 0.58.* The consistency ratio (CR) is $0.045/0.58 = 0.08$, which indicates good consistency.

---

* If numerical judgments were taken at random from the scale 1/9, 1/8, 1/7, . . . , 1/2, . . . , 1, 2, . . . , 9, then using a reciprocal matrix we would have the following average consistencies for different-order random matrices:

Size of matrix	1	2	3	4	5	6	7	8	9	10
Random consistency	0.00	0.00	0.58	0.90	1.12	1.24	1.32	1.41	1.45	1.49

$$\begin{bmatrix} 0.41 \\ 0.64 \\ 2.02 \end{bmatrix} \div \begin{bmatrix} 0.13 \\ 0.21 \\ 0.66 \end{bmatrix} = \begin{bmatrix} 3.15 \\ 3.05 \\ 3.06 \end{bmatrix}$$

Figure 5-8   Determining λ_{max}

A second approximation procedure is to compute the geometric mean of the elements in each row—that is, to multiply the elements and then take their nth root. This step is followed by normalizing the resulting vector so that its components add to unity. In general, the geometric mean is a good approximation, particularly when the consistency is high. The calculation of λ_{max} can proceed as before. The geometric mean for the inconsistent matrix of cars with respect to comfort yields 0.16, 0.20, and 0.64. The exact solution by computer is 0.13, 0.21, 0.66, and $\lambda_{max} = 3.05$, which nearly coincides with the results of the column normalization process described earlier. Note that row averaging followed by a normalization of the resulting vector yields 0.13, 0.23, and 0.64. There are many examples for which this last process yields unsatisfactory results when the matrix is inconsistent.

One way to improve consistency when it turns out to be unsatisfactory is to rank the activities by a simple order based on the weights obtained in the first run of the problem. A second pairwise comparison matrix is then developed with this knowledge of ranking in mind. The consistency should generally be better.

EXTENDING THE PROCESS

To see how the process just described can be extended to an entire hierarchy, consider the problem of a woman who has recently earned her Ph.D. and is being interviewed for three jobs. Which one should she choose? Figure 5-9 shows how she structured the elements of the problem and arranged them in a hierarchy. Level 1, the focus, is overall job satisfaction; level 2 comprises the criteria that contribute to job satisfaction; and level 3 consists of the three job possibilities. The hierarchy is a complete one: Each element in a level is evaluated in terms of all the elements in the next higher level.

The woman compared the level 2 criteria in pairs with respect to job satisfaction and judged the relative importance of each criterion. She felt that research, for example, would be equally as important as location in contributing to job satisfaction, but it would be slightly to strongly more important than colleagues. Figure 5-10 shows the pairwise comparison matrix of the criteria with respect to the focus. The last column gives the

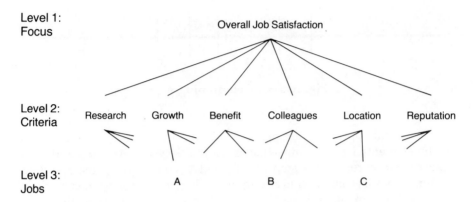

Level 1:
Focus

Level 2:
Criteria

Level 3:
Jobs

Figure 5-9   Hierarchy for Choosing Among Three Job Offers

priorities: Reputation turns out to be the most important criterion, followed by opportunities for growth and benefits.

Next she developed six matrices for comparing the three jobs with respect to each criterion (Figure 5-11). All three entries in the vector of priorities obtained in each of the six matrices and listed in the last column of each are multiplied (weighted) by the priority of the corresponding criterion. These values are shown in Figure 5-12. The results of this operation are then added to yield the overall priorities for the jobs: A = 0.40, B = 0.34, and C = 0.26. The differences made apparent by this synthesis were sufficiently large for the woman to accept the offer for job A.

Although we will not go into the measurement of consistency here, it is important to note that in a hierarchy, the highest-level elements usually have the highest priorities. Inconsistency arising from comparison with respect to these elements is very damaging because of their high priority. The consistency index of a hierarchy is obtained by multiplying the consistency index of each matrix by the priority of the criterion used for the comparison and adding all such quantities. To evaluate the consistency of a hierarchy, compare the consistency index of the hierarchy with its counterpart when the consistency indices of the matrices are replaced by average random judgment consistency indices for matrices of the same size.

INTERDEPENDENCE

So far we have considered how to establish the priority of elements in a hierarchy and how to obtain the set of overall priorities when the elements of each level are independent. But often the elements are interdependent. How do we account for overlapping areas, or commonalities, among such elements? There are two principal kinds of interdependence

Overall Job Satisfaction	Research	Growth	Benefits	Colleagues	Location	Reputation	Vector of Priorities
Research	1	1	1	4	1	1/2	0.16
Growth	1	1	2	4	1	1/2	0.19
Benefits	1	1/2	1	5	3	1/2	0.19
Colleagues	1/4	1/4	1/5	1	1/3	1/3	0.05
Location	1	1	1/3	3	1	1	0.12
Reputation	2	2	2	3	3	1	0.30

Figure 5-10 Overall Satisfaction with Job

Research	A	B	C	Vector of Priorities
A	1	1/4	1/2	0.14
B	4	1	3	0.63
C	2	1/3	1	0.24

Growth	A	B	C	Vector of Priorities
A	1	1/4	1/5	0.10
B	4	1	1/2	0.33
C	5	2	1	0.57

Benefits	A	B	C	Vector of Priorities
A	1	3	1/3	0.32
B	1/3	1	1	0.22
C	3	1	1	0.46

Colleagues	A	B	C	Vector of Priorities
A	1	1/3	5	0.28
B	3	1	7	0.65
C	1/5	1/7	1	0.07

Location	A	B	C	Vector of Priorities
A	1	1	7	0.47
B	1	1	7	0.47
C	1/7	1/7	1	0.07

Reputation	A	B	C	Vector of Priorities
A	1	7	9	0.77
B	1/7	1	5	0.17
C	1/9	1/5	1	0.05

Figure 5-11   Six Matrices for Comparing Three Jobs

	Research (0.16)		Growth (0.19)		Benefits (0.19)		Colleagues (0.05)		Location (0.12)		Reputation (0.30)		Vector of Overall Priorities
A	0.14 (0.16)	+	0.10 (0.19)	+	0.32 (0.19)	+	0.28 (0.05)	+	0.47 (0.12)	+	0.77 (0.30)	=	0.40
B	0.63 (0.16)	+	0.33 (0.19)	+	0.22 (0.19)	+	0.65 (0.05)	+	0.47 (0.12)	+	0.17 (0.30)	=	0.34
C	0.24 (0.16)	+	0.57 (0.19)	+	0.46 (0.19)	+	0.07 (0.05)	+	0.07 (0.12)	+	0.05 (0.30)	=	0.26

Figure 5-12 Determining the Overall Priorities

among elements of a hierarchy level: additive interdependence and synergistic interdependence.

Additive Interdependence

In additive interdependence, each element contributes a share that is uniquely its own and also contributes indirectly by overlapping or interacting with other elements. The total impact can be estimated by examining the impacts of the independent and the overlapping shares and then combining the impacts. The effects of this simpler type of interdependence can be computed precisely since we can usually tell how much of an element's contribution is due to its independent properties and how much to its effect on other elements. Both mechanization and farm size contribute to agricultural productivity, for example, but mechanization also influences farm size by enabling farmers to work larger areas. In practice, most people prefer to ignore the rather complex mathematical adjustment for additive interdependence and simply rely on their own judgment. In the example just given, mechanization would be assigned a higher priority than farm size. The precise value would be determined subjectively from the descriptions in the pairwise comparison scale. Such judgments can also replace the more technical adjustment for synergistic interdependence.

Synergistic Interdependence

In synergistic interdependence, the impact of the interaction of the elements is greater than the sum of the impacts of the elements, with due consideration given to their overlap. This type of interdependence occurs more frequently in practice than additive interdependence and amounts to creating a new entity for each interaction. Power coalitions and the biology of marriage are examples of synergy.

The analytic hierarchy process provides a simple and direct means for measuring interdependence in a hierarchy. The basic idea is that wherever there is interdependence, each criterion becomes an objective and all the criteria are compared according to their contributions to that criterion. This generates a set of dependence priorities indicating the relative dependence of each criterion on all the criteria. These priorities are then weighted by the independence priority of each related criterion obtained from the hierarchy and the results are summed over each row, thus yielding the interdependence weights. By way of validation we find that this approach is compatible with, for example, what econometricians do in calculating input-output matrices. These ideas are illustrated in the mathematical supplement.

With synergistic interdependence, one needs to introduce for evaluation additional criteria that reveal the nature of the interaction. The overlapping element should be separated from its constituent parts. Its impact is added to theirs at the end to obtain their overall impact. Synergy of interaction is also captured at the upper levels when clusters are compared according to their importance. Interactions within and between clusters are better seen and judged higher up in the hierarchy.

Much of the problem of synergistic interdependence arises from the fuzziness of words and even the underlying ideas they represent. The full potential of interaction is never fully understood until it has taken place in practice. The qualities that emerge cannot be captured by a mathematical process. Thus a set theoretical approach using Venn diagrams would not be useful, because we do not have a simple geometric overlap of regions. What we have instead is the overlap of elements with other elements to produce an element with new properties that are not discernible in its parent parts.

Note that if we increase the elements being compared by one more element and attempt to preserve the consistency of their earlier ranking, we must be careful how we make the comparisons with the new element. For example, if we have been comparing apples, oranges, and bananas with respect to taste and then add melons to the problem, this new addition may change the priorities. Once we compare one of the previous elements with a new one, all other relationships are automatically set; otherwise there would be inconsistency and the rank order might change.

PERSPECTIVE

The process of setting priorities captures the feelings and judgments of informed individuals by asking them to make pairwise comparisons among like objects as criteria. The judgments, which represent strength of preference, are simultaneously converted to numerical values to represent their intensity and are laid out in a matrix. The priorities are then derived from all the judgments and the consistency of the judgments is calculated through the deviation of a single number from the order of a matrix. In a hierarchy we synthesize the priorities in a level by weighting the priorities derived from each matrix by the weight of the criterion of comparison. To obtain overall priorities, we add the results for each element. Note that prioritization from the top of the hierarchy downward includes less and less synergy as we move from the larger more interactive clusters to the small and more independent ones.

Independence can be treated in two ways. Either the hierarchy is structured in a way that identifies independent elements or dependence is allowed for by evaluating in separate matrices the impact of all the elements on each of them with respect to the criterion being considered. As before, a weighting process is then used to determine their priorities.

If we already have an idea of the ranking of elements and wish to derive their priorities, the judgments we give must indicate this dominance in rank. Otherwise we must assume that the individual does not fully understand (or is inconsistent in) his or her subjective ranking.

KEY CONCEPTS

☐ To establish the priorities of elements, we have to compare them in pairs according to a criterion. A matrix is the best framework for this comparison.

☐ To obtain the set of overall priorities for a decision, we have to synthesize the results of the pairwise comparisons. That is, we have to combine our judgments to get an overall estimate of the relative rank of priorities.

☐ In a hierarchy, the highest-level elements usually have the highest priorities. They are the clusters that give rise to smaller elements at the lower levels. Their priorities are divided by the weighting process among their descendants.

☐ The consistency of a hierarchy can be measured by multiplying the consistency of each matrix by the priority of its criterion and adding. This result is then compared with a similar number obtained for random matrices of the same size. The ratio should be 10 percent or less. Greater inconsistency indicates lack of information or lack of understanding.

6

Step-by-Step Examples of the Process

This chapter deals with the following questions:

- What are the basic steps of the analytic hierarchy process?

- How can the process be used to analyze high-level decisions like the one to rescue the hostages in Iran?

- How can the process be used to determine consumer preference?

- How can the process be used to estimate the economy's impact on sales?

- How can the process be used to select a stock portfolio?

- How valid is the analytic hierarchy process?

AN OUTLINE OF THE STEPS

We began our study of the analytic hierarchy process by laying out the elements of a problem as a hierarchy. We then made paired comparisons among the elements of a level as required by the criteria of the next higher level. These comparisons gave rise to priorities and finally, through synthesis, to overall priorities. We measured consistency and dealt with interdependence. These basic steps of the process can all be condensed into a brief outline. In broad terms, the process is stable, although certain steps may be given special emphasis in particular problems and, as noted below, repetition is generally necessary.

1. Define the problem and specify the solution desired.

2. Structure the hierarchy from the overall managerial viewpoint (from the top levels to the level at which intervention to solve the problem is possible).

3. Construct a pairwise comparison matrix of the relevant contribution or impact of each element on each governing criterion in the next higher level. In this matrix, pairs of elements are compared with respect to a criterion in the superior level. In comparing two elements most people prefer to give a judgment that indicates the dominance as a whole number. The matrix has one position to enter that number and another to enter its reciprocal. Thus if one element does not contribute more than another, the other must contribute more than it. This number is entered in the appropriate position in the matrix and its reciprocal is entered in the other position. An element on the left is by convention examined regarding its dominance over an element at the top of the matrix.

4. Obtain all judgments required to develop the set of matrices in step 3. If there are many people participating, the task for each person can be made simple by appropriate allocation of effort, which we describe in a later chapter. Multiple judgments can be synthesized by using their geometric mean.

5. Having collected all the pairwise comparison data and entered the reciprocals together with unit entries down the main diagonal, the priorities are obtained and consistency is tested.

6. Perform steps 3, 4, and 5 for all levels and clusters in the hierarchy.

7. Use hierarchical composition (synthesis) to weight the vectors of priorities by the weights of the criteria, and take the sum over all weighted priority entries corresponding to those in the next lower level and so on. The result is an overall priority vector for the lowest level of the hierarchy. If there are several outcomes, their arithmetic average may be taken.

8. Evaluate consistency for the entire hierarchy by multiplying each consistency index by the priority of the corresponding criterion and adding the products. The result is divided by the same type of expression using the random consistency index corresponding to the dimensions of each matrix weighted by the priorities as before. The consistency ratio of the hierarchy should be 10 percent or less. If it is not, the quality of information should be improved—perhaps by revising the manner in which questions are posed to make the pairwise comparisons. If this measure fails to improve consistency, it is likely that the problem has not been accurately structured—that is, similar elements have not been grouped under a meaningful criterion. A return to step 2 is then required, although only the problematic parts of the hierarchy may need revision.

These are the basic steps we will follow in working out the examples of this chapter. In each case we will examine the problem, set up the hierarchy, carry out the pairwise comparisons, determine the priorities, synthesize the overall priorities, and examine the consistency. We begin with a recent application of the method to the Iran rescue operation. An intangible factor played an important role in President Carter's thinking but not necessarily the thinking of his advisors—hence their different conclusions regarding the rescue operation.

The second example challenges us to select the best product to manufacture from three alternatives by using six criteria. The product that is chosen costs more but is more desirable all around. The third example shows how the AHP may be used to estimate the impact of energy, recession, and inflation on a company's sales. Here percentage ranges are prioritized according to likelihood of occurrence. The fourth example illustrates how the AHP can be used to set priorities for stocks according to several criteria. By way of validation, the high-priority stocks did in fact appreciate in value.

ANALYZING THE HOSTAGE RESCUE OPERATION

It is customary for high-level managers and political leaders to make their most important decisions by depending on expert recommendations governed by their own personal judgment and understanding. President Carter once said that when he had to make a really crucial decision between two alternatives, his experts were usually evenly split. In essence, then, the hard decisions were still up to him. If expert opinions were accurate and thorough, leaders would become superfluous. In spite of splitting on their judgments the experts do raise questions that stimulate decision makers and draw their attention to issues they may have neglected to consider.

Background of the Decision

A great shroud of secrecy surrounds the decision to rescue the hostages in Iran. On 28 April 1980 a decision was made to send an American air rescue team to Iran to bring out the fifty-three American hostages from Teheran where they had been held since early November 1979. The mission was a complicated plan involving troops, airplanes, helicopters, a long flight, a landing in the desert, a journey to Teheran, taking out the hostages, and returning to safety.

It appears that not even the upper-level national security staff was informed about how the decision was made. It is said that President Carter had the Joint Chiefs of Staff draw up a couple of plans with different options. He then discussed these plans with his closest advisors. According to *Time* (5 May 1980) these advisors were Brown, Brzezinski, Christopher, Jordan, Mondale, Turner, and Vance. Carter asked for clarification of some of the ideas, but he made the decision on his own. There is no indication that the president resorted to some kind of voting in the discussion on whether the operation should or should not be undertaken. It has been said that this was a typical Carter-style decision in which he asked his advisors for details and then made the decision himself.

There is no question that the likelihood of success of a rescue operation is a compelling factor in deciding whether to go or not to go. Of course, it is crucial how one defines success for such a mission. High success means no deaths among the hostages or military personnel; medium success means a few military and no hostage deaths; low success means a few military and a few hostage deaths. Greater losses could mean anything from failure to disaster. Some experts in the Department of Defense who are familiar with that mission have indicated that it would be generous to assign a medium chance of success to the military operation. They also said that this was known prior to 28 April and is not a question of hindsight. *Time* writes: "Carter himself conceded that 'the operation was certain to be difficult and it was certain to be dangerous.' He insisted that the operation had 'an excellent chance of success.'"

As we will see, the president's decision was consistent with his perception of the situation as it affected him; but it was not necessarily a good decision for the nation. Suppose we do a sensitivity analysis of the subjective factors and the emphasis the president placed on them.

Analysis of the Decision

The decision problem can be divided into two parts. The first part is to identify the best military option among those available and evaluate its likelihood of success. A military option would also have to be examined by experts on foreign relations and intelligence. The second part is the process of making the go/no-go decision based on the body of knowledge provided by the experts. We now examine these two parts in detail.

The likelihood of success was determined by military experts. They considered such factors as:

- Transferability: to the desert, to Teheran, then to the embassy
- Rounding up: getting inside the compound, creating diversion, locating the hostages
- Rescue: subduing the captors, transfer to aircraft, departure (avoiding Iranian forces)

It is not my intention here to analyze the possible details of their deliberations. In this instance the importance of the military factors and the likelihood of the mission's success were probably much more important than the reaction of our allies or the Russians. These factors do appear in the hierarchy for the problem, but one could have construed the medium likelihood of success from other sources. In fact, an analysis of the first part did produce a medium likelihood of success, but a Pentagon expert, when asked, strongly supported these findings. Thus we may assume that a medium likelihood of success was presented to the president, who then made his go/no-go decision. How he did this is what I wish to dwell upon.

The hierarchic structure of both parts of the process is shown in Figure 6-1. We find that the main factors that could have played an important role in President's Carter's mind are:

- Hostages' lives: the president's concern for the safe return of all fifty-three hostages
- Carter's political life: the president's concern about the influence of the decision and his chances for reelection
- Military costs: The president's concern about the loss of soldiers' lives in the operation
- United States prestige: the president's concern about the influence of the decision on relations with foreign states and their subsequent image of the United States

These factors differ in their impact on the president's decision. Moreover, their relative importance changes as the likelihood of success is changed. Now let us assess their priorities based on a medium likelihood of success of the rescue operation. We can carry out a pairwise comparison process by using the pairwise comparison scale (Table 5-1). Figure 6-2 shows, for example, that "hostages' lives" has strong dominance over "military costs" in the president's mind. Thus we assign the value 5 in the first row and third column position and its reciprocal value in the first column and third row position. We always compare the row factors on the left over the column factors on the top.

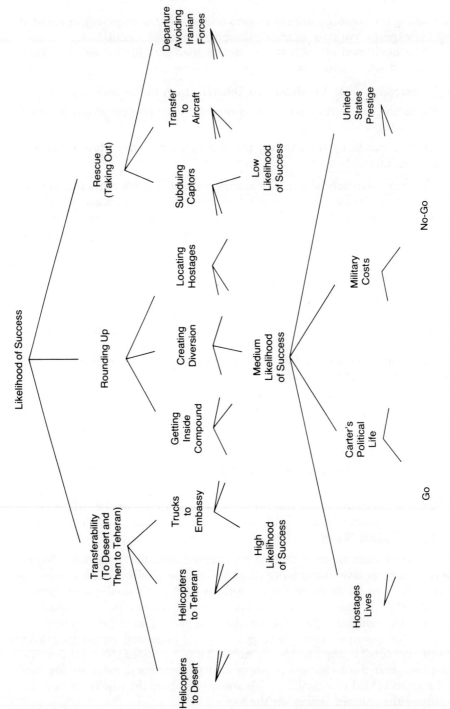

Figure 6-1   Hierarchy for the Go/No-Go Decision

	1	2	3	4	Priorities
1. Hostages' lives	1	1/3	5	1/3	0.15
2. Carter's political life	3	1	7	4	0.54
3. Military costs	1/5	1/7	1	1/6	0.05
4. U.S. prestige	3	1/4	6	1	0.26

Figure 6-2   Relative Priorities of the Factors

As can be seen from the column of priorities in Figure 6-2, the two main factors are "Carter's political life" and "United States prestige." "United States prestige" is important because the United States had to do *something* to assert its power despite the fact that there was a medium chance for success. "Carter's political life," a subjective factor, is the highest-priority factor.

Under each factor we consider this question: Which alternative (go or no-go) is more favorable considering just that factor under a medium likelihood of success? The results are shown in Figures 6-3 to 6-6.

Under "hostages' lives" the decision was evenly split. The rationale for this judgment is that there was no immediate danger to the lives of the hostages. With respect to "Carter's political life," we note that the president was strongly in favor of performing the operation at that time; a few months before the election the polls were not predicting a good chance for his reelection. A successful operation would have resulted in a strong influence on Carter's public image. Failure would be painful to him, but it

Hostages' Lives	G	N	Priorities
Go	1	1	0.5
No-go	1	1	0.5

Figure 6-3   Priority of Hostages' Lives

Carter's Political Life	G	N	Priorities
Go	1	3	0.75
No-go	1/3	1	0.25

Figure 6-4   Priority of Carter's Political Life

Military Costs	G	N	Priorities
Go	1	1/7	0.125
No-go	7	1	0.895

Figure 6-5   Priority of Military Costs

U.S. Prestige	G	N	Priorities
Go	1	4	0.8
No-go	1/4	1	0.2

Figure 6-6   Priority of U.S. Prestige

would not hurt him as much as a success would benefit him. The influences of "military costs" and "United States prestige" on the decision are apparent. Composing the factors' weights with those of the go/no-go alternatives under each factor gives these results:

Go: 69   No-go: 31

It is very easy to appear smart after the events. Yet I am convinced that if the AHP had been applied *before* the decision was made, we would have obtained similar results. Seven people established the priorities presented here. The variance in their judgments was small. It is possible to argue that if those seven people had set the priorities individually, they would have arrived at the same decision.

It is clear that "Carter's political life" dominated that decision. Sensitivity analysis shows that if the 75 percent in favor of go under that factor is changed to 38 percent, the outcome for go/no-go would have been even. I believe that 75 percent is a modest estimate. Carter may not have gone through with the decision to go if his desire to be reelected approximately matched his concern about the hostages.

To pursue the analysis further, my colleagues and I examined the outcome of the decision under a "low likelihood of success" recommendation by the experts. (Presumably this would have been interpreted less optimistically by the president. Recall that he interpreted medium success as "excellent.") Our results are shown in Table 6-1.

Table 6-1   Relative Priorities Given a Low Likelihood of Success

Factor	Priority Given Medium Likelihood of Success	Priority Given Low Likelihood of Success
Hostages' lives	0.15	0.35
Carter's political life	0.54	0.39
Military costs	0.05	0.10
U.S. prestige	0.26	0.16

In this case the "hostages' lives" become a more important issue and "Carter's political life" less important. The influence of these factors on the go/no-go decision is shown in Table 6-2.

The outcome of the decision under a "low likelihood of success" recommendation by the experts leads to the following results:

Go: 0.41   No-go: 0.59

The change from the previous result is due to a greater emphasis on the hostages' lives. Only if the hostages' lives were clearly in jeopardy in Iran would one have decided in favor of go. Moreover, "Carter's political life" would have had to be less important because a military operation with a low chance of success would have had a low chance of helping Carter.

Now let us pull together the observations we have drawn from this analysis of the Iran rescue operation. For President Carter, the subjective factor—namely, his concern with his career—accounted for 54 percent of the total. Perhaps the dominance of this subjective factor was perceived by

Table 6-2   Influence of Factors on the Go/No-Go Decision

Factor	Medium Likelihood Go	Medium Likelihood No-Go	Low Likelihood Go	Low Likelihood No-Go
Hostages' lives	0.50	0.50	0.20	0.80
Carter's political life	0.75	0.25	0.75	0.25
Military costs	0.125	0.875	0.10	0.90
U.S. prestige	0.80	0.20	0.25	0.75

Carter's aides; perhaps it accounts for Secretary of State Vance's resignation. Certainly "Carter's political life" would not have figured as importantly in Vance's analysis of the situation. He would have had to decide against the operation. Of course he may have had other political reasons of his own.

This application of the AHP illustrates its effectiveness in analyzing high-level decisions. There is a value to analysis even after a decision has been made because the method is an efficient tool for deriving a lesson from previous mistakes. In this example the results were consistent with reality. In some situations, as we have seen, media information may be sufficient to indicate what went into a decision. If used by decision makers, the process can sharpen thinking and reveal subjective factors. It can show, for example, that personal interest is weighted much higher than what is good for the business. It can also show that there is not a clear commitment to the important objectives.

DETERMINING CONSUMER PREFERENCE

The AHP is basically a simple, efficient technique for problem solving. The following step-by-step example demonstrates this simplicity; it can also serve as a model for using the process to solve other problems.

A firm wants to determine consumer preferences for three different kinds of paper towel. The attributes considered most relevant from the consumer's perspective are (1) softness, (2) absorptiveness, (3) price, (4) size, (5) design, and (6) integrity. The three kinds of paper towels, X, Y, and Z, possess all these attributes, but at different levels of intensity: high (H), medium (M), and low (L). Given the consumer's "bounded rationality"—that is, the fact that consumers do not act on perfect or complete information and are satisfied with less than the economically most rational choice—we can best distinguish among the attributes by dividing them into this small number of intensity categories. The resulting hierarchy is shown in Figure 6-7. The problem of selecting the product with the greatest overall consumer preference is solved in the following manner:

- *Step 1:* Determine consumer preference among the attributes by developing a matrix that compares attributes in pairs with respect to product desirability (Figure 6-8).
- *Step 2:* Determine consumer preference among the intensities of the attributes by developing six matrices that compare intensity levels in pairs with respect to each attribute (Figure 6-9).

Now we want to synthesize these judgments to obtain the set of overall priorities that will indicate which product consumers prefer. The remaining steps take us through this process:

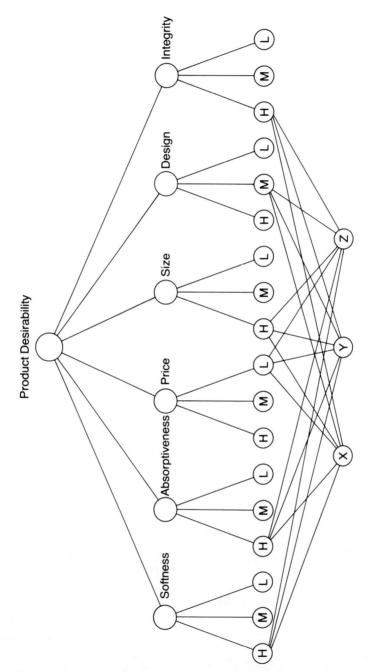

Figure 6-7 Hierarchy for Determining Consumer Preference

Attributes

Product Desirability	S	A	P	SI	D	I	Priority
S	1	1/4	1/5	1/4	5	1/6	0.0570
A	4	1	1/3	3	6	1/2	0.1679
P	5	3	1	4	7	3	0.3837
SI	4	1/3	1/4	1	5	1/5	0.1002
D	1/5	1/6	1/7	1/5	1	1/7	0.0269
I	6	2	1/3	5	7	1	0.2643

$\lambda_{max} = 6.66$; CI = 0.12.

Figure 6-8   Matrix Comparing Attributes

Softness	H	M	L	Priority
H	1	5	8	0.7257
M	1/5	1	5	0.2122
L	1/8	1/5	1	0.0621

$\lambda_{max} = 3.15$; CI = 0.07.

Absorptiveness	H	M	L	Priority
H	1	7	9	0.7608
M	1/7	1	7	0.1912
L	1/9	1/7	1	0.0480

$\lambda_{max} = 3.33$; CI = 0.16.

Price	H	M	L	Priority
H	1	1/7	1/9	0.0480
M	7	1	1/7	0.1912
L	9	7	1	0.7608

$\lambda_{max} = 3.33$; CI = 0.16.

Size	H	M	L	Priority
H	1	3	5	0.6267
M	1/3	1	4	0.2797
L	1/5	1/4	1	0.0936

$\lambda_{max} = 3.09$; CI = 0.04.

Design	H	M	L	Priority
H	1	1/5	2	0.1786
M	5	1	5	0.7089
L	1/2	1/5	1	0.1125

$\lambda_{max} = 3.05$; CI = 0.03.

Integrity	H	M	L	Priority
H	1	7	9	0.7608
M	1/7	1	7	0.1912
L	1/9	1/7	1	0.0480

$\lambda_{max} = 3.33$; CI = 0.16.

Figure 6-9   Matrices Comparing Intensity Levels

Table 6-3   Priorities of the Attributes

	(0.0570) Softness	(0.1679) Absorp.	(0.3837) Price	(0.1002) Size	(0.0269) Design	(0.2643) Integrity
H	0.7257	0.7608	0.0480	0.6267	0.1786	0.7608
M	0.2122	0.1912	0.1912	0.2797	0.7089	0.1912
L	0.0621	0.0480	0.7608	0.0936	0.1125	0.0480

- *Step 3:* Group the priorities of the intensities (H, M, L) for each of the six attributes in columns and enter the priorities of the attributes, taken from Figure 6-8, above the columns (Table 6-3). Then multiply each column by the priority of the corresponding attribute to obtain the weighted vectors of priority for the intensities (Table 6-4).
- *Step 4:* Now select from each column the element with the highest priority to obtain the vector of desired attribute intensities:

H-Soft	H-Absorp.	L-Price	H-Size	M-Design	H-Integrity
0.0413	0.1278	0.2919	0.0628	0.0190	0.2011

Then add this row and divide each entry by the total to get the normalized vector of desired attribute intensities:

H-Soft	H-Absorp.	L-Price	H-Size	M-Design	H-Integrity
0.0556	0.1717	0.3924	0.0844	0.0256	0.2703

- *Step 5:* Determine the perceived product standings by developing matrices that compare the three paper towels (X, Y, and Z) in pairs with respect to the most desired attribute intensities (Figure 6-10).
- *Step 6:* Group the priorities of the paper towels with respect to each desired attribute intensity in columns and enter the normalized priori-

Table 6-4   Vectors of Priority for the Intensities

	Softness	Absorp.	Price	Size	Design	Integrity
H	0.0413	0.1278	0.0184	0.0628	0.0048	0.2011
M	0.0121	0.0321	0.0734	0.0280	0.0190	0.0505
L	0.0035	0.0081	0.2919	0.0094	0.0030	0.0127

H-Soft	X	Y	Z	Priority
X	1	5	7	0.7147
Y	1/5	1	5	0.2185
Z	1/7	1/5	1	0.0668

λ_{max} = 3.18; CI = 0.09.

L-Price	X	Y	Z	Priority
X	1	1/4	1/7	0.0727
Y	4	1	1/5	0.2050
Z	7	5	1	0.7223

λ_{max} = 3.12; CI = 0.06.

M-Design	X	Y	Z	Priority
X	1	2	1	0.4067
Y	1/2	1	3	0.3695
Z	1	1/3	1	0.2238

λ_{max} = 3.37; CI = 0.18.

H-Absorp.	X	Y	Z	Priority
X	1	2	7	0.5659
Y	1/2	1	8	0.3727
Z	1/7	1/8	1	0.0614

λ_{max} = 3.08; CI = 0.04.

H-Size	X	Y	Z	Priority
X	1	2	1	0.4126
Y	1/2	1	1	0.2599
Z	1	1	1	0.3275

λ_{max} = 3.05; CI = 0.03.

H-Integrity	X	Y	Z	Priority
X	1	4	6	0.6817
Y	1/4	1	4	0.2363
Z	1/6	1/4	1	0.0819

λ_{max} = 3.11; CI = 0.05.

Figure 6-10   Matrices Comparing the Three Paper Towels for Desired Attribute Intensities

Table 6-5   Overall Product Attribute Perception

	(0.0556) H-Soft	(0.1717) H-Absorp.	(0.3924) L-Price	(0.0844) H-Size	(0.0256) M-Design	(0.2703) H-Integrity
X	0.7147	0.5659	0.0727	0.4126	0.4067	0.6817
Y	0.2185	0.3727	0.2050	0.2599	0.3695	0.2363
Z	0.0668	0.0614	0.7223	0.3275	0.2238	0.0819

Table 6-6   Weighted Overall Product Attribute Perception

	H-Soft	H-Absorp.	L-Price	H-Size	M-Design	H-Integrity
X	0.0397	0.0972	0.0285	0.0348	0.0104	0.1842
Y	0.0121	0.0640	0.0804	0.0219	0.0095	0.0639
Z	0.0037	0.0105	0.2834	0.0277	0.0057	0.0221

ties above the columns (Table 6-5). Then multiply each column by the normalized priority of the corresponding attribute intensity to obtain the weighted vectors of priority for the desired attribute intensities for each paper towel (Table 6-6).

- *Step 7:* Add each of the three rows to obtain the overall priorities of the three paper towels. This synthesis yields the following priorities:

$$X = 0.3949 \qquad Y = 0.2519 \qquad Z = 0.3532$$

From these results we would select product X as most desirable from the customer's perspective.

Even though low price was the desired attribute intensity with the highest priority, product X, whose priority was very low with respect to low price, was the final choice. The reason for this choice is clear: X dominated Y and Z on all other desired attribute intensities. Thus the firm decided to market a superior but high-priced product, a decision that is not inconsistent with real-world situations.

ESTIMATING THE ECONOMY'S IMPACT ON SALES

The AHP can be used for certain special applications as well as for obtaining sets of priorities in decision problems. In the following example,

Future Sales	EC	R	I	Priority
Energy crisis	1	7	1	0.4667
Recession	1/7	1	1/7	0.0666
Inflation	1	7	1	0.4667

$\lambda_{max} = 3.0$; CI = 0.00.

Figure 6-11   Matrix for Comparing Criteria with Respect to Future Sales

Energy Crisis	0–5	5–10	10–15	15–20	Priority
0–5	1	1/5	1/7	1/5	0.0518
5–10	5	1	1/3	1/4	0.1451
10–15	7	3	1	1/3	0.2904
15–20	5	4	3	1	0.5127

$\lambda_{max} = 4.337$; CI = 0.11.

Recession	0–5	5–10	10–15	15–20	Priority
0–5	1	2	5	7	0.5232
5–10	1/2	1	3	5	0.2976
10–15	1/5	1/3	1	3	0.1222
15–20	1/7	1/5	1/3	1	0.0570

$\lambda_{max} = 4.069$; CI = 0.02.

Inflation	0–5	5–10	10–15	15–20	Priority
0–5	1	2	5	7	0.5232
5–10	1/2	1	3	5	0.2976
10–15	1/5	1/3	1	3	0.1222
15–20	1/7	1/5	1/3	1	0.0570

$\lambda_{max} = 4.069$; CI = 0.02.

Figure 6-12   Matrix for Comparing Sales with Respect to Criteria

the process is extended to estimate the percentage of a company's sales affected by the energy crisis, recession, and inflation.

First the sales of the company—a manufacturer of heavy equipment (oil drills and construction machines)—are divided into intervals: 0–5 percent, 5–10 percent, 10–15 percent, and 15–20 percent. Then a matrix is developed to compare the criteria (energy crisis, recession, inflation) in pairs with respect to future sales (Figure 6-11). Next matrices are developed to compare sales with respect to the criteria (Figure 6-12). The overall priorities of the sales percentage intervals are

$$0.3033 \qquad 0.2264 \qquad 0.2007 \qquad 0.2697$$

To get the expected value of sales affected by the energy crisis, recession, and inflation, multiply the midpoint of each interval by the priority weight of that interval. For example, the midpoint of 0–5 percent is 2.5 and so on. Thus

$$(2.5 \times 0.3033) + (7.5 \times 0.2264) + (12.5 \times 0.2007) + (17.5 \times 0.2697)$$
$$= 9.685\%$$

As this example shows, the analytic hierarchy process can be used to estimate numbers—in this case percentages.

SELECTING A PORTFOLIO

This application is more complex than the preceding one. Here we use the AHP to select a portfolio. Our hierarchical model consists of three separate hierarchies: one based on extrinsic factors, one based on intrinsic factors, and a third based on the investor's objectives. The firms being considered are ranked (weighted) relative to the criteria in each hierarchy. The weights are then combined to get an overall preference list of firms. Figure 6-13 gives an overall view of the model we will use.

The various factors and objectives that influence the selection of firms for the portfolio include:

- *Extrinsic Factors (A):* These are the outside factors or environmental characteristics that affect an industry's (or firm's) performance. The firm, however, has no direct influence on them. These factors are economic, political, social, and technical. By incorporating the analysis of the extrinsic variables we can determine the sensitivity of a firm to changes in these factors.

- *Intrinsic Factors (B):* These are the internal factors or operational characteristics of the firm. They may be considered as a measure of the way the firm is making its decisions or, in general, a measure of the firm's capac-

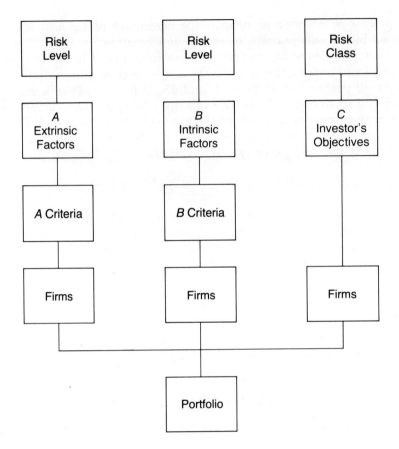

Figure 6-13   Hierarchical Model for Selecting a Portfolio

ity to compete successfully. These factors are profitability, size, technology, and philosophy.

- *Investor's Objectives* (C): These are the values that define the actions the investor undertakes in the business world. We are aware, of course, of the great variety of objectives an investor may have, but to simplify the model we consider four mutually exclusive objectives: profitability, security, excitement, and control.

Since we are dealing with a model that is based on future conditions, we must consider risk—the uncertainty of future events. The model incorporates the uncertainty of the general business environment, the firm's behavior (high, medium, low risk), and the risk class of the investor (high, medium, low).

As our first step we look at the hierarchy of extrinsic factors. At the first level we have the primary extrinsic factors that affect a firm's behavior. At the second level we have the criteria that influence each of the primary factors:

AI: Primary Extrinsic Factors   *AII: Criteria*

Economic	Employment conditions
	Elasticity of demand
	Elasticity of supply
	International economy
	Interest rates
Political	Government regulations
	International exposure
	Employment conditions
Social	Family disintegration
	Age distribution
	Educational achievement
	Employment conditions
Technological	State of technology
	Government involvement

The extrinsic factors are compared pairwise for a high-risk environment, a medium-risk environment, and a low-risk environment (Figure 6-14). In each case we base the comparisons on the questions: Which factor has more impact on a firm's behavior and by how much? We can see that in a high-risk environment the group constructing the matrix believed the technology would have a generally strong influence on a firm's behavior compared to the other factors.

We then compute the priorities for each of the factors for each risk level (Table 6-7). These priorities point out that in a high-risk environment, future technological factors have the greatest impact on a firm's behavior. In a medium-risk environment both the economic and technological factors are most influential; in a low-risk environment the social factors are

Firm	High Risk				Medium Risk				Low Risk			
	E	P	S	T	E	P	S	T	E	P	S	T
Economic	1	3	4	1/3	1	5	7	1	1	5	1/3	4
Political	1/3	1	3	1/5	1/5	1	3	1/5	1/5	1	1/5	2
Social	1/4	1/3	1	1/8	1/7	1/3	1	1/6	3	5	1	5
Technological	3	5	8	1	1	5	6	1	1/4	1/2	1/2	1

Figure 6-14   Pairwise Comparison of Extrinsic Factors

Table 6-7   Priorities for Each Risk Level

Risk	Economic	Political	Social	Technological
High	0.25	0.12	0.06	0.57
Medium	0.43	0.11	0.05	0.41
Low	0.30	0.10	0.54	0.07

	S	G
State of technology	1	4
Government involvement	1/4	1

Figure 6-15   Comparison Matrix for Technology

most important. Economic factors have appreciable impact at all three levels whereas the impact of political actions is rather low.

We could carry through our analysis under each of the three risk levels, but for illustrative purposes we will use the average weight for each factor. A weighted average could be used if we wished to favor one type of future over the other. Averaging, we obtain these weights:

Economic	Political	Social	Technological
0.32	0.11	0.22	0.36

Now we compare the criteria for each factor to see their order of importance. In each pairwise comparison we ask: Which criterion has more impact on the factor and by how much?

In the case of technology and its two criteria, we have the comparison matrix shown in Figure 6-15, which indicates that the state of technology has somewhat more impact on technology in general than does the government's involvement in it. This matrix and three others yield the following sets of weights for the various criteria:

Economic (0.32):

Employment Conditions	Elasticity of Demand	Elasticity of Supply
0.16	0.45	0.07

International Economy	Interest Rates
0.05	0.27

	Government Regulations	International Exposure	Employment Conditions
Political (0.10):	0.24	0.06	0.70

	Family Disintegration	Age Distribution
Social (0.22):	0.30	0.11
	Educational Achievement	Employment Conditions
	0.11	0.48

	State of Technology	Government Involvement
Technological (0.36):	0.80	0.20

To get the final weights for a criterion, we must multiply the criterion weights just found by the weight of the factor associated with that criterion:

	Employment Conditions	Elasticity of Demand	Elasticity of Supply
Economic:	**0.05**	**0.14**	0.02
	International Economy	Interest Rates	
	0.02	**0.09**	

	Government Regulations	International Exposure	Employment Conditions
Political:	0.02	0.01	**0.07**

	Family Disintegration	Age Distribution
Social:	**0.07**	0.02
	Educational Achievement	Employment Conditions
	0.02	**0.11**

	State of Technology	Government Involvement
Technological:	**0.29**	**0.07**

The weights printed in boldface are the largest ones. We will shorten our list to include only these. In order to have the weights total 1, we divide each weight by the total of all the weights in the shortened list. We have our list of extrinsic criteria:

State of Technology	Employment Conditions	Elasticity of Demand
0.33	0.26	0.16

Interest Rates	Family Disintegration	Government Involvement in Technology
0.10	0.08	0.08

The firms being considered (eight in this illustration) are now prioritized relative to each of the six extrinsic criteria. This process is the same pairwise comparison and weighting procedure we have been applying throughout. When comparing the firms pairwise relative to the state of technology, for example, we ask: Which firm will respond more favorably to the technological environment of the future? The matrix for this criterion is shown in Figure 6-16.

Technology	T	IR	IC	AC	R	DG	B	C
Tappan	1	1/3	1/5	4	1/5	1/7	6	5
Ing. Rand	3	1	1/4	4	1/4	1/6	7	6
I.C. Industries	5	4	1	5	1/2	1/4	6	5
Allied Ch.	1/4	1/4	1/5	1	1/6	1/7	4	3
Rockwell	5	4	2	6	1	1/3	7	6
Data General	7	6	4	7	3	1	9	7
Butler	1/6	1/7	1/6	1/4	1/7	1/9	1	1/3
Chemetron	1/5	1/6	1/5	1/3	1/6	1/7	3	1

Figure 6-16   Matrix for Pairwise Comparison of Firms Relative to State of Technology

Table 6-8 summarizes the weights that the eight firms received for each criterion. A glance at the table shows that in a technological environment Data General, Rockwell, and I.C. Industries are heavily favored, as one might expect. Tappan and Rockwell are beneficiaries if employment conditions are good—Tappan's consumer market is in appliances (80 percent of sales) and Rockwell's is in home and auto products (35 percent of sales).

To get an overall prioritized list of firms vis-à-vis the extrinsic factors, we multiply the weights of the firms for a given criterion by the weight of that criterion (shown in parentheses in Table 6-8). Then we add up these new weights for each firm:

Tappan	Ing. Rand	I.C. Industries	Allied Ch.		
0.16	0.07	0.13	0.03		
	Rockwell	Data General	Butler	Chemetron	
	0.20	0.21	0.07	0.13	

For purposes of illustration we will use only the four highest ones with their weights adjusted as we did when shortening the list of criteria. Here is the prioritized list of firms relative to the extrinsic criteria:

Rockwell	Tappan	Data General	I.C. Industries
0.29	0.23	0.30	0.19

Now we turn to the intrinsic factors and go through the same process: Construct a two-level hierarchy of factors and criteria; obtain weights for the factors, then for the criteria relative to the corresponding factor, and then an overall list of weighted criteria; and, finally, prepare a prioritized list of firms. The intrinsic factors hierarchy consists of:

BI: Primary Intrinsic Factors	BII: Criteria
Profitability	Management Quality
	Market share
	Earnings
	Innovativeness
	Diversity
	Payout ratio
Size	Sales
	Labor force
	Assets
	Market structure

Table 6-8 Weights of Firms for Extrinsic Criteria

Firm	(0.33) State of Technology	(0.26) Employment Conditions	(0.16) Elasticity of Demand	(0.10) Interest Rates	(0.08) Family Disintegration	(0.07) Government Involvement
Tappan	0.07	0.36	0.03	0.03	0.45	0.03
Ing. Rand	0.10	0.05	0.07	0.07	0.02	0.10
I.C. Industries	0.17	0.14	0.05	0.05	0.12	0.18
Allied Ch.	0.03	0.03	0.03	0.02	0.02	0.03
Rockwell	0.21	0.23	0.12	0.12	0.21	0.38
Data General	0.38	0.02	0.23	0.23	0.10	0.20
Butler	0.02	0.06	0.17	0.17	0.06	0.02
Chemetron	0.04	0.11	0.31	0.30	0.02	0.06

BI: Primary Intrinsic Factors	BII: Criteria
Technological control	R&D quality
	Age distribution of product
	Energy dependence
	Pollution effects
Business philosophy	Social responsibility
	Participatory decision making

After comparing the four primary factors pairwise in each of the three levels of risk and taking the average of the resulting three weights, we obtain the weighted list of factors:

Profitability	Size	Technological Control	Business Philosophy
0.51	0.17	0.26	0.06

Thus profitability and technological control exert about 76 percent of the total influence on a firm's behavior when we consider only the intrinsic factors. Business philosophy does not seem to have much impact.

After we get the weights of the criteria for each of the factors and multiply them, we obtain a list of sixteen factors. Using the four whose combined weight is about 60 percent of the total, we obtain an abbreviated list of weighted intrinsic criteria:

Innovativeness	Management Quality	R&D Quality	Sales
0.46	0.21	0.17	0.16

The four firms in the extrinsic factors list are now compared pairwise relative to each of the intrinsic criteria. The results are summarized in Table 6-9.

Table 6-9   Weights of Firms for Intrinsic Criteria

Firm	(0.46) Innovativeness	(0.21) Management Quality	(0.17) R&D Quality	(0.16) Sales*
Rockwell	0.34	0.32	0.12	0.25
Tappan	0.27	0.03	0.04	0.05
Data General	0.30	0.55	0.74	0.52
I.C. Industries	0.09	0.10	0.10	0.18

* Sales/assets ratios were used to compare the firms.

The final list of weighted firms relative to the intrinsic criteria (after multiplying and adding) is

Rockwell	Tappan	Data General	I.C. Industries
0.29	0.13	0.47	0.11

The investor's objectives with weights computed under an average risk class are

Profit	Control	Security	Excitement
0.34	0.28	0.25	0.13

Weights of the firms for the investor's objectives are given in Table 6-10. The final list of weighted firms relative to the investor's objectives is

Rockwell	Tappan	Data General	I.C. Industries
0.17	0.05	0.58	0.20

To obtain the final priority of the firms (the portfolio), we weight each criterion (extrinsic, intrinsic, objectives) and perform the multiplication and addition. Table 6-11 shows the final weights for three weighting schemes for the criteria. (The scheme 2 : 1 : 1 means weight of 2/4, 1/4, 1/4, and so forth.) We note that Data General and Rockwell International rank first and second respectively in all the weighting schemes. Moreover, I.C. Industries and Tappan maintain the same relative standing unless the investor's objectives are emphasized. A certain amount of stability is shown here.

What if we want to use these weights for a guideline for allocating funds among the stocks? If we use the criteria weighting scheme (2 : 1 : 1) where the extrinsic criteria are deemed twice as important as each of the

Table 6-10   Weights of Firms for Investor's Objectives

Firm	(0.34) Profit	(0.28) Control	(0.25) Security	(0.13) Excitement
Rockwell	0.27	0.06	0.04	0.38
Tappan	0.03	0.04	0.13	0.03
Data General	0.63	0.75	0.29	0.55
I.C. Industries	0.07	0.15	0.54	0.04

Table 6-11 Final Weights of Firms

Firm	Weights Relative to Extrinsic-Intrinsic Criteria		Investor's Objective	1:1:1	1:1:2	2:1:1	1:2:2
Rockwell	0.29	0.29	0.17	0.25	0.23	0.26	0.26
Tappan	0.29	0.13	0.05	0.16	0.13	0.19	0.15
Data General	0.27	0.47	0.58	0.44	0.47	0.40	0.45
I.C. Industries	0.15	0.11	0.20	0.15	0.17	0.15	0.14

other two, we will invest about 40 percent in Data General, about 26 percent in Rockwell International, about 19 percent in Tappan, and 15 percent in I.C. Industries.

HOW VALID IS THE PROCESS?

The validity of the AHP as a decision-making tool has been confirmed by comparing the priorities derived from the process with those achieved independently by decision makers. For example, the matrix of pairwise comparisons in Figure 6-17 was developed during a discussion with top planners of a large business corporation. They were asked how the chairman of the board viewed the various sectors of the corporation's activity. The relative importance of the sectors in terms of the corporation's allocation of effort was judged and priorities were computed. At the end of this short exercise, two corporate planners left the room and returned with a book containing data on the amount of capital actually invested in each activity. This amount is shown in the last column of Figure 6-17. Clearly the results obtained through the AHP closely approximated those achieved by traditional methods.

	A	B	C	D	E	Priority	Actual Investment
Business A	1	7	6	4	2	0.45	0.45
Business B	1/7	1	1/2	1/3	1/5	0.05	0.04
Business C	1/6	2	1	1/3	1/4	0.07	0.105
Business D	1/4	3	3	1	1/3	0.14	0.145
Business E	1/2	5	4	3	1	0.28	0.25

Figure 6-17   Matrix of Pairwise Comparisons

PERSPECTIVE

The first example in this chapter—the decision to rescue the hostages in Iran—shows how the AHP can be used to put forth a certain point of view and compare the outcome with what is already known. The purpose may be simply to make hypotheses. This application also shows that if a decision maker's priorities are significantly different from those expected, he or she may have important criteria in mind not considered by others.

The second example—determining consumer preference—gives a neat layout dealing with the marketability of a product. Moreover, it clearly shows the usefulness of the AHP to make tradeoffs. With a little higher price, one can make a more desirable product.

The third example—estimating the economy's impact on sales—shows how the AHP can be used to estimate actual numbers (in this case expressed as percentages). Subjective priorities are converted to directly understood numbers.

The fourth example—selecting a stock portfolio—deals with prediction as a result of understanding a problem, its important criteria, their relations, and their priorities. If the understanding is good, prediction can range from good to excellent. Such an approach was used to predict the outcome of the World Chess Championship match of 1978; predictions of the number of games to be played and the number of games won by both players were excellent. The fourth application is being generalized to the entire stock market, but considerable knowledge, understanding, and testing are needed before one can expect to have a representative structure and workable priorities.

7

Planning

This chapter deals with the following questions:

- What are the basic approaches to planning?

- Why is forward-backward planning more effective than forward planning?

- How do hierarchies relate to the problem of planning?

- What is the best way to construct a scenario?

- What are the main advantages of using scenarios to forecast the future?

- How do we test the effectiveness of new policies that appear promising but must be tried out for survival among deeply entrenched ones? Do they help steer the projected future toward the desired future?

CHARTING THE FUTURE

The logic of the AHP acknowledges the important role of experience and intuition in decision making. By now it should be clear that we can trust our intuitive, informed judgments in making decisions. We can also depend on such judgments to chart the future. This chapter shows how to use the AHP to steer a system from a likely outcome to a desired outcome. The procedures we use to project likely futures and plan desirable ones can also be used to produce stable outcomes in conflict situations. The next chapter describes practical applications of the AHP to problems of planning. These applications range from projecting oil prices in 1985 to coping with traffic congestion in the Philippines.

APPROACHES TO PLANNING

Planning is a purposeful, dynamic activity concerned with achieving a desired goal. After observing how a system functions and evolves—and perhaps studying the literature or discussing the system with others—a leader may want to identify a set of goals for the system and to modify the system's evolution to attain these goals. Then the leader would note the result and perhaps modify the goals, modify the evolution of the system toward them, and repeat the process. In this way the system is directed toward a desirable future.

The usual approach to planning is to project forward to what seems feasible or likely. The projected future is determined by the existing state of the system and by the persons or institutions—the "actors"—that pursue certain objectives and implement certain policies to achieve their individual objectives. This descriptive process of estimating the likely future is called *forward planning*.

But sometimes people concentrate on proposing a desired, rather than likely, future and work backward to determine the means to bring about such a future. The desired outcome is achieved by applying policies to influence the actors to remove obstacles in the way of this outcome. This normative, or prescriptive, process is called *backward planning*.

For greater effectiveness in planning, the two processes can be combined. *Forward-backward planning* works in the following way. First the likely future is projected through forward planning. Then a feasible and desired future is hypothesized, and the necessary policies for its attainment are found through backward planning. These policies are added to the set of existing policies to test their effect on a second projection of a likely future—a step that constitutes the second forward planning process. Then a new feasible and desired future is hypothesized, and the necessary policies for its attainment are found in the second backward planning process. Repetition is continued to obtain greater convergence, if possible, of the likely and the desired futures. This forward-backward planning is carried out within two limits. One is fixed in the present by the actors and the available resources; the other is fixed in the future by the desired objectives.

The forward and backward processes need not be symmetric. Take, for example, space travel. Launching a manned craft and returning it to its starting point can be considered a forward-backward problem. The starting point is fixed, and the return point from the orbit is selected so that the vehicle lands near the starting point. However, different considerations are involved. In the forward process, high velocity and the effect of gravity are the critical factors. It is important to know how much gravitational force is exerted on the body. In the backward process, air resistance and the need for parachutes or other deceleration devices, heat, and the tolerance of the nose cone material are the important factors. These factors are present in the launching process, but they are not the critical ones. Both sets of factors must be taken into consideration to solve the problem.

The levels that might be considered in the hierarchies for each of the two planning processes will depend on the group using them. A planner working with a corporate group might use the following levels from top to bottom in a forward-planning hierarchy: uncontrollable environmental constraints, risk scenarios, controllable systemic constraints, overall objectives of the system, stakeholders, stakeholders' objectives (separate for each one), stakeholders' policies (separate for each one), exploratory scenarios (outcomes), and composite or logical scenario (outcome). In the backward-planning hierarchy, the levels from top to bottom might be feasibility and risk discounting, behavior of risk factors, risk scenarios, anticipatory corporate scenarios, problems and opportunities, actors, actor objectives, and corporate policies to influence actors.

In our work with corporations we begin by identifying the appropriate levels of the backward hierarchy that capture the problem at hand. We then fill in the elements of those levels. This step is followed by a process of prioritization to identify the most promising policies a corporation can pursue to reach its goals. These policies must be tested or prioritized in the present milieu of the corporation, however, to see if they are effective and can survive competition with existing policies. To do this we develop the relevant levels of the forward process hierarchy by describing the present situation and then adding the high-priority policies identified in the backward process. We note the priorities of the projected scenarios and their state variables before and after introducing the new policies in the forward process to see if these policies make any difference in shifting the projected future toward the desired future dealt with in the backward process. If they do not, we repeat the backward process by modifying our desired future and identifying new policies to achieve it and again taking these policies to the projected future to test their effectiveness. This process can be repeated. It is a powerful and economical way of trying out ideas.

The forward-backward planning process just described is useful in dealing with systems over which one has control. In other cases, planning may simply involve exploration of the forward or the backward process. No matter which process is used, each entails the construction of scenarios that portray the present and future states of the system in question.

SCENARIOS

For effective planning, scenarios must include an adequate account of the interaction of the system with relevant environmental, social, political, technological, and economic factors. One must consider projections of all these factors to produce a convincing scenario that describes the system's state under various assumptions. In constructing scenarios, one must also guard against free use of undisciplined imagination to avoid falling into a science-fiction type of forecasting.

Two general kinds of scenario are used in planning and conflict resolution: exploratory and anticipatory. *Exploratory scenarios* start from the present and work forward to project alternative outcomes of present trends. To construct an exploratory scenario, we identify the most important components of the system under study and examine events that are logically necessary for a likely future to evolve. The possible alternative outcomes are limited by the existing variety of trends and by a careful examination of the hypotheses of the system's evolution from the present. Planners who construct exploratory scenarios do not rely on theory or methodology. Although they take the conclusions of their scenarios with a grain of salt, they argue that, as far as making errors in predicting the future goes, they are in good company with practitioners of all other methods.

Anticipatory scenarios portray feasible and desirable futures. Unlike exploratory scenarios, they start from the future and work backward to the present to discover what alternatives and actions are necessary to attain these futures. *Normative* anticipatory scenarios determine at the start a set of given objectives and define paths for their realization. *Contrast* anticipatory scenarios sketch feasible and desired futures; each contrast scenario sharply emphasizes a particular range of assumptions. The desired future is derived as a combination of contrast scenarios.

Thus normative and contrast scenarios are synthesized into a *composite* scenario, which retains the properties of each scenario with an appropriate mix or emphasis. Because the future is shaped by a variety of forces or interests, each seeking fulfillment of its particular objectives, the synthesis of a wide-ranging set of scenarios into a composite scenario must include (1) the actors who influence the future, (2) their objectives, and (3) the policies they will pursue in each scenario to attain their objectives. To ensure some success in achieving the desired future, the priority of the actors is measured according to their importance.

The scenario approach to planning and conflict resolution is a unique aid in forecasting the future. Scenario construction is integrated into the AHP in both the process of structuring the hierarchy and the process of establishing priorities and synthesizing. The environment of the problem is first searched for relevant factors. Then the scenarios, actors, objectives, and policies are arranged hierarchically and prioritized. The conclusions of the analysis should lend themselves to reasonable interpretation. The high-priority actions that are to be implemented can be divided into classes according to urgency; the most urgent projects can be implemented first. Later, the planning process may be revised or repeated.

PERSPECTIVE

The AHP provides a useful vehicle for structuring hierarchies for both projected or descriptive and idealized or normative planning. In the normative case one works backward from desired scenarios to feasible policies and, through prioritization, identifies the ones that are likely to lead to the desired future. In the descriptive case one is able to project forward the future that is a logical consequence of existing policies. The high-priority policies of the backward process are then added to the existing ones and a second projection is made to see if the logical future is drawn closer to the desired future. This procedure provides a concrete test of the effectiveness of these hypothetical policies if they were to be put into practice. Repetition of the process makes systematic use of both experience and imagination and offers a procedure for testing their effectiveness to steer toward a desired goal. Moreover, the results of a planning exercise enable one to predict the actual values of the outcome variables such as dollar amount of profit, expected demand, percent increase, and similar important measures.

The next chapter presents examples that illustrate the three planning processes—forward, backward, and forward-backward—and the appropriate kinds of scenarios for each. All the examples are taken from actual applications of the analytic hierarchy process.

KEY CONCEPTS

☐ *Forward planning* is the process of projecting a likely future.

☐ *Backward planning* is the process of identifying a desired future and then working out the details to bring it about.

☐ *Forward-backward planning* is the process of combining backward planning and forward planning by projecting a likely future, identifying a desired future, determining the policies needed for attaining the desired future, and testing their effectiveness to reach the desired future.

☐ A unique aid in forecasting the future is the scenario, which can be integrated into the process of structuring hierarchies and the process of weighing priorities.

8

Practical Examples of Planning

This chapter deals with the following questions:

- How can we apply the concept of forward planning to the future of education in the United States?

- How can we apply the concept of forward planning to the problem of projecting oil prices in 1985?

- How can we apply the concept of backward planning to the development of a transport system in the Sudan?

- How can we apply the concept of forward-backward planning to the future of the steel industry?

- How can we apply the concept of forward-backward planning to the problem of traffic congestion?

FIVE GLIMPSES INTO THE FUTURE

There are times when individuals or corporations have no way of affecting their own future because it is regulated by a larger institution or by factors beyond their control. What they would like to know is how well they are likely to make out and whether a radical change of job, method of production, or markets may be indicated. The way to find out is to attempt a projection of the future by using the best informed judgments available to synthesize one's expectation of a likely outcome. The first example presents just such a projection. The participants in this process were educators concerned about their careers in the educational system. The analysis shows that the future does not warrant undue worry about job security. Their response to the outcome was positive and they tended to accept the process as a means of dealing with a problem.

The second example shows how to convert priorities to dollar values in projecting the energy future and predicting the price of a barrel of oil as a result of that future. This application has received considerable attention by the oil industry. The third example illustrates how one can allocate resources to a large number of contemplated projects to meet desired futures. The fourth example combines the forward and the backward processes in search of effective policies to improve the future of the U.S. steel industry. The fifth and final example is a detailed application that uses both processes to analyze the effectiveness of strategies to deal with traffic problems in Manila.

FORWARD PLANNING: THE FUTURE OF HIGHER EDUCATION

This example is based on an experiment conducted by twenty-eight college-level teachers, most of them from the mathematical sciences. The problem was to construct seven weighted exploratory scenarios and a composite scenario that would describe the future of higher education in the United States from 1985 to 2000.

Constructing the Hierarchy

Figure 8-1 presents the hierarchic structure of the factors, the actors, and the motivating objectives that the group believed would affect the form of higher education between 1985 and 2000. No strict definitions of the various terms will be given, although during the development of the hierarchy (which took approximately nine hours) comments were made on the intended meanings. Seven scenarios were offered:

- PROJ: 1985 projection of the status quo (slight perturbation of present)
- VOTEC: Vocational-technical oriented (skill orientation)

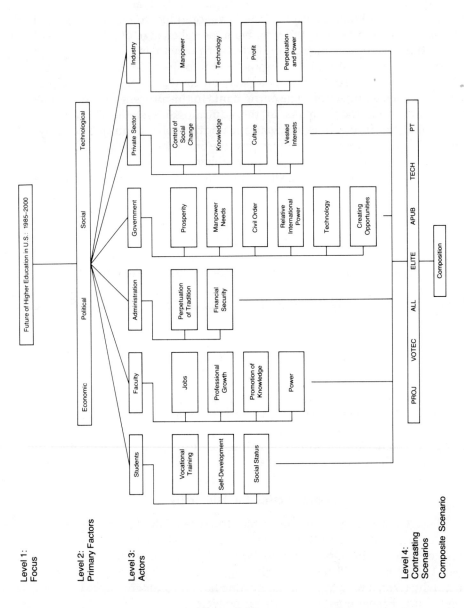

Figure 8-1   Hierarchy of Influences on Higher Education

- ALL: Education for all (subsidized education)
- ELITE: Elitism (education for those with money or exceptional talent)
- APUB: All public (government owned)
- TECH: Technology based (little use of classroom; use of media and computers)
- PT: Part-time teaching (no research orientation)

Setting Priorities and Synthesizing

The scenario characteristics that were considered and measured to prioritize the various scenarios are given in Table 8-1. The measurements are whole numbers between −5 and 5 (changed later to −8 to 8) to correspond to the 1–9 pairwise comparison scale. These measurements were arrived at by consensus.

Zero represents the status quo in the group's opinion. Positive numbers represent the various degrees of increase over the present. Negative numbers represent various degrees of decrease. For example, under "institution—governance" we see a 5 for scenario 6. This means that the group thought there would be a large measure of administrative control (relative to the state of things at present) in a technology-based higher education system in 1985 and after. On the other hand, if scenario 3 (education for all) were to prevail, the value of a degree ("education—value of a degree") would diminish considerably (−2) compared to its value today. The scenario weights and the composite weights should be ignored for the moment but are to be filled in during the course of the discussion.

We first developed a matrix of pairwise comparisons of the factors' relative influence on higher education (Figure 8-2). Which factor has the greater impact on higher education?

The next step was to find the importance of the actors relative to their impact on the factors that affect higher education. This was done by multiply-

Higher Education	E	P	S	T	Priority Vector
Economic	1	4	3	5	0.549
Political	1/4	1	1/3	1	0.106
Social	1/3	3	1	2	0.236
Technological	1/5	1	1/2	1	0.109

CI = 0.02

Figure 8-2 Pairwise Comparison of Factors

Table 8-1   Seven Scenarios and the Measurement of Their Characteristics

Characteristics	(0.096) 1 PROJ	(0.259) 2 VOTEC	(0.191) 3 ALL	(0.174) 4 ELITE	(0.122) 5 APUB	(0.068) 6 TECH	(0.081) 7 PT	Composite Weight
Students								
1. Number	−2	+2	+4	−3	−1	+2	−2	0.42
2. Type (IQ)	−1	−2	−3	+3	−1	−2	−1	1.0
3. Functions	+1	−1	0	+1	0	−2	+2	0.03
4. Jobs	+1	+4	−3	+4	+1	−2	+1	1.32
Faculty								
1. Number	−2	+2	+4	−3	−1	−5	−4	−0.22
2. Type (Ph.D.)	+1	0	−2	+3	+1	+2	−3	0.25
3. Function (role on campus)	−2	−3	−2	+1	−2	−5	−5	−2.12
4. Job security	−2	+1	+2	−3	−1	−4	−4	−0.79
5. Academic freedom	0	−2	0	+2	−1	−4	−5	−0.97
Institution								
1. Number	−1	+2	+2	−3	−1	−4	−1	−0.19
2. Type (academic/ nonacademic)	−1	−4	−3	+3	−1	−3	−3	−1.75

3. Governance	+2	+4	+1	-2	+2	5	5	2.06
4. Efficiency	+2	+3	-2	+4	-1	-1	0	1.09
5. Accessibility	0	+2	+5	-3	+2	+4	+1	1.55
6. Culture–entertainment	0	-2	+3	+3	+1	-3	-1	0.41
7. Available funds and other resources	-1	+2	+2	-2	0	-1	-3	0.64
Education								
1. Curriculum (lifelong learning)	1	-2	+2	+3	+1	+0	-1	0.50
2. Length of study	0	-3	+2	0	+1	+2	0	-0.14
3. Value of a degree	-1	0	-2	+4	-1	-2	-2	-0.20
4. Cost per student	+3	+3	+3	+4	+2	-1	-1	2.43
5. Research by faculty	+1	-1	-1	+3	+1	-3	-4	0.24

Scale: -5 ↔ +5.

ing the matrix of weights of the actors with respect to each factor in level 2 on the right by the weights obtained for level 2:

	E	P	S	T
Students	0.04	0.04	0.10	0.02
Faculty	0.02	0.04	0.07	0.10
Administration	0.06	0.03	0.04	0.03
Government	0.47	0.49	0.41	0.23
Private sector	0.12	0.12	0.12	0.16
Industry	0.28	0.27	0.26	0.44

$$\begin{bmatrix} 0.55 \\ 0.11 \\ 0.24 \\ 0.21 \end{bmatrix} \begin{matrix} E \\ P \\ S \\ T \end{matrix} = \begin{bmatrix} 0.05 \\ 0.05 \\ 0.05 \\ 0.46 \\ 0.14 \\ 0.34 \end{bmatrix} \begin{matrix} S \\ F \\ A \\ G \\ P \\ I \end{matrix}$$

Since government and industry account for 80 percent (0.46 + 0.34) of the impact on the four primary factors that affect higher education, it was decided to use only these two actors to obtain the weights (priorities) for the scenarios. Should one decide to use more actors, the computations follow the same procedure shown below, but the amount of work is increased.

Now we want to find the important objectives of the two actors, government and industry. To do this, we multiply the weights for objectives by the respective actor weight just calculated:

For government:

$$0.46 \begin{bmatrix} 0.20 \\ 0.52 \\ 0.09 \\ 0.11 \\ 0.05 \\ 0.03 \end{bmatrix} = \begin{bmatrix} 0.09 \\ 0.24 \\ 0.04 \\ 0.05 \\ 0.01 \\ 0.01 \end{bmatrix} \begin{matrix} \textbf{Prosperity} \\ \textbf{Civil order} \\ \text{Manpower} \\ \text{Relative international power} \\ \text{Technology} \\ \text{Creating opportunities} \end{matrix}$$

For industry:

$$0.34 \begin{bmatrix} 0.04 \\ 0.08 \\ 0.33 \\ 0.55 \end{bmatrix} = \begin{bmatrix} 0.01 \\ 0.03 \\ 0.11 \\ 0.19 \end{bmatrix} \begin{matrix} \text{Manpower} \\ \text{Technology} \\ \textbf{Profit} \\ \textbf{Perpetuation and power} \end{matrix}$$

From this we see that the most influential objectives are prosperity and civil order for government and profit and perpetuation and power for industry. Using these four objectives and normalizing their weights, we get the following vector of priorities:

$$\begin{bmatrix} 0.15 \\ 0.38 \\ 0.17 \\ 0.30 \end{bmatrix} \quad \begin{array}{l} \text{Prosperity} \\ \text{Civil order} \\ \text{Profit} \\ \text{Perpetuation and power} \end{array}$$

We will use this vector to get our scenario priorities.

The scenarios were weighted with respect to the four objectives. To obtain the scenario priorities, we follow the same process as before:

	Prosperity	Civil Order	Profit	P and P			
1	0.129	0.125	0.067	0.062	0.14		0.096
2	0.329	0.180	0.309	0.306			0.259
3	0.275	0.369	0.028	0.026	0.38		0.191
Scenario 4	0.041	0.033	0.331	0.330		=	0.174
5	0.149	0.177	0.048	0.085	0.17		0.122
6	0.032	0.050	0.129	0.075			0.068
7	0.045	0.065	0.089	0.115	0.30		0.081

Next we use these weights at the top of Table 8-1 for scenario weights to synthesize the values of the variables, yielding the right column of the table. We note that the second scenario has the greatest weight: 0.259. This can be interpreted as the scenario most heavily favored by the group. A description of this scenario could be:

> Higher education in the United States in 1985 and beyond will be vocational-technical oriented. There will be more students who will be less bright (as measured by IQ) and who will be a little less active in influencing the institution, but they will have no problem in getting jobs upon graduation.
> There will be more faculty of about the same intellectual level as today, but they will have considerably less to say about the governing of the university. Their job security will be a little better than it is now, but there will be less academic freedom. As for the institutions, there will be more of them, but with much less academic orientation. The administration will control things to a much greater degree, and the efficiency (less student attrition) will be considerably higher. The schools will be more accessible, but their cultural and entertainment roles will decrease somewhat. The availability of funds and other resources will be greater than at present.
> Finally, the curriculum will be more vocationally (skill) oriented; there will be less of the learning experience that

benefits one for a lifetime. The length of time needed to complete a degree program will be considerably reduced, and the value of a degree will be the same as at present. The cost per student will rise quite a bit. There will be a little less research going on.

We now obtain the composite scenario—a single scenario obtained by finding overall scale measurements for each of the characteristics. The overall scale measurement for a characteristic is obtained by finding the sum of the products of scenario weight and the corresponding characteristic measurement. For example, for the number of students we have

$$(-2)(0.096) + (2)(0.259) + (40)(0.191) + (-3)(0.174) \\ + (-1)(0.122) + (2)(0.068) + (-2)(0.081) = 0.420$$

This measurement is found in Table 8-1 in the last column on the right. A similar process is followed for the other characteristics. An interpretation of the composite scenario from the values of its characteristics might be:

> Higher education in the United States in 1985 and beyond will witness little, if any, increase in total enrollment. Students will exhibit slightly lower performance as measured by the standardized tests we have today and will play about the same role as they do today in setting educational policy in the university. Their chances for jobs upon graduation will be a little better than at present.
>
> The faculty characteristics will be about the same as today regarding numbers, Ph.D. holders, and job security. However, faculty will play considerably less of a role in campus affairs and enjoy a little less academic freedom.
>
> The number of institutions of higher education will not change much, if at all. They definitely will be less academically oriented, and the administration will exhibit more control. There will be some increase in efficiency (less student attrition). Accessibility will be greater, but the cultural and entertainment roles of the institutions will be about the same as today. There will be practically no increase in dollar resources.
>
> The lifelong learning qualities of the curriculum will not undergo much change, nor will the length of study or the value of a degree. Costs will continue to increase significantly. The amount of faculty research will be at a lower level.

Repeating the Process

In the course of the study it was suggested that different results might be obtained by eliminating the level of factors and weighting the actors according to their direct impact on higher education. This produced the following vector of priorities:

Actors:	S	F	A	G	P	I
Weights:	0.09	0.04	0.05	0.44	0.09	0.28

These figures are in close agreement with the ones obtained by keeping the level of factors. In search of a way to make the faculty have greater importance, someone suggested that another primary factor, ideology, be included in the second level. This change did not affect the results significantly, and we decided to omit ideology.

The question sometimes arises as to who will rank the actors according to their power. How can anyone be trusted to do it? If the actors themselves participate in the ranking, each will want a high priority. This problem can be solved by inserting a level in the hierarchy between the actors and the overall objectives. The new level should consist of criteria reflecting a variety of aspects of the conflict so that no actor can claim superiority on all of them without considerable justification. If this step is done well, it may be easy for an outside party to rank the actors according to their abilities.

FORWARD PLANNING: PROJECTING OIL PRICES

Environment of the Problem

Today oil is the world's major energy resource. It accounts for about 54 percent of the world's energy consumption. Because of conservation and the development of alternative resources in the industrialized countries, the share of oil in the world's total energy consumption is expected to decline. But the total volume of oil consumption will still rise, and oil will remain the largest single source of energy for the next two decades.

Despite oil price hikes between 1974 and 1979, the real price of OPEC oil has not increased significantly when adjusted for inflation and depreciation of the dollar. Actually, the devaluation of the dollar against the Japanese yen and the West German mark caused the real price of oil to decline in these countries. However, because of depletion of the world's proved oil reserves, increasing demand, and possible political unrest in the major oil-producing countries, oil prices are expected to rise during the next decade.

There have been a number of projections of world oil prices by major oil companies and government agencies. Most are based on demand and supply. But in today's world, oil market economics and politics are interwoven, and political decisions increasingly influence the levels of oil production, consumption, and prices. In contrast to other methods, the analytic hierarchy process considers all these factors in projecting the real price of oil in 1985.

Constructing the Hierarchy

Figure 8-3 represents the hierarchic model. Elements of the hierarchy are selected after studying the environment of the problem. The goal of the planning effort—projection of increase in oil prices in 1985—is identified at the top of the hierarchy (the focus). Factors influencing price increase compose the second level: (1) world oil consumption increase, (2) world excess production, (3) oil discovery rate, (4) political factors, and (5) development of alternative energy sources. The first three factors are structured into three levels of intensity: high, medium, and low. The fourth element, political factors, is broken down into subfactors of (1) instability of the Persian Gulf region, (2) continuation of the Arab–Israeli conflict, and (3) increasing Soviet influence in the Middle East. Because of the important role of instability in the Persian Gulf region, this element is further decomposed into (1) social strains within countries, (2) tension between individual states, and (3) continuing disorder in Iran. The fifth factor in level 2, development of alternative energy sources, is broken down into three intensity levels: vigorous, moderate, and restrained. The bottom level of the hierarchy consists of five alternative exploratory scenarios: (1) low, (2) medium, (3) substantial, (4) high, and (5) extremely high level of price increase.

Setting Priorities and Synthesizing

The first step in establishing the priorities of this problem is to compare the relative priorities of the level-2 factors (world oil consumption increase and so on) in pairs according to their effectiveness in increasing the price of oil. Then we estimate the relative likelihood of their corresponding subfactors. For oil consumption increase, for example, ask: Which one of the three levels of increase—4 percent, 2 percent, or 1 percent—is more likely for the period under consideration? For instability of the Persian Gulf region, estimate the relative importance of its three subfactors. Then synthesize the priorities to obtain the overall priorities for the subfactors and select the ones with high relative priorities. Compute the relative probabilities for each level of price increase for each selected

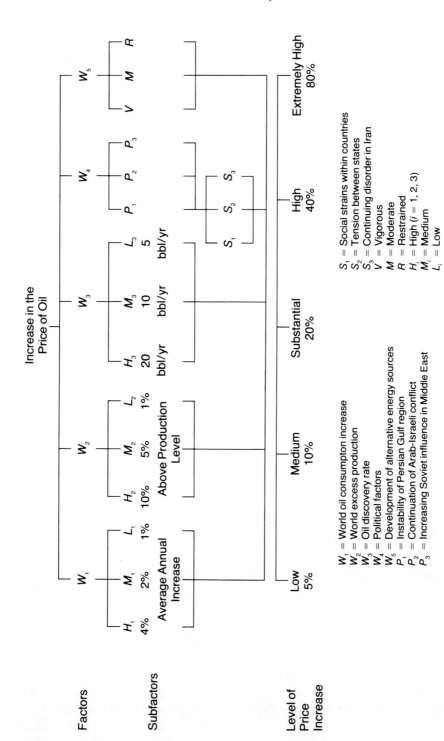

Figure 8-3 Hierarchy for Predicting the Price of Oil in 1985

subfactor. Then compute the overall priorities of the levels of price increase. The result of this step will be a set of numbers representing the likelihood of each price increase. Finally, compute the expected value of price increase by multiplying each price increase level by its corresponding likelihood. The actual computations need not be shown here, but to demonstrate how the comparisons were made, we can proceed to analyze the factors influencing world oil prices according to their relative importance.

Political Factors ($W_3 = 0.631$).   Political factors play an extremely important role in the world oil market. The Arab oil embargo of 1973 and the Iranian revolution and consequent disruptions in the world oil supplies have demonstrated the significance of politics in the supply, demand, and price of oil.

Political factors included in this analysis are the instability of the Persian Gulf region, continuation of the Arab–Israeli conflict, and increasing Soviet influence in the Middle East. Although OPEC itself plays an important political role in the oil market, its stability is very dependent on developments in the Middle East.

- P_1: *Instability in the Persian Gulf region* (0.402)   The region that will continue to be of extreme importance in the future supply and price of oil is the Middle East, particularly the Persian Gulf states. The Persian Gulf is surrounded by a number of major oil-exporting countries such as Iran, Saudi Arabia, Iraq, Kuwait, Qatar, and the United Arab Emirates. These countries are members of OPEC and altogether account for over 80 percent of its proved oil reserves or nearly half of the world's total reserve. Over 30 percent of the world's oil supply comes from this region.

  The stability of the Persian Gulf itself depends on several factors, particularly the social strain due to rapid economic development, industrialization, unstable political systems, and religious movements in the region. Moreover, tensions between the states, especially between Iran and Iraq, could lead to a regional war. Another factor to be considered is the continuation of disorder in Iran, which would not only keep its oil output low but may also increase instability in the region.

- P_2: *Continuation of the Arab–Israeli conflict* (0.163)   The Arab oil embargo of 1973 demonstrated the impact of the Arab-Israeli conflict on the flow of oil to the industrialized world. Long delays in peace will discourage the major Arab oil producers from meeting the demands of the industrialized world. This will put more pressure on the world oil market and consequently oil prices will rise drastically.

- P_3: *Increasing Soviet influence in the Middle East* (0.066)   Although the Soviet Bloc is currently a net exporter of oil, it is projected to become a net importer of oil in the near future because of declining oil production. Therefore the Soviet Union will be competing with Western countries for Middle Eastern oil. Some political observers believe that access to the Persian Gulf, and hence a secure source of oil and gas in the future, lies behind Soviet intervention in Afghanistan and assistance to the rebels in Baluchistan.

Increasing Soviet influence in the Middle East will enhance its position in the oil market vis-à-vis the West. And if it becomes to their advantage, the Soviets would not hesitate to use oil as an economic weapon against the West, particularly the United States. This action would lead to higher payments for oil for the Western countries.

Increase in World Oil Consumption ($W_1 = 0.123$). In 1979, the United States, Japan, and Europe accounted for about 75 percent of the world's oil consumption. No substantial increase in demand is anticipated for these countries, but in the developing countries, particularly the oil-exporting countries, demand for oil is expected to increase significantly due to industrialization and development.

Oil Discovery Rate ($W_3 = 0.099$). Before 1970 oil discovery rates were much higher than oil production rates—in other words, the volume of the world's discovered reserves was increasing. But since the early 1970s, oil discovery declined steadily while production rates increased continuously. This downward trend for discovery rates is expected to continue slowly until 1985 and rather sharply thereafter.

Development of Alternative Energy Sources ($W_5 = 0.051$). A substantial amount of oil could be replaced by synthetic fuels from large coal, oil shale, and tar sands reserves and biomass resources, but due to the long lead times (about six to ten years), large capital requirements, and environmental constraints, these fuels are not expected to make a significant contribution during the next decade. In the 1990s, however, synfuels will play an important role in the world energy market.

World Excess Production Capacity ($W_2 = 0.030$). Today the world's excess production capacity is more than 10 million barrels per day (mbd), two-thirds of which is from the Middle East. At this level of excess capacity only large oil producers can affect oil prices by making their production levels fluctuate. When the excess capacity declines substantially, however, say to 2 to 3 mbd, even small producers can cause a sudden jump in oil prices by cutting back their production (as can large producers by cutting back on a small portion of their production).

**Table 8-2 Probabilities of
Given Levels of Price
Increase by 1985**

Level	%	Composite Probability
Extremely high	80	0.080
High	40	0.281
Substantial	20	0.389
Medium	10	0.190
Low	5	0.059

Projected Oil-Price Increase (1985).   Table 8-2 shows the probabilities of a given oil-price increase for each level under consideration. According to these results, the price increase for 1985 would be

$$(80 \times 0.080) + (0.40 \times 0.281) + (20 \times 0.389)$$
$$+ (10 \times 0.90) + (5 \times 0.059) = 27.6\%$$

Given the present price of Arabian light crude (market crude) of $32 per barrel, a 27.6 percent increase by 1985 means that the *real* price of oil will be

$$32 + (32 \times 0.276) = \$40.80$$

Assuming an average inflation rate of 10 percent in the United States, Americans will pay $40.80(1 + 0.10)^5 = \$65.70$ (or more, depending on the quality of crude oil) for each barrel of imported oil by 1985.

These results are higher than those projected by the Exxon Corporation (*World Energy Outlook* 1980). Based on the price of Arab oil (light crude) in October 1979 of $18 per barrel, the Exxon study projected that the real price of oil would be $25 per barrel in 1985 and $28 per barrel in 1990. The Exxon results are below those assumed by the U.S. Senate Finance Committee in its projections.

BACKWARD PLANNING: THE SUDAN TRANSPORT STUDY

This example is taken from an extensive project to plan alternative strategies for developing a transport system by 1985 for the Sudan—a country of nearly 18 million people and a potential foodbasket for several hundred million people in Africa and the Middle East. A staff of nearly twenty people was intermittently occupied over a period of two years in the definition, analysis, and construction of scenarios. Occasional participants were the foreign minister, the minister of transport, and officials from the Sudan Planning Commission. This part of the study was preceded by a vast attempt to gather information and construct econometric models of the Sudan. The result was a composite anticipatory scenario that provided the basis for determining transport requirements and priorities.

Constructing the Hierarchy

When the national planners of a country have to decide which regional projects they should pursue in the face of limited resources, they start by setting their objectives regarding their future economy, health, education, defense, and the like. Thus they envision a set of anticipatory scenarios for the nation that are prioritized according to their desirability.

Next the regions of the country are prioritized with respect to each scenario so that the contribution of that region is related to the achievement of that scenario. The competing regional projects are then prioritized with respect to the regions they relate to, indicating the extent of the project's contribution to those regions.

The overall priorities of the regional projects show their relative contribution to national welfare. Thus the overall priorities represent the degree of attention the projects should receive and, in the case of limited national resources, also establish priorities for resource allocation.

The hierarchy for the Sudan transport project is incomplete. (Figure 8-4 is a simplified version.) That is, at the fourth level the projects are

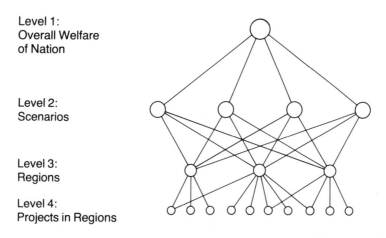

Level 1:
Overall Welfare
of Nation

Level 2:
Scenarios

Level 3:
Regions

Level 4:
Projects in Regions

Figure 8-4   Hierarchy for the Sudan Transport Project

evaluated in terms of their contributions to the regions in which they fall and not to every region. The construction of the projected future was based on the use of pairwise comparison matrices to compare the individual scenarios regarding their feasibility and desirability, taking into consideration the various forces that will shape Sudanese society. First, a reference scenario of the state of the Sudan was constructed to include all major economic, political, social, and transport parameters. The other scenarios comprise variations in the values of these parameters (some of which were given in qualitative terms).

Setting Priorities and Synthesizing

Pairwise comparison of the four scenarios according to their feasibility and desirability by 1985 gave rise to the matrix and priorities presented in Figure 8-5. The priorities of the scenarios in the order they are listed are

I   0.05
II   0.61
III 0.25
IV   0.09

This vector shows the perceived importance of each scenario relative to the others as well as the final priority ratings assigned to each. As can be seen, scenario II dominates and scenario III is next in importance. Since the future is likely to be not one or the other but rather a composition of these scenarios—with emphasis indicated by the priorities—this information was used to construct a composite scenario of the Sudan of 1985.

This composite scenario, which depicts the anticipated actual state of the future, is a proportional mix of the forces that make up the four scenarios just described. The composite scenario takes the main thrust of scenario II, the future given by far the highest priority, and is enlarged and balanced with certain elements from scenarios III and IV. This composition

	I	I	III	IV
Status quo (I)	1	1/7	1/5	1/3
Agricultural export (II)	7	1	5	5
Balanced regional growth (III)	5	1/5	1	5
Arab–African regional expansion (IV)	3	1/5	1/5	1

Figure 8-5   Priorities for the Four Scenarios

indicates the likelihood of a synergistic amplification of individual features.

The Sudan has twelve regions (whose individual economic and geographic identity justifies political division into distinct entities). The regions were compared pairwise in separate matrices according to their impact on each scenario. They comprise the third hierarchy level. Table 8-3 shows a sample matrix for one of the scenarios.

The resulting priorities are arranged as the columns of a matrix that, when multiplied by the vector of priorities of the scenarios, gives a weighted average for the impact of the regions:

Region	% Priority
Bahr El-Ghazal	3.14
Blue Nile	6.55
Darfur	5.37
East Equatoria	1.70
Gezira	12.41
Kassala	5.25
Khartoum	21.40
Kordofan	5.96
Northern	2.94
Red Sea	22.54
Upper Nile	3.37
West Equatoria	9.39

Now the transport projects, the fourth level of the hierarchy, are compared pairwise in twelve matrices according to their impact on the regions to which they belong. Since a project may belong to several regions, this fact has to be considered. The resulting matrix of vectors is again weighted by the vector of regional weights to obtain a measure of the overall impact of each project on the future.

The priorities of the projects (Table 8-4) could have been computed separately according to economic, social, and political impact. However, these attributes were considered jointly in the judgment debate. A number of refinements of the approach along these lines are possible for future revisions of the plan.

The results of prioritization can show not only the relative importance of the regions for possible investment but also the appropriate phase of implementation for each project. There were 103 projects in all appearing in several tables like this.

The priority/cost ratios have been used as a basis for resource allocation to the projects. The plan must be revised every few years to assess the impact of new projects on the perceived future.

Table 8-3   Prioritization of Regions According to Agricultural Export Scenario

Regions	Ge-zi-ra	Blue Nile	Kas-sa-la	Khar-toum	Kor-do-fan	Dar-fur	Bahr El-Gha-zal	East Equa-toria	West Equa-toria	Up-per Nile	North-ern	Red Sea
Gezira	1	1	5	1/3	4	3	6	7	3	5	6	1/4
Blue Nile	1	1	1	1/5	1	1	3	5	1	3	4	1/5
Kassala	1/5	1	1	1/6	1	1	3	5	1/2	3	4	1/5
Khartoum	3	5	6	1	4	5	6	8	4	5	5	1
Kordofan	1/4	1	1	1/4	1	2	4	6	1/2	2	3	1/5
Darfur	1/3	1	1	1/5	1/2	1	3	4	1/2	2	4	1/5
Bahr El-Ghazal	1/6	1/3	1/3	1/6	1/4	1/3	1	3	1/5	1	1	1/6
East Equatoria	1/7	1/5	1/5	1/8	1/6	1/4	1/3	1	1/5	1/4	1/5	1/9
West Equatoria	1/3	1	2	1/4	2	2	5	5	1	4	3	1/5
Upper Nile	1/5	1/3	1/3	1/5	1/2	1/2	1	4	1/4	1	2	1/7
Northern	1/6	1/4	1/4	1/5	1/3	1/4	1	5	1/3	1/2	1	1/7
Red Sea	4	5	5	1	5	5	6	9	5	7	7	1

Table 8-4   Priorities, Costs, and Priority/Cost Ratios

Project	Priority	Cost	Priority/Cost Ratio
Rail			
Port Sudan–Haiya	4.724	9.10	0.52
Haiya–Atbara	3.455	9.50	0.36
Atbara–Khartoum	8.443	11.00	0.77
El Rahad–Babanusa	1.005	12.70	0.08
Road			
Wad Medani–Gedaref	2.840	23.90	0.12
Gedaref–Kassala	0.872	14.20	0.06
Kassala–Haiya–Port Sudan	2.229	50.00	0.04
Wad Medani–Sennar	0.526	14.90	0.04
Sennar–Kosti	0.345	7.20	0.05
Sennar–Es Suki	0.546	7.00	0.08
Ed Dubeibat–Kadugli	1.253	12.30	0.10
Kadugli–Talodi	0.266	6.60	0.04
Nyala–Kass–Zalingei	0.951	11.30	0.08
Juba–Nimuli	0.329	5.30	0.06
Juba–Amadi–Rumbek–Wau	0.494	20.30	0.02

FORWARD-BACKWARD PLANNING: THE FUTURE OF THE STEEL INDUSTRY

Environment of the Problem

The domestic steel industry is in an imbroglio, and its future is uncertain. The industry has been plagued by disruptive labor problems, rising energy costs, market erosion of imports, inadequate cash flow, and inadequate capital to comply with clean air and water regulations. In fact, large integrated steel firms are evaluating the advisability of remaining in the steel business. Approximately 25 percent of U.S. steel companies' revenue is from nonsteel sources, and this proportion will continue to increase. Armco has dropped steel from its name and is slowly reducing its income from steel. The industry is truly at the crossroads. If the U.S. steel industry is to remain a vital entity, key decisions must be made by labor, management, and the government.

A firm that earns a large share of its total revenues by selling equipment to the steel industry, and is therefore deeply concerned about its future, was interested in developing contingency plans based on the steel industry's future over the next ten years. Considering the complex environmental and legislative constraints within which the steel firms compete, it was felt that the analytic hierarchy process could be used to examine potential futures. A forward-backward-forward process was performed to determine the most likely scenario for the ten-year span. The company intended to use the information to develop its strategies to trade with the steel industry.

The U.S. steel industry comprises two major classes of producers: the large integrated steel mill and the mini-mill. The mini-mill produces about 1 million tons of steel per year versus the 20 to 30 million tons produced by the integrated mill. The mini-mill is normally market specific and concentrates on odd-size products or special alloys that the large mills find unprofitable to manufacture due to the small tonnage requirements. Mini-mills account for approximately 20 percent of the steel manufactured in the United States. The other 80 percent is produced by the large integrated steel mills, of which U.S. Steel, National Steel, and J & L are examples. These large mills normally produce low-carbon, low-alloy steels, but some manufacture special alloy products for special markets. These mills are generally older than the mini-mills and some of their equipment is now obsolete. This fact, coupled with environmental regulations, labor unions, and poor cash flow, makes it difficult for the large mills to compete profitably with imported steel. Hence they are feeling the pressure from imports.

Imported steel has been gaining a foothold in the United States since the early 1970s when buyers, in anticipation of possible shortages due to labor strikes, purchased steel from Japan and Europe. Since that time, imported steel has gained an increasing share of the American market. In 1980 it accounted for approximately 25 percent of all the steel used. The domestic steel industry argues that these foreign mills are "dumping" steel in America for less than it costs in their own markets. When a government investigation found that some foreign firms were in fact dumping, Congress introduced tariffs on foreign steel to bring it in line with domestic costs. The tariffs, called trigger price mechanisms (TPM), are based on the estimated production cost for Japanese steelmakers. The Japanese are considered to be the most efficient steel producers in the world and are used as a standard of comparison for imports from other countries.

Steel, which is used extensively in manufacturing, is also experiencing competition from alternative materials (such as plastic and aluminum)—especially in its largest market, automobiles. Cars account for approximately 25 percent of the steel produced. Recent increases in gasoline prices, government-mandated fuel economy requirements discouraging use of the automobile, a general switch to plastics and aluminum—all have been detrimental to the steel industry. Estimates range from a 1 percent to a 5 percent per year decrease in the amount of steel used in automobiles. Although the demand for steel has grown in the building construction and electrical industries, there are other constraints facing these markets, such as the prime lending rate and sluggish national growth. Overall the market for steel is expected to grow at about 1 percent per year for the next decade. Certainly pressure is on management to find new markets for steel or to modernize present operations to increase their profitability.

Competition from imported steel and alternative materials is not the only problem facing the U.S. steel industry. Due to the nature of the steelmaking process, the industry discharges a large amount of pollutants—both in the air and in the water. Government regulations, under EPA and OSHA, have set limits on discharged pollutants, and the steel industry, though at times reluctant, has spent hundreds of millions of dollars to comply with regulations. The estimated expenditures for water and air pollution control equipment for 1980 were $605 million. These expenditures are for nonproductive equipment—that is, equipment which does nothing to decrease the cost of producing steel or to improve the product. The cost of operating the equipment is estimated to be 10 percent of the cost of producing a ton of steel, a sizable figure.

Labor problems have been disrupting the steel industry for years. It was the possibility of a strike and subsequent interruption of supply that gave imported steel its first inroads into U.S. markets. In the early 1970s a nonstrike agreement was signed with the unions to eliminate the problem. This agreement expires in the early 1980s, however, and there may be need for another one. Recently, management has applied pressure in the form of threatened and actual plant closings in an attempt to reduce labor costs. This strategy has been partially successful and may result in improved productivity.

The domestic steel industry uses inefficient equipment and has not kept pace with advancing technology. The current capacity replacement rate is approximately 2 percent per year, or about 2.2 million tons of steel capacity per year. This is well below industry needs. Some sources claim that to remain competitive the steel industry should be modernizing its capacity at 4 percent, or about 4.4 million tons of production capacity per year. Considering the relatively small 1 percent anticipated increase, there is little need for additional capacity.

Reasons for the lack of technological advancement vary. One reason, proposed by the industry, is that the cash flow is poor. The steel industry currently has a 9 percent cash flow/sales ratio (compared to 14 percent for the chemical industry). Cash flow is defined as net income plus depreciation. A big controversy rages over the recommended depreciation schedule for steel mill equipment. At one time steel mills depreciated their equipment over a $14\frac{1}{2}$-year useful life—a long time, compared to other industries. As of August 1979, the steel industry is allowed to depreciate over $12\frac{1}{2}$ years for equipment placed in service after that date. The steel industry thinks this is inadequate for generating sufficient cash flow to allow it to compete with foreign steel. Currently the industry is lobbying for a favorable 10-5-3 depreciation schedule covering different classes of equipment.

Thus the steel industry is undergoing significant changes. The direction and intensity of change depend on the government's response to the industry's needs. They also depend on management's commitment to improve the industry. This is what we will try to assess with the analytic hierarchy process: Where does the industry appear to be going given specific market constraints? Where should it go in a more favorable climate?

Constructing the Hierarchy

Actors and Objectives.   In this phase we identify the major actors concerned with the future of the steel industry and itemize their objectives relevant to the problem:

- *Management:* The management of the steel companies has the following objectives: minimizing risk, increasing the firm's profits and sales, having an equitable market within which they can compete, and, finally, perpetuation of the organization. The target could be either to increase investment in equipment in order to remain in the steel industry or to diversify out of steel.

- *Government:* The United States government represents the most powerful actor. The objectives are sometimes conflicting, as demonstrated by its concern over low inflation and a clean environment. Expenditures for antipollution equipment increase the cost of production and are inflationary. Additional objectives for the government include energy conservation, low unemployment, and providing an equitable marketplace for competition.

- *Users:* Those who buy the steel include automobile manufacturers, construction firms, the appliance industry, and the military. Their objectives are to increase their profits and sales, to minimize the cost of supplies and raw materials used in their product, and to ensure an uninterrupted supply of material. Users want the least expensive steel and are opposed to strong regulations on imports. Prices that are artificially inflated by tariffs increase their material costs relative to foreign competition. This makes it difficult for users to compete domestically and internationally against foreign products. Before the nonstrike agreement between labor and steel management, the possibility of an interruption in supply posed a serious threat to steel users. This was one of the major factors that permitted foreign steel to gain a foothold in the domestic market.

- *Importers:* These actors represent all those who import steel into the United States. They want to maintain their share of the domestic market, but not at the risk of disrupting the market or upsetting the government in a way that could hurt competition. Exporting countries seem to be less interested in the profitability of their own steel firms and more in improving their balance of payments and lowering unemployment. In some way, they are all subsidizing their steel companies.

In our analysis we did not represent all the policies in the first forward process and only used their objectives. In the second forward process, however, we introduce an additional level of policies under the objectives level.

First Forward Process.   The first forward process was carried out to determine what the steel industry will be like over the next five to ten years. The hierarchy and the corresponding pairwise comparisons were developed by consultants investigating the viability of the steel industry. Their judgments were based on their research. The following three scenarios were developed as possible alternatives:

- *Scenario I:* This was the pessimistic scenario. Industry expenditures would decline to the point that the capital equipment replacement rate would be less than the present 2 percent. The consultants also felt that the government would develop a hard-line attitude toward the industry. The depreciation schedule would not change. The EPA would be placing increasing pressure on the industry to improve overall compliance. Expenditures for pollution control equipment would exceed $800 million per year. In addition, unions would resist pressure by management and might reinstate the strike clause in the labor contract. Imports would continue to erode the domestic market, but at a slower pace than in the 1970s. Management would continue to diversify out of steel to more profitable businesses, such as chemicals. A recession and a declining automotive market would soften the demand for steel.

- *Scenario II:* This was the status quo scenario. The consultants thought the capital equipment replacement rate would be 2 percent, or about $2.2 billion per year. The government would develop a more positive attitude toward the industry, realizing that the capital expenditures required for pollution control equipment were hurting it. There would be continued threats against the unions, and the nonstrike clause would continue as part of the labor agreement. Imports would maintain their market share and would have to be continually monitored by the industry. The market would increase at about 1 percent per year.

- *Scenario III:* This was the optimistic scenario. Capital equipment expenditures would be about $3.5 billion per year, or about a 3.4 percent replacement rate. The government would change the depreciation schedule to 10-5-3 to improve the industry's cash flow position. As a result of the industry's political effort, public and government pressure would tacitly force the industry to modernize. Pollution control expenditure would even out at about $600 million per year (1979 dollars). Imports and market growth would maintain the same status as described in scenario II.

Setting Priorities and Synthesizing

The results of the first forward process are shown in Figure 8-6. The hierarchy indicates that the government is the most powerful actor regarding the future of the industry. It received a rating of 0.563 compared to management's 0.289, users' 0.098, and importers' 0.048. This outcome is reasonable considering the government's power to regulate imports, levy taxes, and impose environmental regulations. The result of the forward process weighted scenarios II and III closely: 0.36 and 0.39, respectively. This indicates that, considering the actors and their objectives, the most likely outcome is a fairly even mix of all three scenarios. Clearly it is worthwhile exploring what might have to be done to emphasize the contribution of the optimistic scenario to the outcome. Next a backward process is developed to determine what policies management should use to affect such an outcome.

First Backward Process.   The outcome of the backward process is shown in Figure 8-7. (The pairwise comparison matrices for the hierarchy are omitted here.) The focus of the hierarchy is the desired future of steel companies. The consultants thought that three scenarios would cover the focus: diversification outside the industry, the status quo, and increased investment in the steel industry. These correspond to scenarios I, II, and III in the forward process. The weights of the scenarios are, respectively, 0.57, 0.06, and 0.36.

The third level considers the problems and opportunities (mostly problems) that management would encounter in attempting to realize one of the two more desirable futures. These problems include barriers to entry, increasing energy costs, and cash flow.

Next weights were developed for the actors who are responsible for the problems facing management. These actors include the government, chemical companies, imports, unions, and substitutes for steel. Finally, policies were developed that could be implemented by management either to counteract the problems or to persuade certain actors (the government,

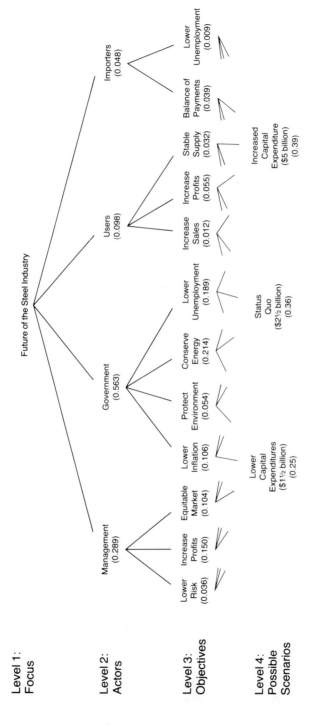

Figure 8-6   First Forward Process

154

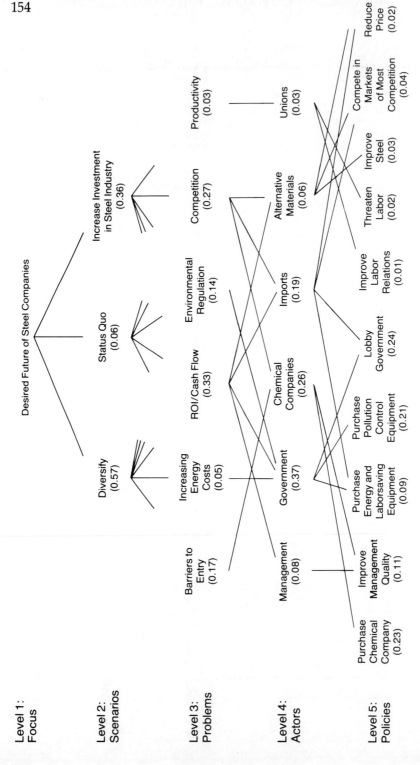

Figure 8-7 Backward Process

for example) to change their policies favorably toward steel. The policies that received the highest weights are these: purchase chemical company (0.24), improve management quality (0.22), purchase pollution control equipment (0.15), and lobby government (0.10). These policies were then used in the second forward process to assess their potential effect.

Second Forward Process.   A second forward process was carried out to determine if there would be any changes in scenario weights as a result of the policies of the backward process. Again the second forward process shows what is most likely to happen considering the power of the actors and the priorities of their policies. The second forward process is shown in Figure 8-8. (Again the pairwise comparison matrices are omitted.) This second iteration indicates a change in the weighting of the scenario from that of the first process. The new weightings are 0.21, 0.24, and 0.55 (Table 8-5). This shows that the policies that could be used by management to influence the major actors would improve the situation in favor of steel. Of these policies, the most effective would be to improve the quality of management and to lobby the government. Because of the difference between the weightings of the two forward processes, additional iterations may be desirable to allow experimentation with different policies for the actors and possibly also with different futures to produce stability. The recommendation made to the firm was that the most likely outcome, considering the present situation in the steel industry, is scenario III. However, it was also noted that this scenario would probably not be realized for about three years, which would give the firm sufficient time to develop strategies to deal with the steel industry. The steel industry itself is actually pursuing policies like those mentioned here. This analysis gives a concrete idea of where the industry is likely to be in a few years.

FORWARD-BACKWARD PLANNING: DEALING WITH TRAFFIC CONGESTION

Environment of the Problem

Metropolitan Manila in the Philippines is by far the country's largest single urban area with its population of 6 million concentrated in 104.2 square miles of land area, about twice the size of Pittsburgh. The center of government, it has the main international port and the only regularly operating international airport; it is also the center of both higher education and cultural activity. This expanding metropolis is a natural attraction for migrants from other parts of the Philippines where there are limited opportunities for material, social, and economic advancement. Because of this, Metro Manila inevitably contains the Philippines' greatest concentra-

Table 8-5 Detail of Objectives, Policies, and Corresponding Weights

Focus: Future of Steel Companies

Actors:	Management (0.31)	Government (0.58)	Users (0.04)	Imports (0.07)
Objectives:	O_1 Minimize risk (0.02)	O_5 Low inflation (0.04)	O_{10} Increase sales (0.01)	O_{13} Improve BOP (0.03)
	O_2 Increase profits (0.06)	O_6 Protect environment (0.03)	O_{11} Increase profits (0.03)	O_{14} Low unemployment (0.01)
	O_3 Equitable market (0.07)	O_7 Conserve energy (0.17)	O_{12} Stable supply (0.01)	
	O_4 Perpetuation (0.15)	O_8 Low unemployment (0.17)		
		O_9 Equitable market (0.17)		
Policies:	P_1 Improve product (0.003)	P_9 OSHA (0.013)	P_{17} Buy foreign steel (0.023)	P_{19} Stable supply (0.010)

P_2 Lobby government (0.117)

P_3 Lower price (0.002)

P_4 Purchase equipment (0.021)

P_5 Purchase PC equipment (0.018)

P_6 Improve management quality (0.122)

P_7 Threaten labor (0.005)

P_8 Close plants (0.018)

P_{10} EPA (0.013)

P_{11} Monitor market (0.105)

P_{12} Regulate energy (0.168)

P_{13} EEOC (0.079)
P_{14} TPM (0.148)

P_{15} Depreciation allowance (0.015)

P_{16} Government spending (0.038)

P_{18} Buy alternative materials (0.023)

P_{20} Dump (0.058)

Scenarios:

I	II	III
(0.21)	(0.24)	(0.55)

Consistency of hierarchy: 0.0182.

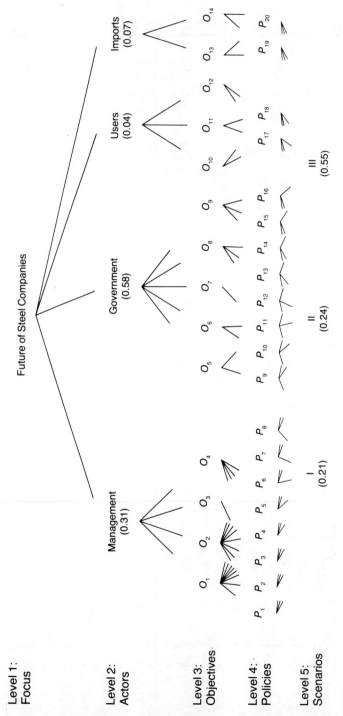

Figure 8-8   Second Forward Process

tion of urban problems—unemployment, inadequate services, wide income disparities, inadequate housing, and traffic congestion.

This example focuses on strategies for dealing with the traffic congestion that occurs in the peak period along all the major roads in the built-up areas and more extensively throughout the day in the central business district. Since in Metro Manila practically everyone who travels does so by road, travelers are all at one time or another affected by congestion and regard it as a major problem.

Constructing the Hierarchy

Forward Process.   A forward-backward planning process will be used in describing the interactions among the different actors who are believed to influence the future of the urban transportation system, the objectives of each actor, future scenarios (both exploratory and anticipatory), problems to be encountered in the achievement of each desired scenario, and policies that the government as the decision maker can effect to achieve the desired state. Figure 8-9 illustrates the hierarchic structure depicting the actors and their motivating objectives that would affect the future transportation system. We note that in a number of cases the objectives of one or two actors conflict with each other. A case in point is the pursuit of cordon pricing by the government, which directly opposes the strong desire of private car owners and drivers to remove physical constraints on car travel.

Four exploratory scenarios are enumerated in the fourth level of the hierarchy:

1. Do nothing/status quo
2. Maintenance of the present system with planned urban expansion in the outer areas
3. Cars and private transport as the predominant mode of transportation
4. Public transport as the predominant mode

Four clusters of characteristics were used to describe each scenario. Using the numbers between −4 and 4, the characteristics were then measured to give quantitative profiles of the four exploratory scenarios (see Table 8-6). The value of zero represents no change, 1 represents a historical change, 4 signifies a very strong change as a direct result of the scenario, 3 represents a strong change as an indirect result of the scenario, and 2 was used in borderline cases. Positive integers represent varying degrees of upward change; negative integers signify downward change.

We note in this forward process that the most probable scenario outcome is the maintenance of the present system coupled with planned urban expansion for commercial and industrial dispersal. The composite scenario can be briefly interpreted as a transportation system characterized

Level 1:
Focus

Level 2:
Actors

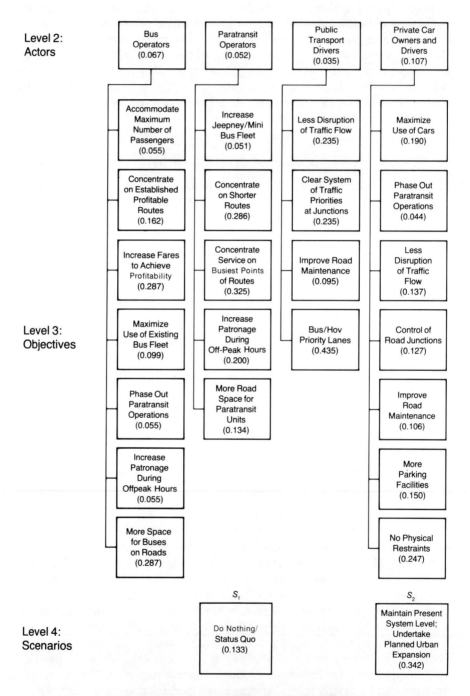

| Bus Operators (0.067) | Paratransit Operators (0.052) | Public Transport Drivers (0.035) | Private Car Owners and Drivers (0.107) |

Level 3:
Objectives

| Accommodate Maximum Number of Passengers (0.055) | Increase Jeepney/Mini Bus Fleet (0.051) | Less Disruption of Traffic Flow (0.235) | Maximize Use of Cars (0.190) |

Concentrate on Established Profitable Routes (0.162)

Concentrate on Shorter Routes (0.286)

Clear System of Traffic Priorities at Junctions (0.235)

Phase Out Paratransit Operations (0.044)

Increase Fares to Achieve Profitability (0.287)

Concentrate Service on Busiest Points of Routes (0.325)

Improve Road Maintenance (0.095)

Less Disruption of Traffic Flow (0.137)

Maximize Use of Existing Bus Fleet (0.099)

Increase Patronage During Off-Peak Hours (0.200)

Bus/Hov Priority Lanes (0.435)

Control of Road Junctions (0.127)

Phase Out Paratransit Operations (0.055)

More Road Space for Paratransit Units (0.134)

Improve Road Maintenance (0.106)

Increase Patronage During Offpeak Hours (0.055)

More Parking Facilities (0.150)

More Space for Buses on Roads (0.287)

No Physical Restraints (0.247)

S_1

Do Nothing/ Status Quo (0.133)

S_2

Maintain Present System Level; Undertake Planned Urban Expansion (0.342)

Level 4:
Scenarios

Figure 8-9   Forward Process Hierarchy

```
┌─────────────┐
│ Projected Future │
│ of Urban     │
│ Transport    │
│ System       │
└─────────────┘
```

Commuters (0.022)	Pedestrians (0.019)	Regulatory Agencies (0.212)	Police/Highway Patrol (0.157)	National and Metropolitan Government (0.329)
Reduce Public Transport Fares (0.536)	Disciplined Drivers (0.750)	Promote Transport Cooperatives (0.072)	Junction Control (0.500)	Cordon Pricing (0.099)
Improve Waiting Conditions (0.081)	More Pedestrian Lanes and Crossings (0.250)	Different Levels of Service at Different Fare Levels (0.392)	Traffic Management (0.500)	Bus/Hov Priority Lanes (0.099)
Improve Vehicle Design for Better Service (0.094)		Driver Behavior (0.464)		Light Rail Transit (0.284)
More Buses and Other Public Transport (0.290)		Vehicle Roadworthiness (0.072)		Highway Construction in Outer Areas (0.518)

S_3

```
┌──────────────┐
│ Cars and      │
│ Private       │
│ Transport as  │
│ Predominant   │
│ Mode          │
│ (0.290)       │
└──────────────┘
```

S_4

```
┌──────────────┐
│ Public Transport │
│ as Predominant   │
│ Mode             │
│ (0.235)          │
└──────────────┘
```

Figure 8-9   (Continued)

**Table 8-6   Four Scenarios and the Calibration
of Their Characteristics**

Scenario Characteristics	(0.133) S_1	(0.342) S_2	(0.290) S_3	(0.235) S_4	Composite Weight
Vehicle composition of traffic flow					
1. Buses	1	3	−2	4	1.519
2. Jeepneys and taxis	0	2	−3	3	0.519
3. Trucks	1	1	0	0	0.475
4. Cars	2	2	4	−3	1.405
5. Nonmotorized travel	−1	−1	0	0	−0.425
Effectiveness of transport regulation					
1. Traffic control	0	1	1	−1	0.397
2. Road maintenance	1	2	1	0	1.107
3. Parking control	0	0	−2	3	0.125
4. Franchising of PU vehicles	1	1	2	0	1.055
5. Vehicle and driver licensing	1	1	2	1	1.290
6. Physical restraint	0	0	−3	3	−0.165
Benefits and costs to passengers					
1. Level of service	0	1	−2	3	0.467
2. Public transport fares	2	2	3	1	2.055
3. Accidents	−1	−2	0	−2	−1.287
4. Pollution	1	0	2	3	1.418
Urban development					
1. Conditions in stress areas	−2	1	−3	−2	−1.264
2. New communities	1	4	1	1	2.026
3. Development controls in inner core	1	3	0	0	1.159
4. Development incentives in outer areas	1	4	0	3	2.206

Scale: −4 ↔ +4.

by a substantial increase in the proportion of buses and cars in the traffic flow, a substantial improvement in traffic regulation, a significant increase in pollution and public transport fares, a decrease in the accident rate, continuing deterioration of conditions in the inner areas, the rise of new communities in outer areas, and more incentives for location in outer areas.

Backward Process.   Given the insight gained from the forward process, the backward process provided a mechanism for identifying policies the government should pursue to attain the desired scenario. The profile of this desired scenario is shown in Table 8-7, and the backward process hierarchy is illustrated in Figure 8-10.

The first level of the hierarchy is now the desired future of the urban transport system. The second level enumerates the three desired scenarios: (1) maintenance of the present system with planned urban expansion, (2) public transport as the predominant mode, and (3) public transport as the predominant mode coupled with planned urban expansion. Level 3 contains the problems that hinder the attainment of each of the desired scenarios. The fourth level names the most influential actors in terms of their ability to affect the future of the transportation system—that is, the actors who received a weight of 0.10 or more in the previous forward process.

The fifth level contains the policies that the government can undertake to achieve the desired scenario with their corresponding composite priorities. The weights suggest that, in order to achieve the desired scenario, the government must pursue most aggressively cordon pricing, highway construction in outer areas (both radial and circumferential), and the development of social infrastructure in outer areas to support the growth of new communities there.

Forward–Backward Process Iterations.   A second forward process was undertaken to incorporate the insights gained from the backward process. Since the government is now pursuing an already defined scenario, the relative importance of the most influential actors changes. The resulting hierarchic structure is shown in Figure 8-11.

The priorities of the actors' objectives with respect to the actors (except for the government) were the same priorities derived in the first forward process. In the case of the government, the priorities were those obtained from the pairwise comparison matrix for government policies in the backward process. The rationale for this strategy is that in the real world, the national and metropolitan government does not immediately involve at the outset the other stakeholders in the formulation and implementation of policies. Hence the other stakeholders act as though nothing is happening. The result of this attitude is a composite scenario that is obviously different

Table 8-7   Desired Scenario Profile

Scenario Characteristic	Composite Weight
Vehicle composition of traffic flow	
1. Buses	3.00
2. Jeepneys and taxis	2.00
3. Trucks	0.67
4. Cars	0.35
5. Nonmotorized travel	−0.67
Effectiveness of transport regulation	
1. Road maintenance	1.50
2. Traffic control	1.00
3. Parking control	1.00
4. Franchising of PU vehicles	1.50
5. Vehicle and driver licensing	1.50
6. Physical restraint	2.00
Benefits and costs to passengers	
1. Level of service	2.00
2. Public transport fares	1.00
3. Accidents	−2.00
4. Pollution	1.00
Urban development	
1. Conditions in stress areas	1.00
2. New communities	3.00
3. Development controls in inner core	2.00
4. Development incentives in outer areas	4.00

from what was intended (see Table 8-8). In brief, the composite scenario depicts a decrease in the number of buses, an increase in the number of cars, and an increase in public transport fares.

From the insights gained in the second forward process, a second backward process was conducted. Since financial incentives for public transport operators to expand their fleet and keep fares low had been overlooked, a new policy calling for public transport subsidies or tax incentives or both was introduced in the second backward process. The resulting hierarchy (Figure 8-12) shows a significant shift in priorities. The attainment of the desired scenario calls for granting subsidies and tax incen-

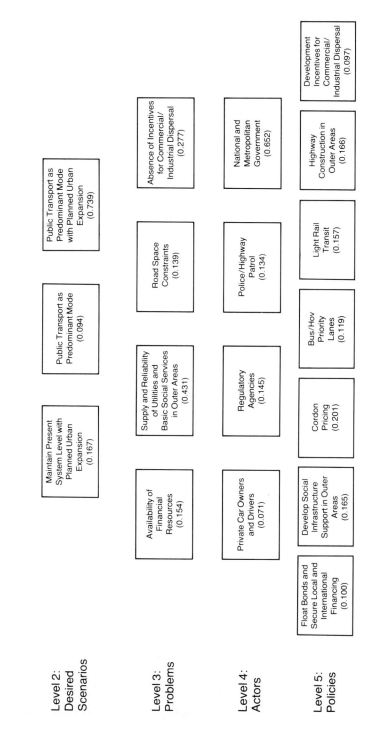

Figure 8-10 Backward Process Hierarchy

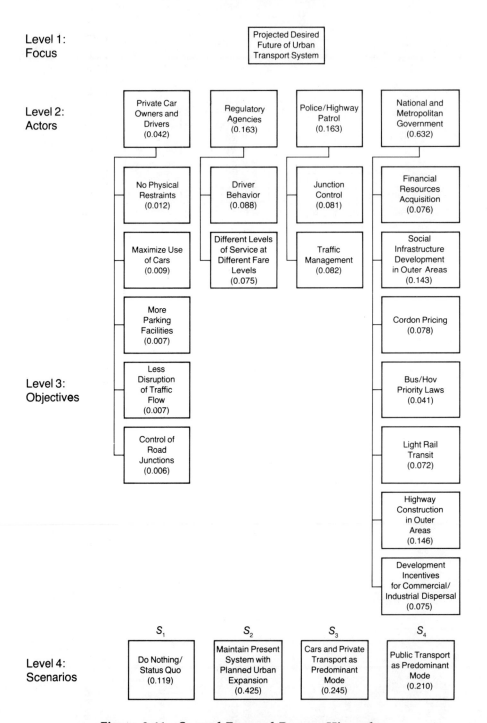

Figure 8-11   Second Forward Process Hierarchy

Table 8-8   Identification of Planning Gap:
Second Forward Process

Scenario Characteristic	Composite Weight	Desired Weight	Variance*
Vehicle composition of traffic flow			
1. Buses	1.499	3.00	1.50
2. Jeepneys and taxis	0.745	2.00	1.25
3. Trucks	0.544	0.67	0.13
4. Cars	1.438	0.35	1.09
5. Nonmotorized travel	−0.544	−0.67	0.13
Effectiveness of transport regulation			
1. Road maintenance	1.214	1.50	0.29
2. Traffic control	0.460	1.00	0.54
3. Parking control	0.140	1.00	0.86
4. Franchising of PU vehicles	1.034	1.50	0.47
5. Vehicle and driver licensing	1.244	1.50	0.26
6. Physical restraint	−0.105	2.00	2.11
Benefits and costs to passengers			
1. Level of service	0.565	2.00	1.43
2. Public transport fares	2.271	1.00	1.27
3. Accidents	−1.389	−2.00	0.61
4. Pollution	1.239	1.00	0.24
Urban development			
1. Conditions in stress areas	−0.492	1.00	1.49
2. New communities	2.274	3.00	0.73
3. Development controls in inner core	1.394	2.00	0.60
4. Development incentives in outer areas	2.449	4.00	1.55

* All variances are unfavorable here—that is, a substantial gap exists.

tives to public transport operators, as well as the aggressive implementation of cordon pricing.

The suggestions from the second backward process were then fed into a third forward process. In the second forward process, private car owners and drivers had a priority less than 0.05; hence they were removed from the list of most influential actors in the third forward process. (See Figure 8-13 for the hierarchy.) Note that most of the objectives of private car

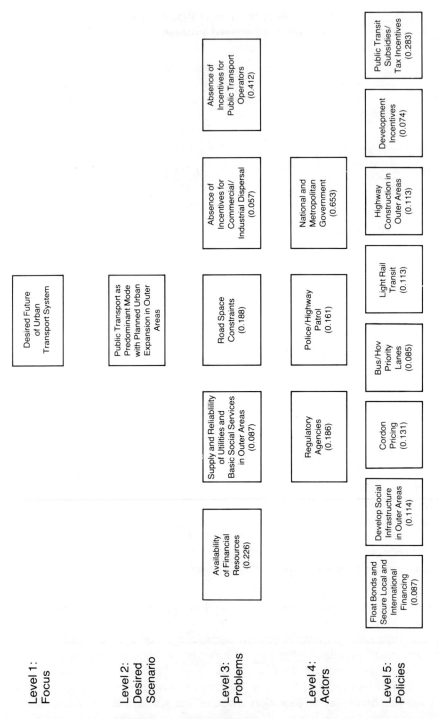

Figure 8-12   Second Backward Process Hierarchy

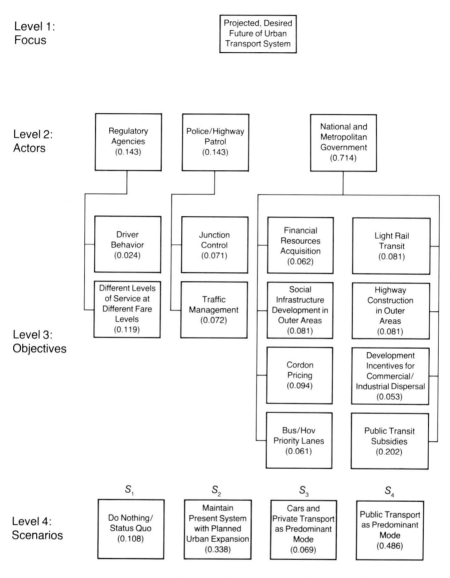

Figure 8-13   Third Forward Process Hierarchy

owners and drivers are contrary to the achievement of the desired scenario. The priorities of the regulatory agencies' objectives were changed because of the unified efforts of the most influential actors in achieving the desired future. Consistency was forced in the pairwise judgment matrix for the government's objectives in order to reflect the composite policy priorities calculated in the second backward process. The

Table 8-9 Identification of Planning Gap:
Third Forward Process

Scenario Characteristic	Composite Weight	Desired Weight	Variance*
Vehicle composition of traffic flow			
1. Buses	2.928	3.00	0.072 S
2. Jeepneys and taxis	1.927	2.00	0.073 S
3. Trucks	0.446	0.67	0.224 U
4. Cars	−0.290	0.35	0.640 F
5. Nonmotorized travel	−0.446	−0.67	0.224 U
Effectiveness of transport regulation			
1. Road maintenance	0.853	1.50	0.647 U
2. Traffic control	−0.079	1.00	1.079 U
3. Parking control	1.320	1.00	0.320 F
4. Franchising of PU vehicles	0.584	1.50	0.916 U
5. Vehicle and driver licensing	1.070	1.50	0.430 U
6. Physical restraint	1.251	2.00	0.749 U
Benefits and costs to passengers			
1. Level of service	1.658	2.00	0.342 U
2. Public transport fares	1.585	1.00	0.585 U
3. Accidents	−1.756	−2.00	0.244 U
4. Pollution	1.704	1.00	0.704 U
Urban development			
1. Conditions in stress areas	−1.057	1.00	2.057 U
2. New communities	2.015	3.00	0.985 U
3. Development controls in inner core	1.122	2.00	0.878 U
4. Development incentives in outer areas	2.918	4.00	1.082 U

* U = unfavorable variance (a substantial gap exists); F = favorable variance; S = within satisfactory range (plus or minus 10 percent of desired change).

result of all these efforts is shown in the composite scenario profile (Table 8-9).

Interpreting the Results

First we note the change in the likelihood of each exploratory scenario in the three forward processes:

Scenario	First	Second	Third
1. Do nothing/status quo	0.133	0.119	0.108
2. Present system with planned urban expansion	0.342	0.425	0.338
3. Cars and private transport as predominant mode	0.290	0.245	0.069
4. Public transport as predominant mode	0.235	0.210	0.486

All of these estimates were brought about by the shifts in priorities made by the most influential actors in order to achieve the desired outcome. It can be inferred from this exercise that the earlier the influential actors work in a unified manner, the fewer iterations it will take for the composite scenario to approximate the desired scenario.

Secondly, the strategies reformulated and made explicit in the third forward process help to close the gap between composite and desired scenarios if we view the planning gap as a multidimensional construct. (In this case, it has $5 + 6 + 4 + 4 = 19$ dimensions.) We are specifically referring to the increase in the number of public transport units (mainly as a result of the subsidies), the decrease (though not substantial) in the number of cars possibly due to the cordon pricing strategy, and the increase in the effectiveness of parking controls attributable to the decline in car traffic.

Nevertheless, many dimensions of the planning gap have not yet vanished. For these, the following reasons and possible solutions can be offered:

- Though transit subsidies were effective in expanding the bus fleet, they did not reduce public transport fares dramatically, although there was a slight decrease from the first scenario. Possibly as a result of this, the shift from nonmotorized travel (cycling and walking) to motorized travel was not substantial.

- As a result of the increase in public transport units, the effectiveness of road maintenance, traffic control, franchising of public utility vehicles, and vehicle and driver licensing did not change significantly as envisioned.

- While the level of service of public transport increased dramatically, it was not as much as originally intended. A possible explanation is that the transit subsidies can be allocated by the operator to at least three competing uses: expansion of the bus fleet, improvement of service, and reduction of fares.

- The effectiveness of physical restraints to car travel increased, but not as much as planned. The bulk of reduced car travel may have been due not to the cordon pricing strategy but to modal shifts brought about by increased attractiveness of public transport services.

- Pollution may have increased as a result of the expanded bus fleet. All travelers on the main roads of Metro Manila suffer from the fumes emitted by improperly maintained engines. Pollution caused by fumes is especially great on roads where large numbers of buses are concentrated.

- The stress areas are, in the main, either extensive areas of makeshift housing or housing that has fallen into disrepair through overuse and multiple occupation. Although transport development is affected by the solution of this problem and vice versa, the solution requires actions extending far beyond the domain of transport planning, actions that have not been accounted for in this analysis.

- Development controls and incentives, as well as the establishment of new communities, have not been very effective. Unlike the other policy tools, they would take some time to have a strategic impact on the metropolis. However, the effectiveness of these measures has substantially increased when the first forward composite weights are used as a base. Another possible reason for their lack of effectiveness is the inadequacy of measures for implementing development controls—for example, zoning ordinances and building regulations.

These new insights can be fed into succeeding backward and forward processes until the planning gap is closed (in the actors' judgment).

PERSPECTIVE

Planning is a process of projecting plausible futures with a prescription to reach desirable futures. A group participates in setting target outcomes—scenarios—and improvising policies to attain them. The set of policies can be improved by iteration, which is like hypothesis making and testing. Each iteration should enhance the effectiveness of the policies in bringing about the desired outcome. A validity check of the outcome with the real constraints can be tested by examining any available descriptions of the situation and appropriate modifications made in both judgments and the existing relationships. Revision may be necessary to reach a compromise between what is desired and what is possible.

Applying the AHP to planning problems saves time over traditional methods. In designing a strategic planning process for a firm, consultants who used the AHP reported the following typical timetable:

- Working with the staff to define the problem and to identify its components required one day of interaction and two days of reading, studying, and background research to consolidate the definition of the problem's environment and to structure the hierarchy.
- In half-day sessions they prioritized the elements of the hierarchy. Different staff members participated in the portion of the hierarchy that related to their expertise. The judgments of other people who exerted influence but could not attend were also included. The total time for this phase, which included computer calculations and writing, was six days.
- Constructing the backward planning problem required one day of interaction and two days of analysis and report preparation.
- Combining the forward and backward planning processes required two days of interaction, meetings, and analysis.
- Preparing the final report and reviewing it with the committee required one week.

The total elapsed time of the project was one month; for such a project, the elapsed time is normally three months. Thus the AHP proved to be a remarkably efficient tool for planning. In the next chapter we will see that it is also a practical method for resolving conflict.

9

Resolving Conflict

This chapter deals with the following questions:

- How can the analytic hierarchy process be used to solve conflict problems?

- How do we apply the forward process to conflicts?

- How do we apply the backward process to conflicts?

- How can the forward and backward processes then be combined to determine the most acceptable outcome all around?

- What compromises would the parties have to make to accept this outcome?

WORKING FORWARD AND BACKWARD

Conflict resolution is the search for an outcome that represents for some participants an improvement from, and for no participants a worsening of, their present situation. Traditionally the outcome sought also had the property of stability—that is, there were constraints that would prevent changes by a participant. However, stability is not initially an essential criterion for resolution of the conflict. Suppose that a solution is shown to be highly likely to emerge, given the characteristics of each party to the conflict, but is also shown to be unstable. If the problem is now embedded in a dynamic framework, stability criteria may change. In other words, suppose that a structure, highly desired by all parties, is implemented. Once it is obvious that basic objectives are being met, it may then become important to all parties to continue their course of action, so that, in fact, stability will now be created in the new conditions.

It is thus important to identify the outcomes that are likely to emerge and that, in large measure, satisfy the objectives of each party. This descriptive process is the forward process. Given the present actors and their current objectives, capabilities, and policies, which outcome is most likely to emerge? This outcome may be a composite of a number of outcomes that have been considered.

There is, however, an alternative approach to the solution of a conflict problem. Given a desired future outcome, what should be done to achieve it? Working backward, one assesses the problems and opportunities that affect this outcome and identifies the policies that would be most effective in producing the desired outcome. This normative approach is the backward process.

FIRST FORWARD PROCESS

To structure a conflict problem as a hierarchy, we place the parties to the conflict on the highest level because their power to influence the final outcome is the dominant factor. Each of these parties has a number of objectives, some more important to them than others. These objectives form the second level of the hierarchy. The political structures that could resolve the conflict will be viewed by each party according to how they might satisfy each of the objectives. Thus the political structures form the third level of the hierarchy. Structuring the levels of the hierarchy in this fashion is natural because this is the way people think and act.

The parties may be compared and prioritized according to their estimated influence on the final outcome. Given two parties, which will have the greater influence on the outcome? The objectives of each party are compared according to their relative importance to the party and the vigor with which one might expect them to be pursued. A typical judgment that has to be made is this: Which of two objectives is the party likely to pursue more, and how much more? We evaluate the objectives in pairs according to their contribution to the relevant party in the level immediately above.

The political structures may similarly be compared and prioritized in a pairwise comparison matrix according to how strongly they would satisfy a given objective in the view of the party in the level immediately above. The process is repeated for each objective of each party. The final priority for each political structure then may be obtained by composite weighting through the hierarchy. Calculations may be eliminated if the contributions to the weights are clearly negligible.

The most likely result has the highest priority. The final priorities for the political structures indicate an ordering of the possible outcomes and also represent the probabilities that the outcomes are stable—and if not, how they can be made stable. Our purpose here is to determine the priorities for a well-known conflict and interpret the numerical values.

FIRST BACKWARD PROCESS

To apply the backward process, it is first necessary to find the desired outcome for each party to the conflict and to evaluate their reactions to all the outcomes. To do this, we can use the weights for the outcomes, which we obtain from the first forward process, and note how much of each weight came from each party. We can determine how much importance each party attaches to each outcome by dividing the final weight it contributes to the outcome by its power.

Essentially, the backward process places bounds on the powers of the actors and their ability to change an outcome. This gives a realistic appraisal of the possible bounds within which the various quantities in the forward process can range. Even when we assign strong objectives for each actor, either to meet that actor's preference for a desired outcome or to counter other actors' moves away from the projected outcome, the final outcome remains essentially unchanged.

SECOND FORWARD PROCESS

We repeat the forward process with the new high-priority objectives from the backward process assigned to the original set and note the outcome. The backward process is repeated with each level of the hierarchy. This time new policies to influence other actors may be introduced and prioritized, and the high-priority policies or their corresponding objectives are again assigned to the forward process.

The forward process is carried out for the third time, and again we note the final result. The result may be regarded as stable if it remains essentially unchanged after two iterations.

SECOND BACKWARD PROCESS

We are ready to repeat the backward process by determining once more how each party views each outcome. As one might expect, each party still has different preferred scenarios and in fact maintains its preference ordering. A further iteration may be carried out to see if this solution can be upset.

PERSPECTIVE

The AHP has been applied on several occasions to analyze conflict situations. The judgments used are those of the parties—either by actual participation, if this is possible, or from their statements and declared positions as known to the group analyzing the problem. The process makes it possible to vary the judgments from the most optimistic to the most pessimistic to show the parties what possible outcomes can be achieved and what responses are available to them to press a point or to check excessive demands made by the opposition. The participation also makes it possible to pinpoint the significant differences and to learn where tradeoffs can be made on other issues in the hierarchy that may be important to one party but not to another. The AHP also sensitizes the parties in a conflict to a whole range of options and tradeoffs.

In the next chapter we will see how the analytic hierarchy process has been applied to two complex problems: the conflict in Northern Ireland and the conflict between Logan Airport and the East Boston community.

KEY CONCEPTS

- ☐ Conflict problems, like other complex problems, can be structured as a hierarchy and then analyzed in terms of priorities.
- ☐ Applied to conflict resolution, the *forward process* involves determining the most likely outcome given the present situation.
- ☐ Another approach to conflict resolution is the *backward process*— finding the desired outcome and then determining how to achieve it.
- ☐ By combining the desired with the likely, a more acceptable outcome may be found that is preferred by all parties to the likely outcome. The process itself can induce people to look beyond the existing conflict.

10

Practical Examples of Conflict Resolution

This chapter deals with the following questions:

- How can the forward-backward process be applied to the conflict in Northern Ireland?

- How can the forward-backward process be applied to the conflict between Logan Airport and the East Boston community?

SEEKING A BETTER WAY OUT

Conflict problems may have causes that are deeply entrenched. Certainly none of the parties likes the conflict; nor do they see an easy way out. They are also reluctant to compromise for fear that one compromise might lead to another, weakening their position and undermining their existence. Such an impasse is hard to resolve and must be either embedded in a larger, more productive debate to enable give and take or be resolved experimentally in small steps that show a better way out. The analysis of the conflict in Northern Ireland presented in this chapter is such an example. It involved travel, contacts, television appearances, talks at conferences, and other ways of both giving and getting information. The analysis was carried out jointly with the author's colleague Dr. Joyce Alexander, who obtained the information and made the contacts.

The second example is a better illustration of what happens often in society. People do something to serve the community at large, only to create problems for a smaller community of mostly innocent bystanders. Such problems may not be seen at the start. Everyone is glad there are jobs and productivity. In the long run, however, a happy operation can turn sour for some of the people who cannot simply leave because the problem is in their homeground. This is the case with a community around an airport in East Boston. What can and what cannot be done?

FORWARD-BACKWARD CONFLICT RESOLUTION: CONFLICT IN NORTHERN IRELAND

Environment of the Problem

The conflict in Northern Ireland, like all conflicts, involves several parties pursuing different outcomes. Some of the parties—perhaps all of them—must make compromises to produce an outcome that is the best compromise for all. This outcome is usually decided after the parties have lived with the conflict and perhaps suffered long enough to accept a fair resolution of benefit to all.

The people of Northern Ireland fall into two main groups. The majority are the descendants of the Scots and English settlers of the early seventeenth century; they are primarily Protestant and wish to maintain the British connection. The minority are the descendants of the original inhabitants; primarily Roman Catholic, some of them wish to unite Northern Ireland with the Republic of Ireland, whose population is almost exclusively Roman Catholic.

When the Irish finally achieved independence from Great Britain in 1921, it was not quite what they wanted. In the revised Government of Ireland Act, passed in 1920, the Northerners exercised the choice of establishing their own political entity of Northern Ireland. This new state would have its own parliament, although certain powers, such as taxation and foreign policy, would be reserved to the British Parliament. Subsequent governments of the Irish Free State, later the Republic of Ireland, refused to recognize this partition and claimed all of Ireland. At the outset most Catholics refused to recognize the de jure existence of the state of Northern Ireland and established a reputation for disloyalty. When it became clear that the new state was not a transient phenomenon, a growing number of Catholics expressed the desire to participate at policymaking levels of government but found they were still regarded as potentially disloyal. The Irish Republican Army capitalized on their increasing resentment. The IRA, a militant group based largely in the Republic of Ireland, believes that violence is the only way to unite the two states and has mounted campaigns of bombing and assassination in Northern Ireland.

The conflict in Northern Ireland escalated. In 1972, Britain suspended the Northern Ireland Parliament and government and instituted direct rule from London through a secretary of state. In 1973, a new constitution for Northern Ireland was passed by the British government, which established a Northern Ireland Assembly with very limited powers. In December 1973, tripartite meetings (between representatives of the British government, the Northern Ireland executive, and the government of the Republic of Ireland) led to the agreement to form a Council of Ireland that would consider problems of interest to both states in Ireland and investigate ways in which the two states might be joined. Above all, it would assume some legislative powers. The agreement was accompanied by a declaration, to which all parties subscribed, that there would be no further change in the constitutional position of Northern Ireland unless a majority in Northern Ireland agreed.

This agreement aroused sharp resentment among the Protestant community. An immediate result was the repudiation of the leader of the executive by his own party (February 1974), followed shortly by a general strike. Supported by most Protestants, this strike brought all activity to a standstill for almost a month and led to the resignation of the executive. At that point began the direct rule of Northern Ireland from Westminster. A Constitutional Convention in Northern Ireland recommended the restoration of parliamentary government and the establishment of legislative committees on the United States model; many important chairmanships would be held by members of minority parties. This report was rejected by the British government and direct rule from London continued.

Constructing the Hierarchy

We structure this problem as a hierarchy by placing the parties to the conflict at the first full level, their objectives at the next level, and the main political outcomes that could be established at the lowest level. The parties to the conflict are identified as the British government (Britain), the Protestant community (Allegiants), the Catholic community (Moderates), the Irish Republican Army (IRA), and the government of the Republic of Ireland (Dublin). The objectives of the parties may be identified as follows:

- Britain wishes to maintain its sphere of influence in the British Isles, to maintain good relations with governments in Northern Ireland and the Republic of Ireland or with any governments in newly formed or combined states, and to ensure that power is shared between the majority and minority communities.

- The Protestant Allegiants are concerned above all that there should be no links with the Republic of Ireland. Many of them want to maintain Northern Ireland as a state separate from both Great Britain and the Republic of Ireland; others want to maintain the British connection. There is a strong feeling that there should be no Irish nationalists in policymaking positions in government, and there is also a concern for the economic well-being of the state.

- The Catholic Moderates want a share in the government as in the power sharing Executive, which collapsed in 1974. Most want the political structure to reflect an Irish dimension even if the two states are not joined. This might be represented by a strong council of Ireland. They share with the Allegiants a desire for economic well-being and take this into account in their attitudes to suggested political structures.

- The objectives of the IRA are to create a United Ireland and to drive the British out of Northern Ireland.

- In Dublin, there is concern about the effects that a political solution in Northern Ireland would have on the stability of the republic, since stability is an important objective. There is also the objective of joining the two countries together. The desire for reelection is strong. (The forces of Irish nationalism must be taken into account.) British markets are important to Dublin, and there is concern that they should not be lost.

The main political structures are:

- A united Ireland
- A totally integrated parliament of Great Britain and Northern Ireland
- A colonial assembly with a strong Council of Ireland
- A colonial assembly without a strong Council of Ireland
- A totally sovereign legislature (independence or Dominion status) with a strong Council of Ireland
- A totally sovereign legislature without a strong Council of Ireland

See the expanded hierarchy in Figure 10-1.

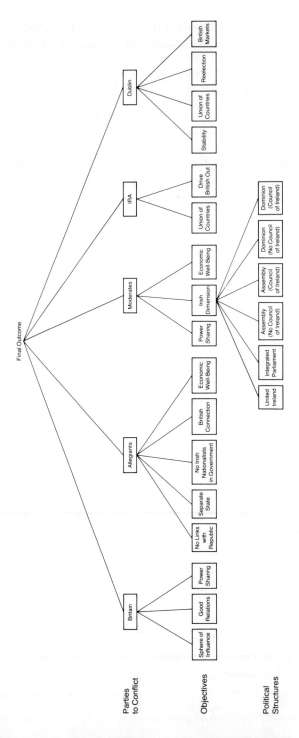

Figure 10-1   Expanded Hierarchy for Conflict in Northern Ireland

Setting Priorities and Synthesizing

The first step in the analysis is to compare the conflicting parties in pairs with respect to their relative power to affect the outcome (Table 10-1). Then we repeat the process to find the strength of objectives for each party (Table 10-2). The priority weights derived from this step are multiplied by the weight of the appropriate party to yield priority weights adjusted for power (Table 10-2). Finally, we evaluate the political structures according to the way they satisfy each objective. One of the seventeen matrices is shown in Table 10-3.

Finally, we add the corrected weights obtained for the political structures from each objective to give the final priorities for each political structure. The vector of priorities is as follows:

United Ireland	0.147
Integrated Parliament	0.156
Assembly without Council of Ireland	0.135
Assembly with Council of Ireland	0.158
Dominion without Council of Ireland	0.236
Dominion with Council of Ireland	0.170

This shows that Dominion (independent) meets the needs of the parties. In fact, the two Dominion structures together account for over two-fifths of the total weighting. Dominion without a Council of Ireland accounts for almost one-quarter of the weight. Given the present power of the parties to the conflict and their current objectives, the most likely outcome will be some form of legislative independence.

Table 10-1 Matrix of Paired Comparisons of Power to Affect Outcome

Party	Britain	Allegiants	Moderates	IRA	Dublin	Weight
Britain	1	2	6	4	9	0.45216
Allegiants	0.50	1	5	3	9	0.30792
Moderates	0.167	0.20	1	0.33	3	0.06768
IRA	0.25	0.33	3	1	5	0.13990
Dublin	0.11	0.11	0.33	0.20	1	0.03234

Note: In this matrix $a_{23} = 5$ says that our study of the events indicates that the Allegiants are *strongly* more important in affecting the outcome than are the Moderates.

Table 10-2   Adjusted Strength of Objectives

Objective	Raw Weight	Weight Adjusted for Power
Britain (power 0.452)		
Sphere of influence	0.705	0.3187
Good relations	0.211	0.0956
Power sharing	0.086	0.0380
Total	1.000	0.452
Allegiants (power 0.308)		
No link with republic	0.645	0.1987
Separate state	0.058	0.0179
No Irish Nationalists	0.183	0.0564
British connection	0.059	0.0182
Economic well-being	0.054	0.0166
Total	0.999	0.308
Moderates (power 0.068)		
Power sharing	0.691	0.0470
Irish dimension	0.160	0.0109
Economic well-being	0.149	0.0101
Total	1.000	0.068
IRA (power 0.1399)		
Union of two countries	0.12	0.0168
Drive British out	0.88	0.1231
Total	1.00	0.1399
Dublin (power 0.032)		
Stability	0.428	0.0137
Union of two countries	0.064	0.0020
Reelection	0.290	0.0093
British markets	0.218	0.0070
Total	1.000	0.032

Note: On occasion it is necessary to carry several decimals because of weighting.

Table 10-3   Allegiants: No Link with Republic

Political Structure	United Ireland	Integrated Parliament	Assembly with No Council of Ireland	Assembly with Council of Ireland	Dominion with No Council of Ireland	Dominion with Council of Ireland
United Ireland	1	0.14	0.17	1	0.11	0.20
Integrated Parliament	7	1	3	9	0.20	6
Assembly with No Council of Ireland	6	0.33	1	7	0.14	3
Assembly with Council of Ireland	1	0.11	0.14	1	0.11	0.20
Dominion with No Council of Ireland	9	5	7	9	1	9
Dominion with Council of Ireland	5	0.17	0.33	5	0.11	1

Repeating the Process

The original solution for the Northern Ireland problem indicated that an independent legislature would best satisfy the needs of all parties. An analysis of the original forward process showed that to all parties (except the Protestant Allegiants themselves) it would seem desirable to weaken the power of the Allegiants in some way, since they oppose the desires of the other parties. Although the Allegiants are the majority in Northern Ireland, there are sanctions that could be applied.

The effects of such a weakening were evaluated by repeating the forward process for the power of the Allegiants set at zero and at a number of levels between zero and the original level. It was found that the Allegiants' power had to be reduced to 44 percent of its original level before a change in the final outcome took place. This is a measure of the strength of feeling held by the Allegiants in respect to self-determination and majority rule. It may also explain why recent policies of the other actors have been directed toward the reduction of the Allegiants' power.

The analysis was then taken further. It was assumed that the Allegiants would not allow themselves to be weakened in this way without some kind of reaction—namely, to maintain their strength. Hence a useful objective for the Allegiants would be to reassure the Moderates of their desire to find a mutually agreeable solution. In consequence, the following objectives were added to the original list:

- Britain: weaken Allegiants
- Allegiants: maintain strength and reassure Moderates
- Moderates: weaken Allegiants
- IRA: weaken Allegiants
- Dublin: weaken Allegiants

The forward process was again repeated; it was found that the preferred outcome remained the same. A more sophisticated set of objectives was assigned after a second backward process was carried out. Even after this third forward process, there was no change in the preferred final outcome. This may be taken as a measure of its stability.

Composite Outcomes

The result of the hierarchic process is a set of weights for a set of final outcomes. We have already noted some ways in which we can interpret those weights. Although there are a number of distinct outcomes that obviously cannot coexist, it seems likely that a final solution, to be completely stable, must incorporate features of the other outcomes whose weights are not negligible. To formalize this process (see Table 10-4), we establish a set of characteristics covering a variation of political, economic, social, and legal factors (control of foreign policy, financing of industry, and so forth). Each of the basic scenarios may be described in terms of the change in each of these variables from the status quo. A difference scale from −8 to 8 was used.

We obtain a composite scenario by applying the final weight to the basic scenarios (outcomes) and adding to give composite weights for each of the characteristics. This gives a measure of the kind of situation that might eventuate. For example, the control of foreign policy is shown to increase considerably, but not quite as much as for a totally independent legislature. This composition of scenarios may be viewed as a composition of forces, and hence it may be regarded as representing what is likely to happen.

Table 10-4   Forward-Backward Process for Conflict in Northern Ireland

Variable	United Ireland	Integrated Parliament	Assembly, No Council	Assembly, Council	Dominion, No Council	Dominion, Council	Composite Scenario*		
							1	2	3
Political									
1. Protection of Protestant community	-6	4	5	-1	8	4	2.843	2.458	2.384
2. Protection of Catholic community	2	1	2	2	4	5	2.830	2.790	2.848
3. Protestant extremist violence (positive if increased)	8	-6	-7	4	-8	-6	-2.981	-2.484	-2.401
4. Catholic extremist violence	-8	8	-2	-4	-7	-8	-3.842	-4.139	-4.317
5. Interference from Britain (positive if increased)	-7	3	-1	-1	-8	-8	-4.102	-4.141	-4.378
6. Interference from Republic of Ireland	8	-6	0	8	-8	2	-0.044	0.428	0.568
7. Control of foreign policy	0	0	0	0	8	8	3.248	3.088	3.244
8. Majority rule (positive if increased)	-7	6	7	2	8	8	4.416	4.004	3.921

(Continued)

Table 10-4 Forward-Backward Process for Conflict in Northern Ireland (Continued)

Variable	United Ireland	Integrated Parliament	Assembly, No Council	Assembly, Council	Dominion, No Council	Dominion, Council	Composite Scenario* 1	2	3
Economic									
1. Financing of industry	0	2	2	0	4	4	2.206	2.150	2.110
2. Unemployment (positive if increased)	2	−2	−2	1	−2	−2	−0.942	−0.808	−0.785
3. Provision of employment in Protestant areas	−5	2	3	−3	2	2	0.320	0.086	0.048
4. Provision of employment in Catholic areas	4	2	2	2	2	2	2.298	2.334	2.378
5. Level of foreign investment	−1	2	2	0	3	2	1.483	1.369	1.347
6. Standard of living	−2	1	1	−1	1	1	0.245	0.149	0.133
7. Balance of payments	−2	−1	1	−1	2	1	0.169	0.080	0.102
Social									
1. Provision of education to Protestant children	−4	0	0	−1	0	0	−0.746	−0.850	−0.875

2. Provision of education to Catholic children	2	0	0	0	0	0.294	0.340	0.356
3. Provision of general education	−5	0	0	1	1	−0.329	−0.464	−0.487
4. Housing in Protestant areas	−3	1	0	1	1	0.160	0.004	0.004
5. Housing in Catholic areas	3	1	1	1	1	1.140	1.194	1.223
6. Integration of communities (positive if increased)	−4	2	−2	3	3	0.896	0.684	0.669
Legal								
1. Power of Protestant church in legal process	−8	0	0	0	0	−1.176	−1.360	−1.424
2. Power of Catholic church in legal process	8	0	0	0	0	1.176	1.360	1.424
3. Prohibition of discrimination against Protestants	−7	0	0	0	0	−1.029	−1.190	−1.246
4. Prohibition of discrimination against Catholics	3	0	0	0	0	0.441	0.510	0.534

* 1 = first forward process; 2 = second forward process; 3 = third forward process.

FORWARD-BACKWARD CONFLICT RESOLUTION: LOGAN AIRPORT AND THE EAST BOSTON COMMUNITY

Environment of the Problem

Logan International Airport in East Boston, with over 800 flights a day, is the eighth busiest airport in the world. The airport's proprietor is the Massachusetts Port Authority (Massport), an autonomous public authority financed by tax-exempt revenue bonds. Massport's expansion programs have resulted in a serious noise problem for the area's 40,000 residents, a problem that is far from unique to Logan.

Constructing the Hierarchy

The primary objective is to increase the welfare of the affected community. The parties to the conflict are Massport, the Federal Aviation Administration (FAA), the citizens, the air transport industry, and the state and local government.

Massport has the legal power to select an airport site, acquire land, assure compatible land use, and control airport design, scheduling, and operations subject to two major prohibitions: Massport may not take any action that adversely affects commerce and it may not discriminate between different categories of airport users. Massport's objectives may be summarized as (1) to promote air transportation at Logan, (2) to carry out rapid and efficient expansion, and (3) to minimize public opposition.

The FAA regulates the use of runways and airways, sets performance standards and equipment requirements, and controls the flight paths. Its authority was extended to include setting and enforcing noise standards. The FAA is oriented toward the needs of the air transport industry. Its objectives can be summarized as (1) to assure human safety, (2) to promote national air commerce, and (3) to minimize environmental harm.

Air transport corporations are interested in reducing operating costs while maintaining the service needed to attract customers. Their objectives can be summarized as (1) to offer the best service, (2) to maximize their financial position, and (3) to promote safety.

Given the federal government's virtual monopoly over air transport regulations, local and state government have very limited powers. Their main objectives are (1) to maximize East Boston land use and development, (2) to enlist voter support, and (3) to protect the local economy.

Much of East Boston's population decline (over 20 percent since 1950) can be attributed to encroachment of transportation facilities. The low-income, working class, residential community now numbers under 40,000. Low-flying aircraft and frequent high noise levels have led to loss of sleep, tension, fatigue, high blood pressure, and loss of hearing. The citizens have been engaged in a long battle with Massport. Their objectives are (1) peace and tranquility in their daily lives, (2) to remain in East Boston, and (3) community health and safety.

Regulations governing noise pollution at the source call for quieter engines or acoustic treatment of the engine casing. Airlines are opposed to large-scale implementation, however, as it would greatly increase their operating costs. Operational techniques such as use of minimum certified flaps or preferential runway systems and night curfews are questioned by the industry as being detrimental to safety and conducive to increased workloads and delays. Policies restricting land use are preventive more than remedial; substantial community disruption or lack of much-needed development may result.

Setting Priorities and Synthesizing

To analyze the alternatives and their priorities, we set up the following forward process. The findings are presented in Figure 10-2. In the forward projection the two most likely outcomes for policy implementation are land use restrictions (weight 0.52) and source regulations (0.24), clearly showing that citizens' preferences are being ignored. The citizens have negligible influence over noise abatement. Moreover, they cannot expect remedial action from the state and local government. The FAA and Massport are the two dominant forces, and their major objectives are in direct conflict with the objectives of the citizens. Therefore, the most likely policy to be adopted is land use restrictions that alter the character of their neighborhood against the people's will.

Next, various backward analyses were performed to test the effect of coalitions. One involved state and local government and citizens but produced no marked change in the outcome. The other also assumed a coalition of the FAA and the EPA. We then analyzed a plan for citizen action from the priorities: source regulations (0.22), land use restrictions (0.29), operating techniques (0.31), and night curfews (0.15). Two possible courses of action emerged: (1) state government takeover of Massport and (2) a shift of federal noise abatement powers from the FAA to the EPA–FAA.

The first course would return accountability of the airport proprietor to the public. While Massport's quasi-public status solves certain financial and political problems, it also eliminates much citizen input from the decision-making process. Private investors have replaced the voter's voice. The first coalition has such low priority that implementation of this course of action would not lead to a significant change in the situation. The second course would introduce the EPA as a significant actor. This course

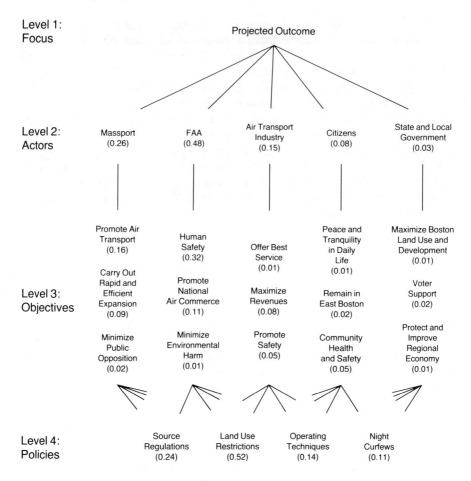

Figure 10-2   Hierarchy for Conflict at Logan Airport

recognizes not only the considerable power of the FAA in promulgating noise abatement procedures but also the EPA's potential to bring greater cooperation with state and local government. The coalition would alter the federal priority structure to give increased emphasis on the single issue of environmental harm. This analysis shows where to concentrate effort to solve a longstanding problem.

PERSPECTIVE

In dealing with short-range and long-range conflicts the AHP helps the participants to highlight in detail all the issues involved and enables them to compare notes and see which outcomes are likely to emerge as most acceptable. The process induces cooperation in less significant areas; on more important issues, it can improve communications. It can also redirect emphasis to the real problem. Finally and significantly, use of the AHP in many conflict examples has demonstrated to third parties the nature of the problem and what they can do to encourage the opponents to compromise through mediation—or, on occasion, through incentives or sanctions. Such analyses can be made even where the parties refuse to participate.

11

Analyzing Benefit/Cost Decisions and Resource Allocation

This chapter deals with the following questions:

- How can the analytic hierarchy process be applied to benefit/cost decisions?

- How can we construct hierarchies of benefits and costs?

- How does the process deal with the problem of separating costs from benefits?

- How does the process deal with the problem of quantifying factors that are intangible?

- How does the process deal with the problem of evaluating mixed resources and activities?

HOW THE PROCESS CAN HELP

In this chapter we apply the AHP to benefit/cost analysis and resource allocation. Benefit/cost (B/C) analysis is a traditional tool for allocating resources among a set of activities. It is a practical method for:

- Deciding whether to undertake specific projects
- Selecting the most productive activities with the highest benefit/cost ratios
- Selecting projects whose benefits can be distributed among the population in specified ways
- Maximizing total benefits within given constraints (such as a budget)
- Reviewing a set of existing projects for possible elimination or reallocation of resources

Applying the AHP to benefit/cost analysis can improve this traditional decision-making tool. First, after structuring benefit/cost problems in an analytic hierarchy, we can use the pairwise comparison scale to quantify intangible, noneconomic factors that so far have not been effectively integrated into decision making. The hierarchy also enables us to make explicit, informed tradeoffs among many criteria for the selection of policies or projects—even when the criteria include multiple performance goals and output activities.

To achieve these extensions of B/C analysis, we construct complementary benefit and cost hierarchies. Ratios of benefits and costs can be projected into the future to identify projects that may be desirable to implement. Thus we will see that B/C analysis can be given an explicit time dimension, which permits a decision maker to apply different discount rates and risk-management strategies at different points in the future.

Moreover, the goal of traditional B/C analysis and economic choice has been to maximize benefits (utility), subject to whatever constraints the economic and political environments impose. Because analysts have not been able to quantify intangible political factors into a common currency to make comparisons and tradeoffs, they have had to seek solutions in various methods of analysis. The procedure offered here, however, fully integrates the economic and political environments as objectives or criteria for evaluating a resource allocation scheme.

Finally, the AHP provides a way to solve complex benefit/cost and resource allocation problems in which sets of mixed resources must be assigned to sets of activities that can be only indirectly measured and compared for evaluation. In the next chapter we will see how the process can be applied to portfolio selection for a corporation. Before we explore specific applications, however, we will consider the problems of separating costs from benefits, quantifying intangible factors, and evaluating mixed resources and activities, as well as the construction of B/C hierarchies.

PROBLEMS OF BENEFIT/COST ANALYSIS

Separating Costs from Benefits

Separating costs from benefits is apparently a natural aspect of human reasoning. Usually, we decide what is a cost and what is a benefit in a piecemeal fashion for each problem we encounter. Although we would prefer to separate costs from benefits systematically, there are several reasons why no general solution has emerged.

First, individuals may disagree not only about the relative magnitudes of costs and benefits but also about their definition. Although masochists may positively value pain (such as paying taxes without receiving benefits in return), criteria for evaluating choices reflect fairly normal values. If Detroit were to place a regulator on cars to prevent them from exceeding 55 mph, who would derive benefits and who would incur costs—and of what kinds? A number of pragmatic solutions to determine which consequences are costs and which are benefits can, however, be applied:

- Aggregation of individual preferences (perhaps by voting)
- Definition of a social welfare function
- Expansion of the problem's scope (expansion to a choice among alternative transport and energy policies in the example above) in the hope of gaining more complete agreement

However, none of these solutions touches a deeper analytic difficulty in separating costs from benefits.

This difficulty arises from the apparent structure of many scalable quantities as ranges in which the endpoints represent opposite extremes and the midpoint represents a neutral value or lack of the quantity being scaled. Cooperation–conflict, friendliness–hostility, and—perhaps—cost-benefit appear to be such conceptual ranges. To my knowledge, no technique exists for constructing, as a single ratio scale, a range of this sort from stimuli or measurements obtained by direct observation. In other words, we do not know how to make scales with "center" points representing neutrality, absence, indifference, and so forth.

Situations arise in which all the objects to be scaled lie to one side of a hypothesized midpoint on a range. For instance, we are able to deal with the comparison of several different sets of costs. Yet when some items are costs and others benefits, it is generally not possible to construct questions that allow us to compare the relative merits of costs and benefits directly in pairs.

Here a third kind of difficulty arises. Consider a choice to be made among a number of vacation sites. One could list the benefits of vacationing at alternative sites and include them in a single hierarchy. One could also place costs—transportation costs, travel time, and the like—in a hierarchy. This strategy yields one hierarchy for benefits and another for costs. If people disagree about which factors constitute costs and which constitute benefits (say, travel time), the same elements can be included in different roles in both hierarchies.

Alternatively, in this restricted problem one could redefine some monetary costs as benefits in order to evaluate vacation sites with respect to their economy of travel or other criterion. In effect, this strategy reverses the direction of an implicit scale of monetary costs and takes the most expensive site as a baseline for comparison with the alternatives. One can see that this solution to integrating costs and benefits would fail in more complex problem settings.

Suppose that a new government program is undertaken to conserve energy by paying vacationers a subsidy to stay at home. A new vacation site—let's call it the backyard pool—enters as an alternative, except that its cost is negative, say −$50. Now costs of travel can no longer all be included within a single hierarchy, because the person supplying judgments is required to estimate the relative contribution to economy of one trip costing −$50 with another costing, say, +$200.

Because the attributes of alternative policies or projects generally involve both positive and negative contributions to several criteria (and because the same criteria may not be meaningful in a single hierarchy), a better strategy for characterizing B/C problems with analytic hierarchies is to construct separate hierarchies for benefits and for costs and then to investigate their possible integration in a restricted problem.

Quantifying Intangible Factors

In the extensive work done on B/C analysis, there is widespread recognition that many relevant factors escape quantification. More serious, they may succumb to traditional operations research techniques. Most practitioners resign themselves to these limitations and leave to the decision maker the problem of coping with the lack of a measure for intangibles. This situation does not guarantee that the decision maker integrates quantitative and qualitative factors better than would the analyst alone, however. It also greatly dilutes the value of the quantitative analysis because the choice of relevant measurable factors is deliberately inadequate.

Evaluating Mixed Resources and Activities

In many problems, resources can be valued in a common unit of measurement, a single dimension of exchange. A convertible currency, such as the dollar, is usually adequate for measuring the costs of performance at a specified level of an activity. Evaluation by a common currency presumes that exchange among units of different resources can be made freely by using the ratio of their costs. Of course, these currencies are not readily available in noneconomic areas. Particularly when an allocation problem extends to social, political, or (nonmarket) environmental issues, the heterogeneity of the resources and laws against their exchange prevent expression in terms of a currency. There are three measurement problems affecting tradeoffs among resources and activities: lack of a common currency, inadequate exchange for establishing prices, and short-term horizons.

- *Lack of a Common Currency:* Resources may be priced directly through the use of exchange rates or indirectly as shadow prices, which represent some internal mechanism or rule for effecting tradeoffs. Despite the possibilities of shadow pricing, the valuation of all inputs in a single predetermined currency may not be practicable or desirable. For some resources, no market may exist—perhaps because the resource is unique, because it has only recently been created (or recognized as useful to the productive process), or because its exchange is thought to be immoral or socially debilitating. Even when exchange is physically and morally possible, the resource may be so exotic that participants in the system are unable to set any but the most approximate value on it. The valuation of human talent is a case in point.

- *Inadequate Exchange for Establishing Prices:* Valuation of resources may be difficult if some are fixed, such as existing physical assets, and regulated as to use. For example, constraints may be imposed on the employment, promotion, and distribution of manpower through the Civil Service Code. Physical and human capital may take the form of an existing "inventory" whose flexibility of use is small but whose marginal costs for use are also small. Other items of the inventory may be valued at a premium over market prices if there are restrictions on replacement. These phenomena are, in some sense, failures of an existing or potential market. But from the perspective of the person charged with the efficient allocation of such resources, trying to value them through a hypothetical market is not very useful.

- *Short-Term Horizons:* In the very short term, a market may not exist or may inadequately reflect the exchange rates of large volumes of resources. In this situation, resources take on values reflecting their comparative usefulness or, in a loose sense, "opportunity costs" for the performance of the specified set of activities of the system. The alternative uses may be hypothetical or may lie in the future. Such would be the value of resources husbanded or hoarded for future use. Furthermore, in the short term the "internal" valuation by the system of some resources, such as specialized skills or knowledge crucial to several activities, may greatly exceed valuation by an "external" market.

For these reasons, the decision maker who can select among alternative combinations of resources and alternative levels of system performance must develop a way to evaluate potential resources in a dynamic fashion that is highly sensitive to the actual context of the system. Because a market is unlikely to extend to all the relevant resources or to adequately measure their contributions to the performance of a system in a given context, the decision maker must acquire methods for comparing mixed resources by using all available information. One flexible, extensive, and efficient approach to evaluation is the analytic hierarchy.

STRUCTURING BENEFIT/COST HIERARCHIES

In resource allocation problems, analytic hierarchies useful for measuring costs or benefits are typically constructed as follows. The highest levels include the overall objectives of the organization or system. Criteria for assessing benefit/cost allocations may appear in another level. A subordinate level may clarify these criteria in the context of the problem by itemizing specific objectives or tasks that are to be accomplished at some level of performance specified in advance. Then the relative impacts of specific tasks on general allocation objectives, such as aggregate consumption and redistribution, can be measured. Once benefits and costs have been obtained, ratios of benefits to cost (priority ratios) and of appropriate differences possibly using discounting are formed and the resources are allocated accordingly. It is recommended that long-range benefit/cost analyses consider the individual periods of time (short, medium, and long range) in the second level. The third level should itemize the overall benefit criteria (or cost criteria for the costs hierarchy). The elements in the second and third level are prioritized in terms of each other, thus creating a loop between the time periods and the criteria. Two types of questions are answered here: Given a time period, which criterion is the most desired? Given a criterion, in which time period is the criterion most important?

Using the priorities obtained from both questions, one then derives priorities for the horizons and for the criteria without having to answer such a difficult question as which time horizon is more important to attain the overall objective of the corporation. The final priorities of the horizons and the criteria are obtained by using the supermatrix method of the AHP. The remaining questions in the hierarchy proceed downward from the level of criteria.

At lower levels of the hierarchy, usually between the criteria and the alternatives, policies are often listed to evaluate the contribution anticipated from each potential policy to each objective. Policies can be further subdivided into projects or packages of related projects whose relative importance may differ depending on which policies are adopted. Still more specifically, clusters of resources are listed as elements on a subordinate level—similar to the way in which alternative allocation packages are evaluated in zero-based budgeting—in order to measure the importance of these finite allocations with respect to the accomplishment of individual projects. Ultimately the decision maker seeks the best allocation of resource packages to perform a set of high-priority objectives under specified constraints.

Figure 11-1 presents a simple illustration of benefit/cost hierarchies. The overall objective for both hierarchies is to choose an optimum fuel heating system. The benefit criteria are efficiency, reliability, and adaptability to the addition of a solar heating component. Several alternatives are then compared with respect to these criteria or refinements of them if so desired. Similarly, the cost hierarchy includes criteria of fuel and equipment costs, maintenance and service costs, and environmental impact costs.

PERSPECTIVE

In making a decision on a short-range or long-range profit, a decision maker (particularly an elected one) has been observed to follow one of three alternative courses of action: (1) to examine short-run and long-run benefits and pains (both economic and intangible) associated with the activity and choose the best option available, (2) to put personal concerns first and formulate the decision in serving his or her personal interests, and (3) to hedge a little by projecting personal interests with an altruistic concern for the success of the activity to reap the maximum benefit. Particularly in the social and political fields, the AHP offers the decision maker a way to choose a course of action which places less emphasis on personal interest.

In general, the following questions are dealt with in the analysis of benefits and costs:

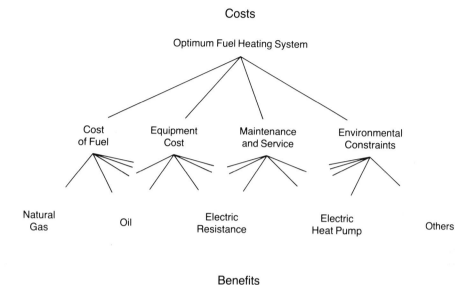

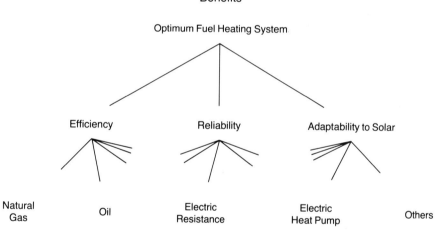

Figure 11-1   Typical Benefit/Cost Hierarchies

- Given a time period, which criterion is most likely to yield the greatest benefits (costs) to the welfare of those concerned by choosing one of the options considered?

- Given a criterion, during which time period is that criterion most likely to yield the greatest benefits (costs) to the welfare from the choice of an option? (The first two levels yield a cycle from which the priorities are derived.)

- Given a benefit (cost) criterion, which subcriterion is important to that criterion? (This is done for each period.)
- Given a benefit (cost) subcriterion, which option is the most important—that is, yields the greatest benefits or incurs the greatest costs? (This is again done for each time period.)

Benefits and costs are often observed to have greater value in the future than in the present. Nevertheless, these values have a certain worth in the present that affects the decision being made. Thus the output of both the benefits and the costs hierarchies is often discounted in terms of its utility in the present. This discounting decreases over the time horizon considered.

Discounting (which is a weighting process) of both tangible and intangible factors is done in a similar fashion to discounting money—that is, by estimating the worth of benefits and costs in present value. This process is carried out before forming the preference ratios, which for lack of better words I call benefit/cost ratios.

KEY CONCEPTS

☐ The analytic hierarchy process, unlike conventional benefit/cost analysis, is capable of converting intangible factors into a common currency that permits comparisons and evaluation.

☐ The analytic hierarchy process can also be used to solve complex benefit/cost decisions and resource allocation problems involving mixed resources and activities.

☐ Two hierarchies are constructed for this purpose. One deals only with the criteria that relate to evaluation of the benefits of the alternatives; the other deals with criteria relating to costs.

12

Practical Examples of Benefit/Cost Analysis and Resource Allocation

This chapter deals with the following questions:

- How can the analytic hierarchy process be used to allocate resources for an R&D program?

- How can the process be used to decide on a home computer system?

- How can the process be used to select a portfolio for a corporation?

SHORT-TERM AND LONG-TERM DECISIONS

There seem to be two types of decisions in the business world. One type is concerned with short-range alternatives whose consequences can be foreseen. The first and third examples in this chapter are of this kind. Annual investment or evaluation is needed so that the most promising alternatives will materialize while the less promising ones are eliminated. The other type of decision deals with alternatives whose life span is not determined. These alternatives require a long-range view of the consequences of their implementation, and their realization calls for ongoing investment. The second example is of this kind: an immediate problem requiring a decision on the best computer available. But that is not enough. Since the resources may be needed for other alternatives, two sets of benefit/cost hierarchies are required for this decision. Now let us see how the AHP can be applied to three practical examples involving benefit/cost analysis and resource allocation.

ALLOCATING RESOURCES FOR AN R&D PROGRAM

Figure 12-1 shows a benefit hierarchy constructed to guide resource allocation in research and development by a research institute (RI). In analyzing the benefits that may be derived from various projects in research, development, testing, and evaluation, one must acknowledge RI's responsibility to ensure that an integrated energy system—for generation, storage, conversion, transmission, and distribution—is created to meet anticipated demands. Thus the measurement of potential benefits from a specific project and technology exceeds in scope the financial return on that project and encompasses its contribution to the overall system of the future. It is RI's responsibility to support progress in areas that are, taken individually, cost ineffective.

After examining RI's current operations and plans, its mandate from its clients, its cooperative arrangements with other R&D institutions, and contemporary assessments of technological, economic, and social alternatives, we constructed the hierarchy pictured in Figure 12-1. In level 1 of the hierarchy, we charted RI's activities for three future dates and applied a discount to the return (that is, benefits) in each.

The sources of electric power in each of the three target years have been projected by a number of industry and government sources. At level 2 we enumerated power sources, reasoning that the technological options for the electric utilities are primarily driven by fuel availabilities. The projected proportions of electric power from each source can be taken directly from existing projections, under an implicit assumption of a "most likely" scenario. Two elements at this level were ignored in the subsequent analysis. Petroleum and natural gas were judged to have such a short

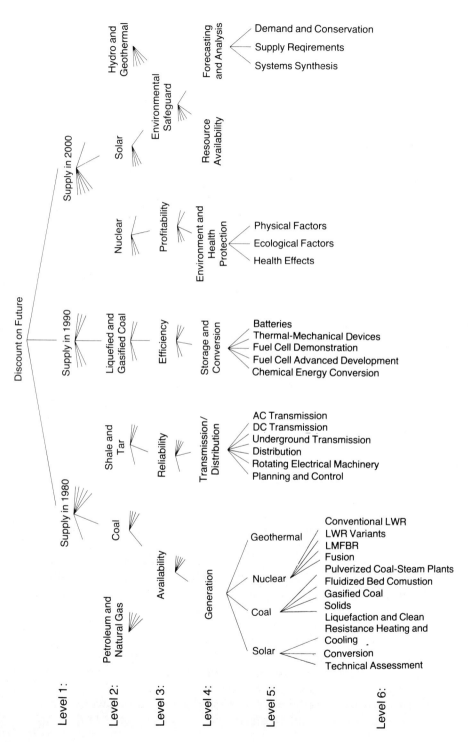

Figure 12-1 Hierarchy of an R&D Program for a Research Institute

useful life for electric power generation that investments to improve the efficiency of their use will have little or no return. Hydro and geothermal power were projected to have such localized benefits that their exploitation should be left to the utilities and other interests that would benefit directly. Thus the critical elements around which RI's allocations must be made are coal, shale and tar, liquefied and gasified coal, nuclear power, and solar power.

The research institute's current planning takes as objectives five operational criteria that may be summarized by the elements on level 3. These are availability of supply, reliability of power generation from each fuel, efficiency of the use of the fuel for production of electric power, profitability of power production from the fuel, and safeguarding the environment from damage caused by generation of power with the fuel. From the literature and from discussions with specialists in the power industry and academia, we hazarded judgments about the relative challenge posed by each of these objectives, given the projections about fuel usage derived from level 2. We scaled the objectives at level 3 to derive priorities of their importance as targets for, or sources of problems to be overcome by, the institute's R&D program.

At level 4, we listed the various aspects of supplying electric power. Again using the judgments of specialists in the field, we prioritized these elements to measure the importance of each operational area to future power production. Elements at this level correspond closely to RI's divisions, and the priorities we assigned to these elements indicate the proportion of total resources that should be allocated to each. Subordinate levels 5 and 6 comprise more detailed breakdowns of activities that may be carried out to permit the analyst to determine resource allocations for individual projects or technologies—for example, for the conventional boiling or pressurized water reactors versus the fast breeder reactor at level 6. One of the elements at level 4, assuring the availability of fuel resources, falls outside RI's mandate and was therefore not subdivided further.

Priorities at the lower levels represent benefits to be derived from the individual project or technology as a proportion of total benefit to the electric power system. The benefits integrate all the factors enumerated in the hierarchy—for example, the objectives on level 3—under the hypothesis of a projected discount rate of level 1 and distribution of fuel sources of level 2. An analyst can, of course, vary the assumptions at the topmost levels to investigate how the benefits of individual projects and technologies vary in response. Those that evince high benefits under a wide variety of plausible conditions are obviously prime candidates for R&D support. Note that the use of multiple, nonfinancial objectives on level 3 assures that benefits will accrue to relatively expensive projects that are, however, crucial ingredients of an integrated electric power system.

If we assume that the only costs are the dollars allocated to develop-

ment of the technologies, we can compare RI's current budgetary allocations to technologies in order to determine which areas of R&D deserve
more support and which deserve less. In other words, taking the ratio of
priorities (derived from the hierarchy for Figure 12-1) to current budgetary
allocations, we get a first cut at assessing benefit/cost ratios. These data are
presented in Table 12-1, on the next page.

In most comprehensive analyses of large social systems, costs are not
limited to dollars. As benefit/cost analysts are well aware, there may also
be substantial components of "externalities" that escape the price system.
The next illustration of the AHP approach introduces separate hierarchies
for benefits and costs in a very simple problem.

DECIDING ON A HOME COMPUTER

A middle-class family consisting of children of grade school age, a
professionally computer-oriented wife, and a college professor husband
considered buying a programmable home computer. Their intention was
to have a source of education, to be able to enter checking accounts, rec-
ipes, addresses, and the like, and even to carry out computations in the
husband's line of work. Their choice had to be made among three types
available in the market: Apple II, Radio Shack, and Texas Instruments.
The husband could connect a computer terminal in the house to a university computer to satisfy his needs, but the family would thereby lose
the home computer's educational value for the children and the domestic
needs would remain. While examining the costs of the computer, the
family—which at the time was incurring considerable expenses in ren-
ovating an old house—also wished to consider keeping the money in
the bank (to gather interest), donating it to charity, or cementing the
driveway.

Here we need two benefit/cost hierarchies. One is to determine the
most desirable computer from the standpoint of the family. The other is to
decide which alternative to follow: the computer, the bank, charity, or the
driveway.

Figures 12-2 to 12-5 show the computer benefits and computer costs
hierarchies and also the diagrams for the alternative benefits and alternative costs hierarchies. It is important in Figures 12-4 and 12-5 to cluster the
criteria into economic, psychological, and ideological categories to facilitate comparison. Since the psychological concerns received a priority of
only 0.08, these criteria were not pursued further.

In each case the family had to answer the correctly formulated question. In the benefits hierarchy, we sought relative benefits in the pairwise
comparisons; in the costs hierarchy, we sought the relative costs in the
pairwise comparisons. An overall benefit weight was divided by the over-

**Table 12-1   RI's Proportionate Funding for 1977
Compared with Priorities of Benefits***

Program	I Percentage of RI's Budget	II Priority $\times 10^2$ (from Figure 12-1)*
Generation	54	46
Nuclear	28	26
Coal	22	30
Solar	5	2.5
Geothermal	2	2.5
Transmission/distribution	18	7
AC transmission	4	4.1
DC transmission	6	2.7
Underground transmission	4	0.8
Distribution	3	0.3
Rotating electrical machinery	0	0.3
Planning and control	1	1.1
Storage and conversion	8	14
Batteries	2	9.6
Thermal-mechanical	1	4.5
Fuel cell demonstration	3	1.3
Fuel cell advanced development	2	2.3
Chemical energy conversion	0	1.1
Environment and health	15	6
Physical factors	11	0.5
Ecological factors	2	1.5
Health effects	2	6.1
Forecasting and analysis	5	1
Demand and conservation	1	0.8
Supply requirements	2	0.3
Systems synthesis	2	0.2
Resource availability		27

* Where necessary, some of RI's expenditures have been reallocated from their actual division to the category most descriptive of the activities they support. Analysis and software pertinent to a single program are included in that program category. Analysis pertinent to systems integration is allocated to forecasting and analysis.

Level 1:
Focus

Level 2:
Objectives

Level 3:
Attributes

Level 4:
Computer
Types

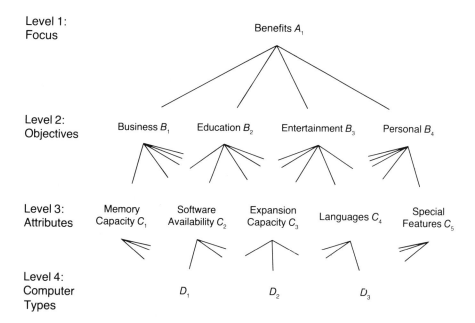

Figure 12-2   Hierarchy of Computer Benefits

Level 1:
Focus

Level 2:
Objectives

Level 3:
Alternatives

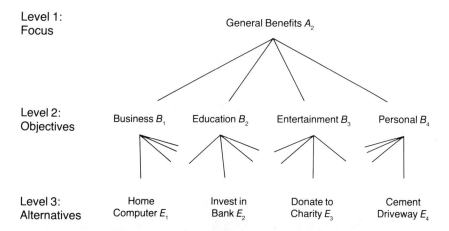

Figure 12-3   Hierarchy of Benefits from Alternatives

210 BENEFIT/COST ANALYSIS AND RESOURCE ALLOCATION

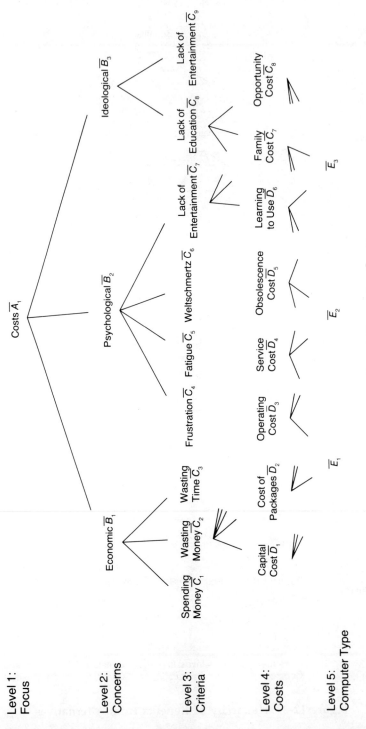

Figure 12-4 Hierarchy of Computer Costs

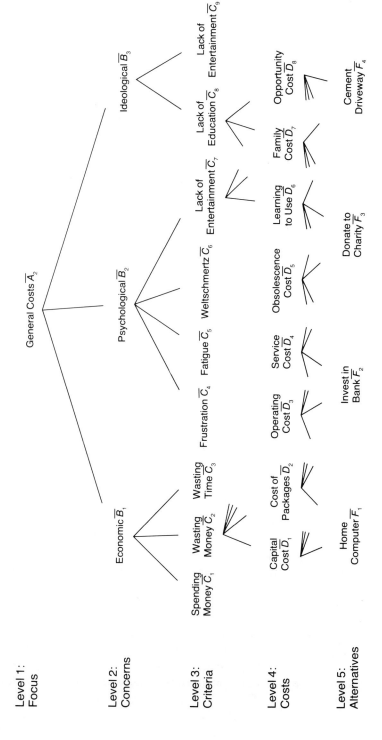

Figure 12-5 Hierarchy of Costs of Alternatives

Table 12-2   Benefit Weights, Cost Weights, and Benefit/Cost Ratio

	Benefit Weights	Cost Weights	Benefit/Cost Ratio
Computer			
I.	0.243	0.383	0.634
II	0.443	0.381	1.163
III	0.314	0.236	1.389
Alternatives			
Computer	0.348	0.405	0.859
Bank	0.195	0.113	1.726
Charity	0.220	0.282	0.780
Driveway	0.237	0.200	1.185

all cost weight to obtain the benefit/cost ratio. Table 12-2 shows that if the family were to buy a home computer, computer C would be the most desirable. If they were to select the best of the four alternatives, however, the benefit/cost ratios say that the money should remain in the bank. This is also the result one would get by using marginal analysis of differences of consecutive costs and their corresponding benefit differences. It took nearly two working days to carry out this exercise and write the report. The project involved three students and nearly five hours of interviews with the family. The cost priorities of the alternatives were evaluated in terms of the three highest priority costs: $\bar{D}_1$, $\bar{D}_7$, and $\bar{D}_8$. I call this process *telescoping* or truncating.

SELECTING A PORTFOLIO FOR A CORPORATION

In this application, rather than discussing an analysis completed by others, we consider a strategic management blueprint for working out a portfolio based on evaluating benefits and costs. The solution is open-ended: This example provides only the directions for using the AHP approach.

An executive officer of a large corporation once gave his simple definition of strategic management: "Take money out of a bad business and put it into a good business." On pursuing the subject further he found that by a good business he meant one that accrues benefits and by a bad business one that incurs pains. Traditionally people have interpreted pains as costs, but costs often refer to money and a bad business can have other pains besides financial problems.

An important idea emerges from these considerations—namely, that for a good business the benefits usually exceed the costs and for a bad business the converse is true. Of course, in starting any operation, the costs will exceed the immediate benefits for some time. Nevertheless, by looking at the future one can generally estimate how much benefit can be expected over the long run. Such thinking leads one to focus on benefits and costs as the basic ingredients in selecting a business portfolio.

Most large businesses consist of several companies, each specializing in a different activity. The total set of activities usually complement each other in a way that produces a coherent framework to satisfy corporate objectives. Sometimes complementarity is not possible because of diversity. The object is to evaluate these companies according to their overall benefits and costs. This is done directly by comparing them according to their relative strengths (benefits) and their weaknesses (costs). Often the number of companies is large. (There are corporations with nearly two hundred companies.)

Clustering Benefits and Costs

The first step in comparing benefits and costs of a large number of companies in a corporation is to examine alternative ways in which they can be put into clusters. The resulting clustering schemes should be designed to reflect both desirable (benefit) and undesirable (cost) properties. In practice one would focus on a few clustering methods that, in the evaluation process, turn out to be the most significant for aggregating the companies. Here are some typical clustering schemes:

- Type of manufacturing or service
- Market-end use
- Driving force
- Distribution channels
- Investment intensity
- Market share
- Cyclicality
- Sensitivity to technological change
- Inherent cash flow
- Labor intensity

- Growth rate/potential
- Product life cycle
- Geographic segmentation
- Internationalization
- Financial leverage
- Nuclear sensitivity
- Knowledge sensitivity
- Risk classification
- Financial performance
- Environmental impact

In each clustering scheme the companies are divided into five to seven groups ranging from very low to very high according to how strongly a company benefits that clustering property. For example, a company that is highly automated would be put in the "very low" group under the labor intensity cluster whereas an assembly line operation with considerable manpower would fall in the "very high" group of this clustering scheme. The groups of the scheme are then compared among themselves according to benefits and costs.

Ranking Benefits and Costs

The benefits of a business are themselves ranked according to their impact on the major objectives of the operation. The same process is repeated for the costs. The criteria are subdivisions of the overall objectives and are in turn compared as to their relative impact on the objectives. Finally the objectives are ranked according to their significance to the success and survival of the organization.

This process is done once to project the outcome of existing trends of benefits and costs; then their ratios and marginal ratios are formed. With a plan for the future, the process is repeated by altering the emphasis on the importance of the objectives and subobjectives. This alteration would be reflected in the adoption of new policies leading to the expansion of certain companies, the acquisition of new ones, and the sale of old ones whose overall benefit/cost ratio is deemed too low. The combined benefit and cost hierarchies are depicted in Figure 12-6.

Figure 12-7 outlines the steps of the prioritization process for a benefits hierarchy and a costs hierarchy. Level 2 splits the concentration of effort over time. Level 3 identifies the major corporate concerns, which are clustered into two categories: (1) growth, sales, and earnings and (2) survival of the organization and management. Level 4 identifies the corporation's objectives. Possible subobjectives for level 5 are given in Table 12-3. Level 5 is followed by a set of criteria for benefits and another set for costs. This level is then followed by clustering schemes that may be used in both hierarchies or may be separated according to their utility in evaluating benefits and costs. The clustering schemes are followed by business units and then by a level in which the companies themselves are listed.

Identifying Benefits and Costs

Our objective here is to identify the benefits and the costs that the corporation accrues from its business segments. To be able to identify some of the benefits and costs, we must first identify criteria to which the

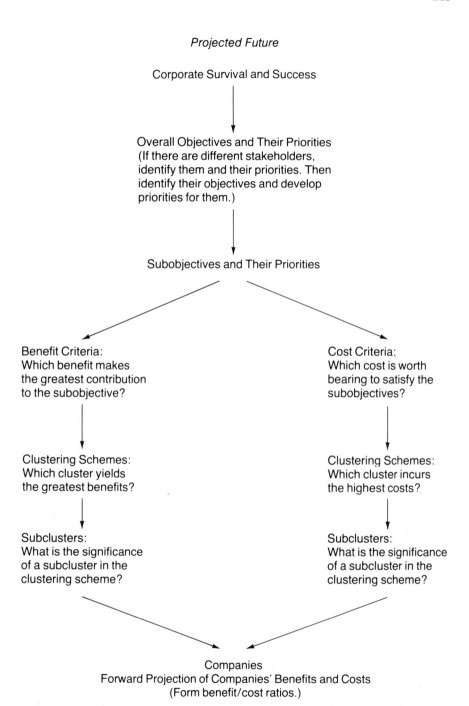

Figure 12-6   Combined Benefit and Cost Hierarchies

Level 1:			Focus		
Level 2:		Short Range		Long Range	
Level 3:	Shareholder Improvement	Growth	Survival	Management Perpetuation	
	Growth, Sales, Earnings		Survival of Organization and Management		

Level 4:

Market Standing · Innovation · Ability to Manage Physical and Financial Resources · Productivity and Added Value · Corporate Commitment · Worker Performance and Attitude · Management Development · Public Responsibility

Level 5:	Subobjectives
Level 6:	Benefit or Cost Criteria
Level 7:	Clustering Schemes
⋮	⋮
Level n:	Business Segments

Figure 12-7   Analytic Hierarchy for Strategic Planning

benefits and costs are related. Thus, whatever the objectives may be, we look at the business segments and ask:

- Are they increasing in value?
- What are the different rates at which they are increasing in value?
- Is their size significant?
- What is the relative pain associated with increasing the value of one business over another at the same rate?

These questions are the criteria for setting policy. The value of the system is what someone else is willing to pay for it.

With these criteria in mind, we identify four major actors that interact with the corporation:

- The managers or operators
- The system (the corporation itself)
- Other systems (other corporations or potential competitors)
- The environment (government, EPA, and so on)

Thus to identify the benefits we ask: What are the benefits to the managers or operators, the system, other systems, and the environment resulting

Table 12-3   Subobjectives

Market standing	*Productivity and added value (constant $)*
Market share	Value added per employee
Relative	5% increase per year
Absolute	Capital expenditure
Concentration ratio	Value added (% sales billed)
Defensibility of market share	$ per employee and equipment
Service	*Corporate commitment*
Image	Operating profit (% sales)
Distribution effectiveness	IAT (% sales)
Coverage	ROI
Market share trends	Earnings growth
Product synergy	Sales growth
Size	Absolute IACC
Growth rate	*Worker performance and attitude*
Innovation	Representation
Number of product "firsts"	Work stoppages
Number of patents	EEO
Engineering expenditures	Size of plant
Number of engineers	Plant age
Ability to manage physical and financial resources	Turnover
Age of facilities	*Management development*
Inventory/sales ratio	*Public responsibility*
Investment turnover	
Receivable ratios	
Debt/equity ratio	

from economic, social, political, technological, and environmental changes reflected through an increase of the system's value? At what rate does the system increase its value? Is the size significant in these benefits?

Suppose we look at the benefits in greater detail. We begin with the economic benefits accrued by the managers or operators from the corporation (system):

1. Salary
2. Employee compensation:

- Increases in per capita market value reflecting increases in productivity as shown by average salary increases
- Percentage of employees participating in increases reflecting scope of productivity increases
- Percentage increase in revenues per employee reflecting per capita productivity increase

3. Fringe benefits affecting the quality of life:
   - Health
   - Health insurance coverage
   - Life insurance coverage
   - Employment and disability coverage
   - Education
   - In-house courses
   - Company-supported external program

4. Recreation:
   - Athletic program
   - Day care services
   - Food services
   - Holidays and vacations

5. Career advancement

6. Growth of the employee

Economic benefits of the managers or operators from other systems include:

1. Job opportunities
2. Volunteer service
3. Value of reputation

Economic benefits accrued by the system from the managers or operators include:

1. Productivity
2. Effort

Economic benefits accrued by the system from other systems include:

1. Competition
2. Licensing technologies (royalties)

Economic benefits accrued by the system from its business segments include:

1. Potential to make money
2. Acceptable growth potential
3. Acceptable investment turnover
4. Invulnerable to unmanageable controlling factors
5. Opportunity to occupy a strong position in the market
6. Size
7. Good value-added opportunities
8. Strong position as major elements of a cost chain

Economic benefits accrued by other systems from the corporation (system) include:

1. Competition
2. Licensing technologies (royalties)

Social benefits accrued by the managers or operators from the system include:

1. Ego benefits (social status)
2. Promotion to positions of greater responsibility
3. Reputation

Social benefits accrued by the managers or operators from other systems include volunteer service.

Social benefits accrued by the managers or operators from the environment include volunteer service.

Social benefits accrued by the system from other systems include good product differentiation.

Social benefits accrued by the system from the environment include the image of a socially responsible corporation.

Social benefits of the environment from the corporation (system) include:

1. Equality of opportunities
2. Increased employment
3. Contributions to knowledge
4. Public education
5. Awards
6. Unpaid services to public institutions
7. Training
8. Stimulation of minority business enterprises

Political benefits of the managers or operators from the system include more power.

Political benefits accrued by the system from the environment include influence in the political arena.

Technological benefits of systems from the managers or operators include:

1. Retention of employees capable of autonomy
2. Promotion of technologies that give a unique market position

Technological benefits accrued by the system from other systems include:

1. Perpetuation of power
2. Investment in many technologies to identify the right one and avoid the wrong one

Technological benefits accrued by the environment from the system include greater industrial efficiency.

Now we consider the costs associated with the actions of the four parties. The costs are determined by asking: What are the pains associated with the actions of the managers or operators, the corporation, other systems, and the environment when economic, social, political, technological, and environmental changes take place? In listing the costs we must keep in mind the criteria discussed earlier. What are the pains of increasing the value of a business? What are the costs associated with different increasing value rates? Is the size of the business significant to the positive costs associated with increasing or decreasing its size? The following paragraphs summarize the costs resulting from the analysis.

Economic pains accrued by the system from the managers or operators include:

1. Loss of productivity due to strikes
2. Decline in productivity due to less time spent on the job

Economic pains accrued by the system from the business segments include:

1. Low return on the cost of capital (long-term return)
2. Low or uncertain growth potential
3. Unmanageable cyclicality
4. Small size with poor growth potential
5. Poor market position with low potential (or unjustified cost) for significant improvement
6. Poor opportunities for product differentiation

7. Returns not commensurate with risks
8. Low value-added opportunities
9. Weak position of business segments as major elements of a cost chain
10. Operating costs
11. Strategic costs
12. Costs incurred to attain benefits
13. Intrinsic costs that give rise to benefits

Economic pains accrued by the system from the environment include:

1. Depreciation
2. Interest
3. Capital charge
4. Negative market impact

Social pains accrued by managers or operators from the corporation (system) include:

1. Staff turnover
2. Staff layoff
3. Industrial accidents
4. Occupational diseases
5. Female and child labor
6. Competitive depletion of energy resources and the tendency to shift the overhead costs of labor to individual workers

Social pains accrued by the system from within itself include:

1. Unsafe, impure, and defective products
2. Deceptive promotion
3. Return per unit of effort to make the business succeed

Social pains accrued by the system from the environment include:

1. Monopoly: wastes and inefficiencies of excessive duplication of retail services
2. Mandatory costs to maintain a license
3. Required protection at high costs
4. Negative public image (more important than positive public image)

Political pains accrued by the system from the environment include:

1. Loss of corporate autonomy
2. Bribery of public officials

3. Conflicts between corporate freedom and public interest
4. Antitrust laws

Technological pains accrued by the system from within itself include:

1. Insufficient knowledge to start a business
2. Investment in undeveloped technologies

Technological pains accrued by the system from the environment include:

1. Urbanization
2. Increasing complexity
3. Risk of societal breakdown
4. Increasing dehumanization
5. Unemployment
6. Distress from adjustment to technological change
7. Cost of disseminating technological benefits

Environmental pains accrued by the system from the environment include:

1. Air pollution controls
2. Water pollution controls
3. Solid waste controls
4. Noise control
5. Reputation
6. Environmental changes that render a product obsolete
7. Catastrophic event from one of the company's products
8. Strong environmental impact like that of steel mills

Synthesizing the Data and Selecting the Business Units

To obtain the relative benefits and costs of the business segments, we follow these steps:

1. Rank the main corporate objectives.
2. Rank the subobjectives according to each of the main corporate objectives. Then select only the most relevant subobjectives of each cluster.
3. Cluster the benefits (and costs) into four major groups: economic, social and political, environmental, and technological.
4. Rank these clusters according to each relevant subobjective. Then rank benefits (and costs) according to their importance in each major cluster.

The next step is to select a reasonable number of economic (seven), social and political (three), technological (three), and environmental (three) benefits and costs.

5. Rank the clustering schemes according to the benefits (and costs). Select 7 ± 2 clustering schemes with the highest priorities.

6. Cluster the business units according to the relevant clustering schemes in five groups of seven business units each.

7. Select the business units with the highest priorities (7 ± 2). (Had we considered all the business units, ranking the business segments according to their contribution to the business units would have required between two and three months of three-hour-a-day sessions.)

8. Rank the surviving segments according to the 7 ± 2 clustering schemes. Relative benefits and costs are then obtained in the usual manner. A benefit/cost ratio framework is used to allocate the available resources.

A shorter process is also available if desired. The business units can be clustered and compared according to the surviving subobjectives. In this case, the decision maker has to keep in mind all the benefits (costs) accrued by the corporation from each business unit.

PERSPECTIVE

A major problem in benefit/cost analysis is comparing intangible factors with tangible ones involving money, tons of materials, numbers of people, and other measurables. The AHP makes it possible to lay out all the relevant factors of concern to the decision maker, tangible and intangible. The decision maker can then develop priorities for their benefits and their costs and use their ratios as an overall measure for appropriate allocation of resources. Similarly, if a resource is to be allocated to projects in which only benefits are seen to occur at the start, the priorities for these projects may be weighted by their individual resource requirement in order to distribute a limited amount of that resource among them or to satisfy all the requirements of the most cost-effective one first. This is a particularly useful way to organize a new undertaking in which many activities are listed by people with differing judgments. A limited resource can then be allocated according to the general consensus on need, urgency, and benefits.

13

Making Group Decisions

This chapter deals with the following questions:

- How can we use the analytic hierarchy process in a group session?

- What about special problems like differing levels of experience and status in a group?

- What happens when group members change their opinions?

- What if people are unwilling to reveal their true preferences?

- How can we control the quality of results in a group session?

- What is the value of using questionnaires in group sessions?

- What are the basic steps to introducing the process in your organization?

GROUP SESSIONS: THE PROMISE AND THE PROBLEMS

The AHP can be used successfully with a group. In fact, brainstorming and sharing ideas and insights often leads to a more complete representation and understanding of the issues than would be possible for a single decision maker. But group sessions can also pose special problems. In this chapter I make a few observations about group processes; in the next chapter I illustrate them in some detail with a real-life application.

When the analytic hierarchy process is used in a group session, the group members structure the problem, provide the judgments, debate the judgments, and make a case for their values until consensus or compromise is reached. In an ideal situation, the group is small and the participants well informed, highly motivated, and in agreement on the basic question being addressed. They are also willing to participate fully in a rigorous, structured process whose outcome will partly determine their future activities, no matter what differences of opinion still surround the results of the process. Again ideally, the group is patient enough to reconsider the subject so that, through iteration, the remaining differences of opinion are debated and an agreement is reached or at least the range of differences is narrowed.

But such a scenario is the exception. Often the participants are unequal in their expertise, influence, and perspective, and cooperation may take some coaxing by the leader. Patience on the part of the leader and the group is highly desirable; an unhurried, structured group discussion can yield a more satisfactory outcome than one achieved quickly and with little debate.

CONDUCTING GROUP SESSIONS

The process of group interaction and policy choice cannot be reduced to a set of rules. As in any activity that broadens people's views and stimulates their thinking, flexibility is essential. What I offer here are suggestions based on experience in conducting many group sessions.

Preliminary Steps

First make sure that the participants are comfortable and well provided with writing materials, refreshments, adequate lighting, and so on. If the AHP is being used for the first time, explain how it works and illustrate it with simple applications. Large flip charts are convenient for this purpose. Allow for a question-and-answer period.

It may be helpful to have two discussion leaders with one or two assistants. A group session that lasts for two days, typical for planning, is quite taxing, and much of the pressure on either leader is reduced by having the other carry on when necessary. A computer terminal makes it possible to obtain answers immediately and to test the consequences of judgments with respect to sensitivity and consistency.

A good way to begin the session is by brainstorming the overall focus of the problem or plan. Several suggestions may be made, from which one is selected as most representative of the current overall concern. The important thing is to define the objective of the discussion clearly at the very beginning.

Constructing the Hierarchy

With the focus determined, the group defines the issues to be examined and constructs the hierarchy as richly as possible to cover the issues. The discussion should be relaxed and unhurried. The leader reminds the group that the purpose of the meeting is to construct the hierarchy and, through discussion, debate, and the use of pragmatic imagination, to make pairwise comparisons from which priorities are set for the elements at the lowest level of the hierarchy. Overhead transparencies may be used to record entries in the hierarchy and matrices. After the hierarchy is completed, it should be drawn, typed, and distributed to all the participants. Before proceeding to the judgments, revisions are made and the hierarchy is retyped and redistributed.

Breaking down a complex issue into different levels is particularly useful for a group with widely varying perspectives. Each member can present his or her own concerns and definitions, no matter what the level may be. Then the group is assisted in identifying the overall structure of the issue. In this way agreement can be reached on the higher-order and lower-order aspects of the issue through a clustering and ordering of all the concerns that members have expressed.

The group then agrees on how it will proceed to make decisions. The whole group might start at the top level and then progress to lower ones. It may delegate to subgroups the responsibility of considering, subdividing further, or setting priorities on a particular level. Or it may choose a combination of these alternatives.

Setting Priorities and Synthesizing

Group priority setting is by nature interactive and noisy and involves bargaining and persuasion. This lively interaction need not be perfectly orchestrated—the participants may feel regimented and intimidated. Those who have no patience for the process should be allowed simply to observe or, if they wish, to leave the room and return when the process is completed. A leader should also be sensitive to the unspoken words of group members. Some need coaxing and encouragement to participate or to express their feelings. In a large group the process of setting priorities is easier to handle by dividing the members into smaller, specialized subgroups, each dealing with an issue of particular interest or one in which members have special expertise. When the subgroups rejoin for a final justification, the values in each matrix can be debated and revised if desired.

The debate could be eliminated and individual opinion taken by questionnaire, a method that is described later. The final values are derived from the geometric mean of the judgments. Recall that to compute the geometric mean, the values are multiplied and a root equal to the number of individuals who provided the values is taken. For example, the geometric mean of 2, 3, and 7 is $\sqrt[3]{2 \times 3 \times 7}$, which is 3.48 (3 in the pairwise comparison scale).

Taking the geometric mean of individual judgments is one way to resolve a lack of consensus on values after debate. Another method of resolving conflict is to vote on the proposed values. The final solution can also be obtained as a range of values that represents the range of judgments.

The AHP does not subvert or force human nature. There is no guarantee that all aspects of dissent can be harnessed, nor should they be. Dissent is a valuable basic process that should not be banned in group interaction. But dissent must eventually lead to some kind of cooperation if anything is to be accomplished.

Special Problems

The leader of a group session should be prepared to deal with such problems as inequality of power and expertise among members, unequal desire to express preferences, frequent change of expressed preferences, and the unwillingness of some to reveal their true preferences or the true strength of their preferences.

Unequal Power and Expertise. Groups are often composed of people with different levels of status, knowledge, and experience. A superior might be unwilling to participate in a process that equalizes his or her judgment with that of subordinates. The chances that such a person would abide by the outcome of the process are slim indeed.

One way to handle this problem is by weighting votes according to the importance or expertise of the participants. The group can design a hierarchy to judge the relative power and merit of the individuals who will be voting. All factors that bear on the particular issue to be voted on should be included, such as power, experience, political favors, fame, wealth, and ability to disrupt or withhold participation. The individuals can then be compared according to their relative influence with respect to these factors. Consensus on such matters or a structured debate will result in a set of priorities for weighting the judgments of individuals. The final solution is obtained not by consensus but by the relative power and merit of individuals, which will shift as the issues change.

But votes do not have to be weighted if the interaction process itself, combined with the participants' knowledge of each other, allows individuals to exercise their influence through reasoned debate—even though the votes are equally weighted. Shared decision making exposes leaders of an organization to a broader range of views and arguments than is typically filtered up to them. The AHP thus serves a useful intelligence-gathering function.

Variable Preferences.   In groups that must make decisions on a large number of complex and varied issues, some individuals may be much more interested in particular questions than others are. Such people are often willing to bargain for votes or support on issues of importance to themselves by trading their own votes on less important questions. Bargaining helps a group come to an agreement and speeds the process. But when trading of political favors determines the outcome, and a majority is willing to allow the outcome to bear no relationship to facts and informed judgment, then there is little point in using the AHP. The group should have a positive interest in understanding the complexity of the problem and possible approaches to its solution.

Changes in Preferences.   People may change their opinions and judgments as a result of new information or changes in external factors such as the state of the economy and other conditions. Such change complicates the problems of planning, allocating resources, and predicting the behavior of people and organizations. The question arises whether the AHP can be useful if priorities and the outcome of decisions are subject to change within a relatively short time.

Of course, the AHP does not change reality. It does not impose stability on an unstable environment. But the AHP does try to make reality more comprehensible. It can also provide an opportunity to identify variables subject to change and to attach certain probabilities to those changes.

It is important to view the AHP not as a tool for isolated, one-time application but as a process that has ongoing validity and utility to an organization or group. It permits iterations and adaptations that can incorporate changing environmental factors. Thus the question of the AHP's usefulness in the context of changing views may reduce itself to one of how people value the time required to participate in the process. Does the expenditure of personal and organizational resources seem justified? Or would people rather rely on "seat-of-the-pants" techniques of decision making and problem solving?

Unwillingness to Reveal Preferences. Sometimes people are not willing to reveal their true preferences and the strength of their attachment to these preferences. They may even wish to hide their most important "agenda item," because an explicit statement might lead to its demise by exposing it as a focus for opposition. If people are unwilling to state their preferences, the definition of issues will be incomplete and the analysis and priority setting will be inadequate.

One strategy for coping with hidden agendas is to include enough members in the group session to produce a broad range of ideas. In such a situation people may be able to anticipate hidden agendas and put them out on the table for discussion. Another strategy is to design the rules of the game so that the outcome—the list of priorities or programs—can emerge only from the set of stated issues.

If a particular person is intent on disrupting the process—perhaps by distorting his or her preferences—that person can be isolated by dividing the group into smaller subgroups so that the majority can proceed without interruption. Clearly groups should be prepared in advance to use the AHP. If the organization is committed to the use of the AHP because of the benefits it expects, the group will probably regulate itself.

GETTING THE BEST RESULTS

When applying the AHP in a group session, several factors may affect the quality of the results. Some have to do with the individuals involved, some with the process itself.

The number of people in the work group is significant. It is desirable to have many people participate in constructing the hierarchy. The more ideas offered, the richer the representation of relevant issues. But analyzing the elements of the hierarchy can become unwieldy if too many people with diverse points of view are included. It is better to form smaller subgroups for priority setting.

The status and expertise of the group leader or a member can influence the outcome. Usually this is to the good, because experience and informed judgment contribute to a better understanding of complex situations. But everyone should be encouraged to participate, even if the range of judgments widens. As a group becomes more experienced in using the AHP, consistency should improve.

The stake of group members is another important factor. Generally the AHP should be used for group interaction only when a majority have a genuine interest in the outcome of the process and are willing to be open-minded about the possibilities.

In constructing the hierarchy, the number of levels in the design may affect the quality of the results. The levels should relate naturally to each other. If necessary, a level may be expanded into two or more levels or eliminated. The criteria employed in each level should be of the same order of magnitude and relate to at least two elements in the level immediately below. A study may be required to identify and characterize elements that are relevant to the issue in question.

Most of the problems in applying the AHP occur in the priority-setting stage. Particularly when the process is being used for the first time, the number of elements being compared and the order in which the comparisons are made should be carefully monitored. The more elements in a level, the greater the chance of inconsistency and the more taxing the comparison process. On the other hand, a sufficient number of elements (7 ± 2) should be listed to represent the issue adequately. As a rule, it is best to compare the strongest and the weakest elements in a level first. The resultant value serves as a guidepost for the other comparisons.

Attributes perceived through the senses can be evaluated more precisely than those recalled from memory or abstract ideas. The meaning of the values in the pairwise comparison scale must be clearly understood. As suggested earlier, it is best to state the verbal judgment first (*A* is strongly or weakly more important than *B*) and then translate it into its numerical value. Allowing enough time for debating priorities is critical. The more carefully the judgments are made, the more valid the conclusions. Consensus is not essential at the lower levels of the hierarchy, but it is needed at the higher levels, where the priorities drive the rest of the hierarchy.

USING QUESTIONNAIRES

Participants in group sessions sometimes remark that the judgmental process strained their minds and their patience over a short period of time. To remedy this problem, a questionnaire can be given in which only a minimum number of judgments are asked for rather than the usual number for making all possible comparisons. The minimum number of judgments must interconnect so that every element in a level of a hierarchy is compared, directly or indirectly, with every other element. If one row is used, the element of that row is related to all others, making it possible to obtain relationships among the other elements indirectly. Thus $A = 7B$ and $A = 5C$ leads to $7B = 5C$ or $B = 7/5C$. One way to make this kind of comparison is to use a *spanning tree*. Figure 13-1 shows a spanning tree that connects nine criteria. If, for example, nine elements are being examined,

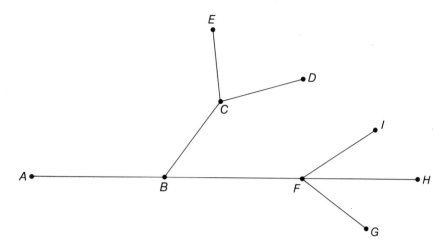

Figure 13-1   Spanning Tree

eight comparisons (line segments) are the minimum. The judgments in one row are a minimum number if we ignore the unit entry.

In a spanning tree all the elements are connected—in one and only one way to prevent ambiguity—and we can travel from any element to any other. Such a connection makes it possible to derive all other comparisons in the matrix from just a few of them. This matrix is consistent because it is entirely derived from a minimal set of judgments.

For each pair, a questionnaire asks for a judgment expressing the intensity of dominance with respect to the criterion: "Does A dominate B or does B dominate A with respect to this criterion? Indicate how strongly next to the proper alternative." (See Figure 13-2.) The same process is followed for the remaining pairs.

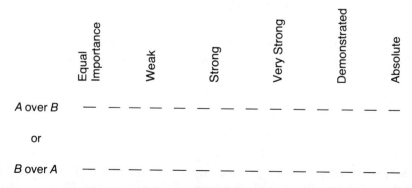

Figure 13-2   Questionnaire for Paired Comparison

If there are several individuals, we can ask each of them to provide a minimum number of judgments, but the spanning tree for each would be different in order to enrich the information. The spanning tree would be generated by a computer program that randomized the selection of the elements to be compared.

The final step is to take all these matrices, each constructed completely from its minimum number of judgments, and develop a single matrix whose entries are obtained by taking the geometric mean of all the entries from the matrices that are in the corresponding position to the entry in question. We then construct another matrix from the entries of the spanning trees and their geometric means and fill in any gaps from the previously constructed matrix. This matrix is generally inconsistent and provides an overall representation of the judgments of the group. The process can be done rapidly through prior preparation.

Since the questionnaires are prepared in advance and calculations are made after the interviews, little burden is placed on the participants. Nevertheless, it is worthwhile to encourage discussion and debate on issues, even if this means more work for the group. The next chapter shows how a good decision can be reached through the intense participation of group members.

INTRODUCING THE AHP IN YOUR ORGANIZATION

Despite the problems inherent in a group decision-making process, the AHP is an effective tool for organizations. Introducing the AHP in an organization requires the same kind of tact, patience, and fortitude needed in conducting group sessions. The following suggestions may be helpful:

- Persuade the leader of the organization to try the process.
- Ask, in a talk to a large audience, how the organization does its priority setting, its resource allocation, and its planning.
- Explain the process to interested parties and present simple, practical examples.
- Offer to help people structure their problems in an informal atmosphere.
- Prepare one level of judgments and return to the problem at intervals. Too much pressure may cause people to resist.
- Prepare good examples for presentation.
- Work (perhaps independently) with several departments of an organization and with innovative personnel.
- Leave the arithmetic to specialists.
- Ask the management committee and chief executive officer to participate in defining the overall objectives of the corporation. They can also

supply the judgments for the top objectives. With their interest stimulated in this way, they can be shown the rest of the hierarchies and priorities developed by other groups who may participate in the relevant aspects of the process. This approach reduces tedium for upper management and creates a dynamic interaction on all major issues.

PERSPECTIVE

The AHP creates a systematic framework for group interaction and group decision making. In that setting people have an opportunity to define the problem in different ways and structure its solution together. They can interact to debate, justify, and modify their personal judgments. They can also test the sensitivity of the chosen alternative to variations in their individual judgments. A few differences of opinion are sometimes observed not to have a significant impact on the best alternative. The AHP offers an opportunity to represent various interests in a balanced participation. It also enables the participants to use hard data along with their carefully deliberated judgments. If time is limited, it is possible to use a questionnaire to elicit the judgments and obtain a wide representation. The consistency test provides feedback on the coherence of available information. Finally, the process of synthesizing the judgments of many people to select an alternative is a practical and lasting contribution of the AHP.

In conducting a group session, the leader should be concerned about the problem, willing to share without dominating, encouraging the participants, and setting targets to reach on time. This leader should be willing to listen to suggestions and dissent and to modify the approach accordingly. The leader should also encourage reticent individuals to express themselves.

The room should be large and comfortable. Participants should be able to face, hear, and see each other easily. Minutes should be taken and the debate recorded for the final report. Thus the environment should be the best conceivable place to encourage camaraderie and break down the barriers of formality. The problem and its solution should be seen as the work of all involved.

KEY CONCEPTS

☐ When the analytic hierarchy process is used in a group session, the group structures the problem, provides the judgments, debates the judgments, and makes a case for their values until consensus or compromise is reached. Occasionally people feel so certain about their judgments that they want them documented.

- ☐ The ideal group is small. Its members are well informed, patient, and highly motivated.

- ☐ The greater the number of people involved in constructing the hierarchy, the greater the range of ideas. If too many people are involved in establishing priorities, however, the analysis may become unwieldy and time consuming.

- ☐ The objective of the discussion should be clearly defined at the outset. Once the focus has been determined, the group defines the issues and constructs the hierarchy.

- ☐ Priorities are established through group discussion or by means of a questionnaire. Although questionnaires can be used to sidestep the heat of debate, discussion often brings more worthwhile results.

- ☐ It is best to compare the strongest and weakest elements in a level first. The resulting value can then serve as a benchmark for other comparisons.

- ☐ Consensus is reached by taking the geometric mean of individual judgments or by voting on the proposed values. Consensus is not as important at the lower level of the hierarchy, where averaging can be used to better advantage, but it is essential at the higher levels. Yet, even here ranges of differences can be used to estimate the variability in the outcomes.

- ☐ The more carefully judgments are made, the more valid the conclusions.

14

A Practical Example of Group Decision Making

This chapter deals with the following question:

- How can a group set priorities for health care research projects?

WORKING TOWARD CONSENSUS

A useful feature of the AHP is that it enables a group to structure a hierarchy jointly and then participate in a discussion to provide the judgments. Usually people need time to identify the real problem. There may be several that need to be prioritized before the most important one is selected for consideration. The group then constructs a hierarchy and debates the problem, a process that usually takes two to four hours. Often a secretary is asked to draw the hierarchy and type up the levels and elements. The result is copied and circulated so that each participant can comment on it to obtain consensus.

The debate begins with the judgments. All that is said can be recorded. Although people will often accept the geometric mean of their judgments, sometimes they are adamant in their opinion. It is possible to resolve such differences by selecting the judgments that are most consistent with the judgments on which there is general agreement. Even then, however, there are occasions when people would rather hold their ground than yield to the consistency test. In that case, different priorities are obtained because of the range of differences. In the end people often accept averaging the final answers because participating in the process gives greater confidence that other people's judgments may also be sound despite differences. The following application illustrates some of the highlights of the process in operation.

SETTING PRIORITIES FOR HEALTH CARE
RESEARCH PROJECTS

The Regional Advisory Committee (RAC) of the National Health Care Management Center (NHCMC) met in two full-day sessions, one in June and one in August of 1978, to identify problem areas for research affecting health care in the United States. They first structured a hierarchy of actors who would have influence on the research but then decided to focus on those who provide health care rather than those who use it or regulate it or do research.

The major objectives of providers of health care were separated into two groups as shown in Figure 14-1. Initially, RAC members estimated the relative weights of economic and service objectives to be one-third and two-thirds, respectively. As the day progressed, however, members felt that these groups should have equal weights. To corroborate this feeling, RAC members cross-weighted selected objectives from among the two groups. This, however, produced implied weightings of two-thirds (economics) and one-third (service).

Figures 14-2 and 14-3 give the pairwise comparisons of the providers'

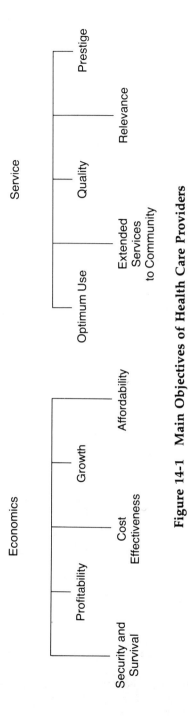

Figure 14-1   Main Objectives of Health Care Providers

Economic Objectives	1	2	3	4	5	Priority
Security and survival (1)	1	7	3	6	2	0.44
Profitability (2)	1/7	1	1/5	5	1	0.102
Cost effectiveness (3)	1/3	5	1	7	1	0.237
Growth (4)	1/6	1/5	1/7	1	1/9	0.033
Affordability (5)	1/2	1	1	9	1	0.188

Figure 14-2   Matrix of Economic Objectives

Service Objectives	1	2	3	4	5	Priority
Optimum use (1)	1	1/8	1/4	1/5	5	0.078
Extended services to community (2)	8	1	1*	1	7	0.331
Quality of care (3)	4	1	1	1	7	0.272
Relevance (4)	5	1	1	1	7	0.286
Prestige (5)	1/5	1/7	1/7	1/7	1	0.033

* Three hospital administrators voted together here, assigning a value of 1/3.

Figure 14-3   Matrix of Service Objectives

objectives. In these two figures, the shaded areas represent conflict; in those cases, the reciprocal value was nominated. Conflict is defined as (1) a four-unit difference between the highest and lowest values nominated by RAC members (for example: 5 and 1; 1/3 and 1/8) or (2) an integer accompanied by a reciprocal value (for example: 1, 1/3, and 1/7).

The economic objectives were ranked as follows:

Security and survival	0.44
Profitability	0.10
Cost effectiveness	0.24
Growth	0.03
Affordability	0.19

Then RAC members assigned priorities to the service objectives:

Optimum use	0.08
Extended services to the community	0.33
Quality of care	0.27
Relevance	0.29
Prestige	0.03

Objectives with low priorities were dropped from further consideration, and the priorities of the remaining objectives were renormalized to express their relative importance with respect to one another. This produced the final list of important objectives and their priorities shown in Table 14-1.

Table 14-1   Weighted Objectives

Objective	Original Within-Group Weight	Renormalized Weights Within Each Group
Economic		
Security and survival	0.44	1
Service		
Extended services	0.33	0.37
Quality of care	0.27	0.31
Relevance	0.29	0.32

Note: Cost effectiveness, an economic objective with a reasonably high weight (0.24), was omitted because of time considerations.

General Health Management Problems

The RAC then developed an extensive list of specific issues in the health care field. These, in turn, were grouped into six general health care management problems:

1. Institutional management/governance
   - Operations management
   - Institutional planning
   - Systems approach
   - Organization, direction, and control
2. Financial management
   - Reimbursement
3. Service delivery
   - Evaluation
4. Environmental control and regulation
5. Consumer behavior/health education
6. Manpower and industry structure
   - Manpower
   - Industry structure
   - Medical education

Each of the six areas represented issues that the RAC had identified previously.

Establishing Priorities Among Problems

The RAC then compared the six problem areas, one at a time against each other, with respect to their relative impact on each of the four objectives. This process produced a set of relative weights for each of the six problem areas (Table 14-2). In Table 14-2, the last two columns indicate the overall relative impact of the six problem areas on the economic and service objectives. (The last column is obtained by multiplying the problem area weight, with respect to each of the three service objective columns, by the weight of that service objective and then adding the results.) From these last two columns we can determine the final weights assigned to each of the six problem areas—specific to the three variations in the relative importance of economic to service objectives (that is, $1:2$, $1:1$, and $2:1$). Table 14-3 summarizes these findings.

The last column of Table 14-3 notes the *final* weights assigned to each problem area with respect to the values assigned to economic and service

Table 14-2 Relative Weights of Problem Areas

Problem Area	Economic Objectives Security and Survival	Service Objectives Extended Services (0.37)*	Quality of Care (0.31)*	Relevance (0.32)*	Overall Weight Relative to Economic Objectives	Overall Weight Relative to Service Objectives
Institutional management/governance	0.36	0.09	0.33	0.06	0.36	0.15
Financial management	0.29	0.30	0.16	0.07	0.29	0.18
Service delivery	0.13	0.19	0.27	0.19	0.13	0.21
Environmental control and regulation	0.12	0.15	0.11	0.16	0.12	0.14
Consumer behavior/health education	0.04	0.16	0.03	0.28	0.04	0.16
Manpower and industry structure	0.06	0.11	0.10	0.24	0.06	0.15

* Renormalized weight with respect to the other two service objectives.

Table 14-3   Problem Area Rankings

| Problem Area | Economic/Service Ratio | | | Rank |
	1:2	1:1	2:1	
Institutional management/governance	0.22*	0.26	0.29	1
Financial management	0.22†	0.24	0.26	2
Service delivery	0.19	0.17	0.16	3
Environmental control and regulation	0.13	0.13	0.13	4
Consumer behavior/health education	0.12†	0.10†	0.08	6
Manpower and industry structure	0.12*	0.10*	0.09	5

Note: Before rounding off, ratios marked with an asterisk slightly dominated those marked with a dagger.

objectives. It is noteworthy that irrespective of the value assigned to economic versus service objectives, the rank ordering of problem areas remains unchanged:

Rank Order	Problem Area
1	Institutional management/governance
2	Financial management
3	Service delivery
4	Environmental control and regulation
5	Consumer behavior/health education
6	Manpower and industry structure

It appears that even if cost effectiveness were returned to the economic objectives, the rank order of problem areas would probably not be changed.* At most, the weights of institutional management/governance and financial management would probably increase slightly while closing the gap between the relative weights of these top-ranked problem areas. Generally, there tended to be greater agreement among RAC members than disagreement with respect to the relative value placed on various problem areas vis-à-vis particular objectives. There was greater RAC disagreement when weighting problem areas with respect to *lower-order* objectives—such as extending services to the community, relevance, or quality of care—than with respect to high-priority objectives such as secu-

---

* Within the service objectives, security and survival was assigned a weight of 0.44. Cost effectiveness (which was dropped from further consideration) received a relatively high weight of 0.24. If we add cost effectiveness, the renormalized weights of these two would be 0.65 (security and survival) and 0.35 (cost effectiveness).

rity and survival. These lower-order service objectives averaged more conflict zones, and an increased percentage of votes were reciprocals.

Relative Weighting of Projects

To develop the matrices required for the analytic hierarchy decision process, each project was assigned to the most appropriate of three problem areas: institutional management, financial management, and management of service delivery. One project, work measurement, was assigned to both the first and third categories.

1. Institutional management
   - Conflict in institutional management
   - Fixed-cost analysis
   - MIS
   - Work measurement
   - Long-range planning methodologies
   - Continuing education strategies
   - Interorganizational relationships
   - CEO–CMO relationships
   - Matrix organization
   - Internal/external capability analysis
   - Financial incentives
   - Alternative management styles
   - Governance
2. Financial management
   - Budget development process
   - Present-value analysis
   - Financial feasibility methodology
   - Reimbursement incentives
   - Simplification of reimbursement procedures
3. Management of service delivery
   - Work measurement
   - Quality control measures for patient outcome
   - Measuring services to patients
   - Service utilization payoff guides
   - Analysis of service addition/deletion decisions
   - Alternative delivery systems

Matrix I: Institutional Management.   Because so many projects fell into the category of institutional management, the group was divided into two subcategories: structural/interpersonal relations and operations management. The RAC then voted on the relative importance of the areas. One man argued that structure is largely a function of the particular group of personalities in an organization at a given time and that operations management offers more promise for projects and real help for managers. Others took exception to this view, suggesting that structural concerns are dominant for several reasons—importance of structural problems in multi-institutional systems, for example, and greater possibility of learning from experience rather than mechanical classroom education. The range of votes was 1/5 to 7.

	Structural	*Operations*
Structural	1	2
Operations	1/2	1

One person suggested that years of sociological research have not had much effect on improving health care management. Instead, modern management techniques are needed. On the contrary, noted a doctor, social change in hospitals has been far-reaching; certainly health care is much more accessible to the poor.

Matrix IA: Operations Management.   Discussion on the pairing of MIS and fixed-cost analysis revealed two points of view (Figure 14-4). The first was that fixed-cost analysis was a greater problem because so little work has been done, whereas considerable effort has been put into MIS. The opposing view held that since management information systems are fundamental to direction and control of organizations, they present more significant problems. Also receiving brief debate was the pairing of MIS and financial incentives. Discussion focused on a definition of financial incentives for employee and medical staff performance. One person noted that financial incentives of the reimbursement system work against optimum use. Another questioned whether enough was known about this topic to warrant a priority rating. Then someone suggested that fixed-cost analysis is subordinate to MIS because MIS would be necessary to determine where financial incentives are necessary.

Matrix IB: Structural/Interpersonal Relations.   Matrix IB (Figure 14-5) was the last matrix developed during the first meeting. There was no significant discussion of any of the matrix pairings. Unfortunately, one

	MIS	Fixed-Cost Analysis	Work Measurement	Financial Incentives
MIS	1	2 (1/5–5)*	2 (1/3–5)*	3 (1/7–5)*
Fixed-cost analysis	1/2	1	3 (1/5–5)*	1 (1/3–3)*
Work measurement	1/2	1/3	1	1/2 (1/5–7)*
Financial incentives	1/3	1	2	1

* Range.

Figure 14-4   Matrix IA: Operations Management

project area that had engendered much interest in the morning discussion was inadvertently left out of the institutional management matrices. This project was long-range planning methodologies. While it is impossible to determine through hindsight what relative weighting this project would have obtained, its similarity to several projects that did receive high priorities should be noted. In fact, it could be argued that the following topics are actually subsumed under long-range planning methodologies: management of conflict in institutional planning, management/development of interorganizational relationships, budget development process, methodologies for analyzing service addition/deletion, and analysis of alternative delivery systems. All in all, it appears that NHCMC should give careful consideration to R&D activities relating to long-range planning methodologies for institutions and community-based agencies.

Priorities Among Projects

A computer was used to determine the relative weight of each project within its category. Then the top choices were identified and a composite ranking across categories was prepared. The results are as follows.

Matrix II: Financial Management.   Matrix II (Figure 14-6) was originally a four-project matrix. Partway through the voting, however, the two reimbursement-related projects were combined, necessitating some new votes. Only the pairing of budget development versus reimbursement received much discussion. Most RAC members appeared to agree that

	Conflict in Institutional Planning	Inter-organizational Relationships	CEO–CMO	Matrix Organization	Governance	Management Style
Conflict in institutional planning	1	3 (1/5–7)*	5 (1–9)*	7 (3–9)*	1/2 (1/7–7)*	5 (1/2–9)*
Inter-organizational relationships	1/3	1	7 (5–9)*	7 (3–9)*	1/2 (1/4–1)*	6 (3–9)*
CEO–CMO	1/5	1/7	1	1 (1/5–3)*	1/3 (1/9–3)*	2 (1–5)*
Matrix organization	7	1/7	1	1	1/5 (1/9–3)*	(1/9–3)*
Governance	2	2	3	5	1	4 (1–9)*
Management style	1/5	1/6	1/2	1	1/4	1

* Range

Figure 14-5   Matrix IB: Structural/Interpersonal Relations

	Budget Development	Financial Feasibility	Reimbursement
Budget development	1	3 (1–5)*	1/4 (1/9–3)*
Financial feasibility	1/3	1	1/5 (1/9–3)*
Reimbursement	4	5	1

* Range.

Figure 14-6   Matrix II: Financial Management

since an institution's approach to budgeting is a function of the reimbursement system, problems with the latter are more significant than those with the former. One doctor's vote for a reverse weighting stressed the importance of the budget process as a significant planning tool for health care managers.

Matrix III: Management of Service Delivery.   Matrix III was then considered. At the outset of the discussion, RAC members agreed that they were not voting on the intrinsic importance of project topics but rather on which areas posed greater problems for health care managers and providers. It was also agreed that the issues of feasibility and NHCMC competence to address a project would not be considered during the matrix voting. These and other criteria would be decided on after the projects had been ranked for priority. Then the criteria could be chosen and used to select a subset of projects for full-scale development as NHCMC activities utilizing internal or external resources.

Only the first pairing, quality control outcome measures versus measurement of service to patients, received much discussion during the rating. Two divergent points were represented in lengthy discussion of this issue. The first argued that an institution's ultimate survival is a function of patient and staff satisfaction. The opposing view held that the health care system must address needs (because wants are infinite) and that quality is of central importance. The results of the voting on relative weights of project areas are presented in Matrix III (Figure 14-7). In almost every pairing in this matrix, and in other matrices as well, a considerable range of values was proposed. The range of votes is indicated below the geometric mean score in each cell.

	Quality Control Outcome Measures	Service to Patients	Service Use Payoff	Service Addition/ Deletion	Alternative Delivery Systems	Work Measures
Quality control outcome measures	1	2 (1/3–7)*	6 (5–7)*	3 (1–5)*	2 (1–5)*	4 (1/7–7)*
Service to patients	1/2	1	1/2 (1/5–4)*	1/2 (1/5–1)*	1/2 (1/5–3)*	1/5 (1/7–1/3)*
Service use payoff	1/6	2	1	3 (1/3–5)*	1 (1/5–5)*	3 (1/7–7)*
Service addition/deletion	1/3	2	1/3	1	1/2 (1/5–3)*	3 (1/5–7)*
Alternative delivery systems	1/2	2	1	2	1	3 (1/5–7)*
Work measures	1/4	5	1/3	1/3	1/3	1

* Range.

Figure 14-7   Matrix III: Management of Service Delivery

Table 14-4   Priorities of Projects in Each Area

Institutional management

Operations management (1)*

MIS	$0.43 \times 1/3 = 0.14$
Fixed-cost analysis	$0.25 \times 1/3 = 0.08$
Work measurement	$0.12 \times 1/3 = 0.04$
Financial incentives	$0.20 \times 1/3 = 0.07$

Structural/interpersonal relations (2)*

Conflict in institutional planning	$0.31 \times 2/3 = 0.21$
Interorganizational relationships	$0.23 \times 2/3 = 0.15$
CEO–CMO relationships	$0.06 \times 2/3 = 0.04$
Programmatic matrix/organization	$0.04 \times 2/3 = 0.03$
Governance	$0.31 \times 2/3 = 0.21$
Management style	$0.05 \times 2/3 = 0.03$

Financial management

Budget development process	0.23
Financial feasibility	0.10
Reimbursement	0.67

Management of services

Quality outcome measures	0.37
Alternative delivery systems	0.17
Service use payoff	0.17
Addition/deletion service analysis	0.11
Work measurement	0.10
Service to patients	0.07

* Within the category of institutional management, structural/interpersonal relations was given twice the weight of operations management. Hence, to normalize the project scores in this category, the structural scores are multiplied by 2/3 and the operations management scores by 1/3.

Overall Ranking

The project scores were normalized across all three categories, and the seven top projects were selected:

Reimbursement	0.24
Quality outcome measures	0.11
Budget development process	0.08

Conflict in institutional planning	0.07
Governance	0.07
Interorganizational relations	0.05
Service use payoff	0.05

Each of these high-scoring projects is related to one of the top three out of six problems defined during the session in June. At that meeting it was recognized that the problems had different impacts on economic and service objectives and that the weights assigned to the problems would depend on the importance assigned to economic and service objectives. Three ratios of the relative importance of economic versus service objectives were proposed—1 : 1, 1 : 2, and 2 : 1—and the effect on problem area weight was calculated.

The scores of the projects vary according to the different economic/service ratios. To determine the scores under each of the different ratios, the project scores were multiplied by the appropriate values in Table 14-4 and the results were normalized. Table 14-5 shows that varying the economic/service ratio had a very slight impact on project scores. The overall ranking of the seven projects was not significantly affected.

Table 14-5   Project Rankings

	Economic/Service Ratio		
Project	*1:1*	*1:2*	*2:1*
Reimbursement	0.35	0.36	0.36
Quality outcome measures	0.17	0.14	0.12*
Budget development process	0.12	0.12	0.12*
Conflict in institutional planning	0.11	0.12	0.12*
Governance	0.11	0.12	0.12
Interorganizational relations	0.08	0.09	0.09
Service use payoff	0.08	0.06	0.06

* Before values were rounded off, the projects were ranked in the following order: conflict in institutional planning, quality outcome measures, and budget development process, by several thousandths of a point.

PERSPECTIVE

People who are anxious for quick, dependable answers are often concerned whether the same problem structured by the same group more than once leads to the same hierarchy and priorities. The answer clearly is no. Stable results are produced from broad knowledge and understanding derived from experience. People who do not make a process of solving the problem are apt to identify too narrow or too broad a hierarchy. They may give judgments conditioned by the feeling, emotions, and problems sensed at the time of the meeting and by the incisiveness of the logic expressed then. To stabilize a process, we need to analyze it according to well-founded experience, to use a variety of criteria, and to take into consideration variations in judgment. Only repetition of the process and continued interaction with the real world can bring the AHP closer to a true representation of the problem—whether it concerns priority setting, planning, or resource allocation—and ensure the quality of the results.

Appendix: Computer Programs

The Basic, Fortran, and APL programs are interactive. In other words, once they are introduced in the computer the user is asked to decide among the following alternatives:

- Whether one is processing a single matrix or an entire hierarchy
- In the latter case, whether the hierarchy is complete or incomplete
- The number of levels
- The number of elements in the levels
- The judgments
- When introducing the judgments, reciprocal values are input as negative numbers.

These alternatives will vary according to the language used. The output is usually the priorities for each criterion λ_{max}, the consistency index (CI), the consistency ratio (CR), and the hierarchic consistency (CH). For a small programmable calculator the program is not interactive due to the lack of memory, but similar inputs must be made.

BASIC COMPUTER PROGRAM

```
50 REM   PRIORITY HIERARCHY PROGRAM
60 REM
70 DIM A(60),B(60,60),N(60),Y(60),R(10),S(60),C(60,60),W(60),W2(60),C7(60),Z(60)
80 MAT READ R
90 DATA .0,.0,.58,.9,1.12,1.24,1.32,1.41,1.45,1.49
100 REM
110 REM 2ND LEVEL
120 REM
130 L=2
```

252

```
140 PRINT "ENTER THE # OF FACTORS IN 2ND HIERARCHY LEVEL."
150 INPUT N1
160 PRINT N1;" ? IF WRONG > '9', ELSE > '0'.";
170 INPUT Y9
180 IF Y9>5 GOTO 150
190 SI=N1
200 GOSUB 5000
210 MAT A=W
220 REM T9=TOTAL RANDOM CONSISTENCY FOR THIS HIERARCHY
230 REM T3=TOTAL CONSISTENCY OF THIS HIERARCHY
240 REM R()=RANDOM CONSISTENCY TABLE
250 L=L+1
260 MAT B=ZER
270 PRINT "ENTER THE # OF FACTORS IN LEVEL "L".  IF YOU WANT TO STOP HERE, > '0'."
280 INPUT N2
290 PRINT N2 "? IF WRONG > '9', ELSE > '0'.";
300 INPUT Y9
310 IF Y9 > 5 GOTO 280
320 IF N2 < 1 GOTO 830
330 REM
340 FOR N6=1 TO N1
350 PRINT "ENTER ALL FACTORS IN LEVEL "L" RELATED TO ELEMENT "N6" OF LEVEL "L-1"."
360 MAT N=ZER
370 MAT INPUT N
380 N3=NUM
382 FOR X=1 TO N3
384 PRINT N(X);
386 NEXT X
388 PRINT
400 PRINT "? IF WRONG > '9', ELSE > '0'.";
410 INPUT Y9
420 IF Y9 > 5 GOTO 380
430 IF N3 > 1 GOTO 470
440 REM ONLY 1 ELEMENT RELATED
450 B(N(1),N6)=1
460 GOTO 550
470 S1=N3
480 GOSUB 5000
490 MAT Y=W
500 T3=T3+A(N6)*C8
505 T9=T9+A(N6)*R(N3)
510 REM ONLY RELATED ELEMENTS HAVE WEIGHTED VALUES
520 FOR I=1 to N3
530 B(N(I),N6)=Y(I)
540 NEXT I
550 NEXT N6
560 PRINT "***LEVEL "L" WITH RESPECT TO LEVEL "L-1"."
562 PRINT "WEIGHT:";
564 FOR X=1 TO N1
566 PRINT A(X);
568 NEXT X
570 PRINT
580 FOR I=1 TO N2
590 PRINT I;
600 FOR J=1 TO N1
610 PRINT B(I,J);
620 NEXT J
630 PRINT
640 NEXT I
650 REM COMPOSITE
660 FOR I=1 TO N1
670 FOR J=1 TO N2
680 B(J,I)=B(J,I)*A(I)
690 NEXT J
700 NEXT I
710 FOR I=1 TO N2
720 S9=0
730 FOR J=1 TO N1
740 S9=S9+B(I,J)
750 NEXT J
760 A(I)=S9
770 NEXT I
780 PRINT "***COMPOSITE PRIORITIES FOR LEVEL "L"."
782 FOR X=1 TO N2
784 PRINT A(X);
```

```
 786 NEXT X
 788 PRINT
 800 N1=N2
 810 GOTO 260
 820 REM CONSISTENCY OF THE HIERARCHY
 830 PRINT "$$CONSISTENCY OF ALL HIERARCHY=" T3/T9
 840 STOP
5000 PRINT "ENTER THE UPPER TRIANGULAR PART OF THE MATRIX,
     DO NOT ENTER THE ELEMENTS IN THE MAIN DIAGONAL."
5005 PRINT "THE ELEMENTS IN A ROW SHOULD BE ON THE SAME LINE.
     FRACTIONAL ELEMENTS LIKE 1/3, SHOULD BE ENTERED AS -3."
5010 FOR I=1 TO S1-1
5020 PRINT "ROW" I ":";
5025 MAT INPUT Z
5030 FOR J=I+1 TO S1
5040 C(I,J)=Z(J-I)
5050 NEXT J
5060 FOR J=I+1 TO S1
5070 PRINT C(I,J);
5080 NEXT J
5090 PRINT "? IF WRONG > '9', ELSE > '0'.";
5100 INPUT Y9
5110 IF Y9>5 GOTO 5020
5120 FOR J=I+1 TO S1
5130 IF C(I,J)>=0 GOTO 5150
5140 C(I,J)=-(1.0/C(I,J))
5150 C(J,I)=1.0/C(I,J)
5160 NEXT J
5170 NEXT I
5180 FOR I=1 TO S1
5190 C(I,I)=2
5200 NEXT I
5210 REM
5220 REM FIND INITIAL WEIGHT
5230 T4=0
5240 FOR I=1 TO S1
5250 S=0
5260 FOR J=1 TO S1
5270 S=S+C(I,J)
5280 NEXT J
5290 W2(I)=S
5300 T4=T4+S
5310 NEXT I
5320 FOR I=1 TO S1
5330 W2(I)=W2(I)/T4
5340 NEXT I
5350 REM
5360 K=0
5370 T4=0
5380 K=K+1
5390 FOR I=1 TO S1
5400 S=0
5410 FOR J=1 TO S1
5420 S=S+C(I,J)*W2(J)
5430 NEXT J
5440 W(I)=S
5450 T4=T4+S
5460 NEXT I
5470 D=0
5480 FOR I=1 TO S1
5490 W(I)=W(I)/T4
5500 D=D+ABS(W(I)-W2(I))
5510 NEXT I
5520 IF K>10000 GOTO 5570
5530 IF D<1.E-15 GOTO 5570
5540 MAT W2 = W
5550 GOTO 5370
5570 FOR I=1 TO S1
5580 C(I,I)=1
5582 FOR J=1 TO S1
5580 C(I,I)=1
5582 FOR J=1 TO S1
5584 PRINT C(I,J);
5586 NEXT J
5588 PRINT
```

```
5590 NEXT I
5610 REM
5620 FOR I=1 TO S1
5630 S=0
5640 FOR J=1 TO S1
5650 S=S+C(I,J)*W(J)
5660 NEXT J
5670 C7(I)=S
5680 NEXT I
5690 S=0
5700 FOR I=1 TO S1
5710 S=S+C7(I)/W(I)
5715 NEXT I
5720 Y5=S/S1
5730 C8=(Y5-S1)/(S1-1)
5735 PRINT "WEIGHTS:"
5740 FOR I=1 TO S1
5742 PRINT W(I);
5744 NEXT I
5744 PRINT
5750 PRINT "LAMDA(MAX)=" Y5 "  C.I.="C8"
5760 RETURN
5790 END
```

PROGRAM FOR TEXAS INSTRUMENTS HOME COMPUTER IN TI BASIC LANGUAGE

```
95 CALL CLEAR
100 PRINT " ANALYTIC HIERARCHY P
ROCESS      SOLUTION ALGORITHM"
101 PRINT
102 PRINT
103 PRINT
110 REM   THOMAS SAATY / ROD A
     NDERSON / STEVE HART
120 REM   REVISION 0 12/10/80
130 DIM A(6),B(6,6),N(6),Y(6),R(
10),C(6,6),W(6),U(6),Q(6),Z(6)
140 FOR I=1 TO 5
150 READ R(1)
160 NEXT I
170 DATA 0.0,0.0,0.58,0.90,1.12,
1.24,1.32,1.41,1.45,1.49
180 REM  2ND LEVEL
190 L=2
195 PRINT
200 PRINT "ENTER THE # FACTORS I
N 2ND HIERARCHY LEVEL"
210 INPUT N1
220 S1=N1
230 FOR I=1 TO N1
240 A(I)=0
250 W(I)=0
260 U(I)=0
270 NEXT I
280 GOSUB 1015
290 FOR I=1 TO N1
300 A(I)=W(I)
310 NEXT I
320 REM   T9=TOTAL RANDOM CONSIST
ENCY FOR THIS HIERARCHY
330 REM   T3=TOTAL CONSISTENCY OF
THIS HIERARCHY
340 REM   R()= RANDOM CONSISTENCY
   TABLE
350 L=L+1
355 PRINT
360 PRINT "ENTER THE # OF FACTOR
S IN LEVEL";L;" OR 0 TO END"
370 INPUT N2
380 IF N2<1 THEN 1000
390 FOR I=1 TO N2
400 W(I)=0
410 U(I)=0
420 FOR J=1 TO N1
430 B(I,J)=0
440 NEXT J
450 NEXT I
460 FOR N6=1 TO N1
465 PRINT
470 PRINT "ENTER #OF FACTORS IN
LEVEL";L;" RELATED TO ELEMENT";N
6;" OF LEVEL";L-1
480 INPUT N3
485 PRINT
490 PRINT "ENTER ALL FACTORS IN
LEVEL";L;" RELATED TO ELEMENT";N
6;" OF LEVEL";L-1
500 FOR I=1 TO N3
510 INPUT N(I)
520 NEXT I
530 IF N3>1 THEN 570
540 REM   ONLY 1 ELEMENT RELATED

550 B(N(1),N6)=1
560 GOTO 650
570 S1=N3
580 GOSUB 1015
590 T3=T3+A(N6)*C8
```

```
600 T9=T9+A(N6)*R(N3)
610 REM   ONLY RELATED ELEMENTS H
AVE WEIGHTED VALUES
620 FOR I=1 TO N3
630 B(N(I),N6)=W(I)
640 NEXT I
650 NEXT N6
660 PRINT "LEVEL";L;" WITH RESPE
CT TO LEVEL";L-1;"."
670 PRINT "WEIGHT:"
680 FOR I=1 TO N1
690 PRINT A(I);
700 NEXT I
710 PRINT
720 FOR I=1 TO N2
730 FOR J=1 TO N1
740 PRINT B(I,J);
750 NEXT J
760 PRINT
770 NEXT I
780 PRINT
790 REM   COMPOSIT
800 FOR I=1 TO N1
810 FOR J=1 TO N2
820 B(J,I)=B(J,I)*A(I)
830 NEXT J
840 NEXT I
850 FOR I=1 TO N2
860 S9=0
870 FOR J=1 TO N1
880 S9=S9+B(I,J)
890 NEXT J
900 A(I)=S9
910 NEXT I
920 PRINT " ***COMPOSITE PRIORIT
IES FOR LEVEL";L;"."
930 FOR I=1 TO N2
940 PRINT A(I);
950 NEXT I
960 PRINT
970 N1=N2
980 GOTO 350
990 REM   CONSISTENCY OF THE HIER
ARCHY                        .
1000 PRINT "$$CONSISTENCY OF ALL
  HIERARCHY = ";T3/T9
1005 PRINT
1010 STOP
1015 PRINT
1020 PRINT "ENTER CRITERION NAME
"
1030 INPUT C$
1035 PRINT
1040 IF L>2 THEN 1070
1050 PRINT "ENTER THE UPPER TRIA
NGULAR PART OF THE MATRIX, WITHO
UT UNITY ELEMENTS IN THE MAIN DI
AGONAL."
1060 PRINT "ELEMENTS ARE ENTERED
  ONE AT A TIME. FRACTIONAL ELEME
NTS LIKE 1/3, ARE ENTERED AS -3.
"
1070 PRINT "ENTER UPPER TRIANGLE
"
1080 FOR I=1 TO S1-1
1085 PRINT
1090 PRINT " ROW ";I;":"
1100 FOR J=1 TO S1-I
1110 INPUT Z(J)
1120 NEXT J
1130 FOR J=I+1 TO S1
1140 C(I,J)=Z(J-I)
1150 NEXT J
1160 FOR J=I+1 TO S1
1170 IF C(I,J)>=0 THEN 1190
1180 C(I,J)=-(1.0/C(I,J))
1190 C(J,I)=1.0/C(I,J)
1200 NEXT J
1210 NEXT I
1215 PRINT
1220 FOR I=1 TO S1
1230 C(I,I)=2
1240 NEXT I
1250 REM
1260 REM   FIND INITIAL WEIGHT
1270 T4=0
1280 FOR I=1 TO S1
1290 S=0
1300 FOR J=1 TO S1
1310 S=S+C(I,J)
1320 NEXT J
1330 U(I)=S
1340 T4=T4+S
1350 NEXT I
1360 FOR I=1 TO S1
1370 U(I)=U(I)/T4
1380 NEXT I
1390 REM
1400 K=0
1410 T4=0
1420 K=K+1
1430 FOR I=1 TO S1
1440 S=0
1450 FOR J=1 TO S1
1460 S=S+C(I,J)*U(J)
1470 NEXT J
1480 W(I)=S
1490 T4=T4+S
1500 NEXT I
1510 D=0
1520 FOR I=1 TO S1
1530 W(I)=W(I)/T4
1540 D=D+ABS(W(I)-U(I))
1550 NEXT I
1560 PRINT "K=";K;" D=";D
1570 IF K>100 THEN 1630
1580 IF D<1.E-5 THEN 1630
1590 FOR I=1 TO S1
1600 U(I)=W(I)
1610 NEXT I
```

```
1620 GOTO 1410                1800 S=S+C(I,J)*W(J)
1630 PRINT K;" ITERATIONS D=";D    1810 NEXT J
1640 PRINT                    1820 Q(I)=S
1650 PRINT "CRITERION= ";C$    1830 NEXT I
1660 FOR I=1 TO S1            1840 S=0
1670 C(I,I)=1                 1850 FOR I=1 TO S1
1680 NEXT I                   1860 S=S+Q(I)/W(I)
1690 FOR I=1 TO S1            1870 NEXT I
1700 FOR J=1 TO S1            1880 Y5=S/S1
1703 SUBA=C(I,J)              1890 C8=(Y5-S1)/(S1-1)
1705 SUBB=INT(SUBA*100)       1900 PRINT "WEIGHTS:"
1710 SUBC=SUBB/100            1910 FOR I=1 TO S1
1715 PRINT SUBC;              1920 PRINT W(I):
1720 NEXT J                   1930 NEXT I
1730 PRINT                    1940 PRINT
1740 NEXT I                   1950 PRINT "LAMBDA(MAX)=";Y5;"CO
1750 PRINT                    NSITENCY INDEX =";C8
1760 REM                      1960 PRINT
1770 FOR I=1 TO S1            1970 RETURN
1780 S=0                      1980 END
1790 FOR J=1 TO S1
```

AHP-7 PROGRAM FOR THE TI-59
PROGRAMMABLE CALCULATOR

Program Description

AHP-7 receives data and performs calculations on a matrix of comparisons for decision making through the analytic hierarchy process. This program for the TI-59 will accommodate up to a 7×7 matrix. It requires $[n(n-1)]/2$ data entries from the keyboard for an $n \times n$ matrix. The priority weights, matrix λ_{max} (i.e., the largest eigenvalue of the matrix), consistency index (CI), and consistency ratio (CR) are calculated and stored for recall. All matrix elements and calculated values are listed when a printer is used.

Program Use

The program is stored on magnetic card and read with the initial TI-59 partitioning of 479.59. Repartitioning is under program control during execution.

The two user-defined keys intended for operator use in this program are:

(A) Store entered value "x." During normal program execution R/S may be used instead of A.

(E) Execute calculations, store, and print values.

Step	Procedure	Enter	Press	Display
1	* Clear data memories.		RST R/S	
2	(Program displays "0" and waits for matrix size to be entered.) * Enter matrix size "m" = 2, . . . , 7; for example, enter "3" for a 3 × 3 matrix.	m	R/S	0
3	(Program displays "RC" = row number–column number location of next value "x" to be entered; for example, "RC" = 12 for row 1, column 2.) * Enter value "x." (Program stores "x," calculates and stores "$1/x$," and enters 1 in matrix diagonal. Program repeats step 3 until the matrix is completed; then it displays "6.")	x	A or R/S	"RC" 6
4	* Execute calculations for priority weights, matrix λ_{max}, CI, CR, and store and print values. (Program displays "7" when done.)		E	7

The following data registers are used:

Register	Use
00	Working register/λ pointer
01	Mean total/weight pointer
02	Matrix size "m"
03	Row counter
04	Column counter
05	P pointer
06	P' pointer
07	Matrix λ_{max}
08	CI
09	CR
10,20,30	—
40,50,60	Priority weights for respective matrix rows, 1, 2, . . . , 7

70	—
11–17	
21–27	
31–37	
41–47	Values of matrix elements in "RC" = row number–column number location
51–57	
61–67	
71–77	
19,29,39	—
49,59,69	Row for respective matrix rows 1, 2, . . . , 7
79	—
80–85	Table CR values for $m = 2, . . . , 7$

Program Code

Location	Code	Key	Comments
000	61	GTO	Go to instructions for clearing data memories
001	01	01	
002	96	96	
003	76	LBL	Execute calculations and store/display values
004	15	E	
005	43	RCL	Initialize counters, pointers, and calculation register
006	02	02	
007	71	SBR	
008	59	INT	
009	01	1	
010	00	0	
011	42	STO	
012	06	06	
013	01	1	
014	42	STO	
015	00	00	
016	76	LBL	Calculate geometric mean of current row
017	70	RAD	
018	73	RC*	
019	05	05	
020	49	PRD	
021	00	00	
022	69	OP	
023	25	25	
024	97	DSZ	
025	04	04	
026	70	RAD	
027	43	RCL	
028	00	00	
029	22	INV	
030	45	Yˣ	
031	43	RCL	
032	02	02	
033	42	STO	Store value for later counter use
034	04	04	

Location	Code	Key	Comments
035	95	=	
036	72	ST*	
037	06	06	Store geometric mean for current row
038	44	SUM	Add current row geometric mean to total for matrix
039	01	01	
040	01	1	Increment P and P' pointers for next row
041	00	0	
042	44	SUM	
043	06	06	
044	43	RCL	
045	06	06	
046	85	+	
047	01	1	
048	42	STD	Initialize calculation register for later use
049	00	00	
050	95	=	
051	42	STD	
052	05	05	
053	97	DSZ	
054	03	03	Perform for all rows
055	70	RAD	
056	01	1	Initialize P' pointer
057	00	0	
058	42	STD	
059	06	06	
060	76	LBL	Normalize eigenvector (priority weights "w")
061	80	GRD	
062	43	RCL	
063	01	01	
064	22	INV	
065	64	PD*	
066	06	06	
067	01	1	
068	00	0	
069	44	SUM	
070	06	06	
071	97	DSZ	
072	04	04	
073	80	GRD	Perform for all row values
074	43	RCL	Initialize counters and pointers
075	02	02	
076	71	SBR	
077	59	INT	
078	01	1	
079	00	0	
080	42	STD	
081	01	01	
082	01	1	
083	09	9	
084	42	STD	
085	00	00	
086	76	LBL	Perform matrix multiplication with current row to calculate $\lambda_{max} w$
087	38	SIN	
088	73	RC*	
089	05	05	
090	65	×	
091	73	RC*	
092	01	01	
093	95	=	
094	74	SM*	
095	00	00	

Location	Code	Key	Comments
096	69	OP	
097	25	25	
098	01	1	
099	00	0	
100	44	SUM	
101	01	01	
102	97	DSZ	
103	04	04	
104	38	SIN	Perform for all columns in current row
105	01	1	Initialize weight pointer and column counter
106	00	0	Increment λ pointer, P and P′ pointers
107	42	STO	Decrement row counter
108	01	01	
109	44	SUM	
110	00	00	
111	44	SUM	
112	06	06	
113	43	RCL	
114	06	06	
115	42	STO	
116	05	05	
117	43	RCL	
118	02	02	
119	42	STO	
120	04	04	
121	97	DSZ	
122	03	03	
123	38	SIN	Perform for all rows
124	01	1	Initialize weight pointer, λ pointer, row counter
125	00	0	Point P′ pointer to table CR location
126	42	STO	
127	01	01	
128	01	1	
129	09	9	
130	42	STO	
131	00	00	
132	43	RCL	
133	02	02	
134	42	STO	
135	03	03	
136	42	STO	
137	06	06	
138	07	7	
139	08	8	
140	44	SUM	
141	06	06	
142	76	LBL	Calculate λ_{max} for current row, add in matrix λ_{max}
143	39	COS	
144	73	RC*	
145	00	00	
146	55	÷	
147	73	RC*	
148	01	01	
149	95	=	
150	44	SUM	
151	07	07	
152	01	1	
153	00	0	
154	44	SUM	
155	00	00	
156	44	SUM	

Location	Code	Key	Comments
157	01	01	
158	97	DSZ	
159	03	03	
160	39	COS	Perform for all rows
161	43	RCL	Calculate and store eigenvalue (average λ_{max})
162	02	02	
163	22	INV	
164	49	PRD	
165	07	07	
166	43	RCL	Calculate and store CI
167	07	07	
168	75	-	
169	43	RCL	
170	02	02	
171	95	=	
172	55	÷	
173	53	(	
174	43	RCL	
175	02	02	
176	75	-	
177	01	1	
178	54	)	
179	95	=	
180	42	STO	
181	08	08	
182	42	STO	Calculate and store CR
183	09	09	
184	09	9	
185	69	OP	
186	17	17	
187	73	RC*	
188	06	06	
189	22	INV	
190	49	PRD	
191	09	09	
192	07	7	If connected to printer, list registers 07–89 (registers 80–85
193	22	INV	are table CR values, and 86–89 are program code data)
194	90	LST	
195	91	R/S	Display 7 (execution completed)
196	08	8	Clear data memories 00–79
197	69	OP	
198	17	17	
199	47	CMS	
200	00	0	
201	91	R/S	Display 0 (wait for matrix size to be entered from keyboard)
202	71	SBR	Use subroutine to initialize counters and pointers
203	59	INT	
204	61	GTO	
205	02	02	
206	60	60	
207	76	LBL	Subroutine to initialize counters and pointers
208	59	INT	Store matrix size
209	42	STO	Initialize row and column counters
210	02	02	Position P and P' pointers to register 11 (matrix location 1, 1)
211	42	STO	
212	03	03	
213	42	STO	
214	04	04	

Location	Code	Key	Comments
215	01	1	
216	01	1	
217	42	STO	
218	05	05	
219	42	STO	
220	06	06	
221	92	RTN	
222	76	LBL	Increment P pointer to location for next "x" entry
223	16	A'	Increment P' pointer to location for next "$1/x$" entry
224	69	OP	
225	25	25	
226	01	1	
227	00	0	
228	44	SUM	
229	06	06	
230	43	RCL	
231	05	05	
232	91	R/S	Display P (wait for the "x" for location P to be entered from keyboard)
233	76	LBL	Store entry value "x"
234	11	A	Calculate and store "$1/x$"
235	72	ST*	
236	05	05	
237	35	1/X	
238	72	ST*	
239	06	06	
240	97	DSZ	
241	04	04	
242	16	A'	Perform for remaining columns in current row
243	69	OP	Position P and P' pointers to next matrix diagonal position
244	33	33	
245	43	RCL	
246	03	03	
247	42	STO	
248	04	04	
249	75	−	
250	01	1	
251	01	1	
252	95	=	
253	22	INV	
254	44	SUM	
255	05	05	
256	43	RCL	
257	05	05	
258	42	STO	
259	06	06	
260	01	1	Store 1 in current P pointer location
261	72	ST*	
262	05	05	
263	97	DSZ	
264	04	04	
265	16	A'	Perform through last row and last column
266	06	6	
267	91	R/S	Display 6 (wait for execution instruction from keyboard)
268	00	0	
269	00	0	
270	00	0	
271	00	0	

Procedure for Storing Table CR Values

Key	Comments
9	Use this sequence to repartition and load table CR values in registers 80–85. Complete the
OP	sequence by repartitioning to the initial TI-59 partition. Then record banks 1 and 2 on a
17	magnetic card. On subsequent use this eliminates the need to repartition the TI-59 before
0	reading the magnetic card.
STO	
80	*Note:* This sequence is performed *out* of the LRN mode.
.	
5	
8	
STO	
81	
.	
9	
STO	
82	
1	
.	
1	
2	
STO	
83	
1	
.	
2	
4	
STO	
84	
1	
.	
3	
2	
STO	
85	
6	
OP	
17	

Contents	Register	Comments
0.	80	The listing or recalling of data registers 80–85 shows the table CR values that are permanently
0.58	81	stored with the program. Registers 86–89 are the "data values" of program codes in program
0.9	82	locations 240–271. This results from the repartitioning of registers 80–89 to become
1.12	83	data registers.
1.24	84	
1.32	85	
9.1061 -68	86	
-9.7057201 54	87	
5.442295 -51	88	
-4.2034334 -49	89	

Location			Comments
272	00	0	When registers 80–89 become program locations through repartitioning, the program codes for
273	00	0	locations 240–271 are as previously listed. However, the table CR values stored as data are
274	00	0	interpreted as "program code" values shown in listing program locations 272–319.
275	00	0	
276	00	0	
277	00	0	
278	20	CLR	
279	13	C	

```
280  00  0
281  00  0
282  00  0
283  00  0
284  00  0
285  00  0
286  40  IND
287  12  B
288  00  0
289  00  0
290  00  0
291  00  0
292  00  0
293  00  0
294  20  CLR
295  11  A
296  14  D
297  00  0
298  00  0
299  00  0
300  00  0
301  00  0
302  00  0
303  90  LST
304  14  D
305  00  0
306  00  0
307  00  0
308  00  0
309  00  0
310  00  0
311  58  FIX
312  00  00
313  00  0
314  00  0
315  00  0
316  00  0
317  00  0
318  00  0
319  00  0
```

Sample Problem: Wealth of Nations Through Their World Influence

	U.S.	U.S.S.R	China	France	U.K.	Japan	W. Germany
U.S.	1	4	9	6	6	5	5
U.S.S.R.	0.25	1	7	5	5	3	4
China	0.11	0.14	1	0.2	0.2	0.14	0.2
France	0.17	0.2	5	1	1	0.33	0.33
U.K.	0.17	0.2	5	1	1	0.33	0.33
Japan	0.2	0.33	7	3	3	1	2
W. Germany	0.2	0.25	5	3	3	0.5	1

The first row in this table compares the wealth influence (Marshall Plan, AID, and so on) of the U.S. with the other nations. For example, it is of equal importance to the U.S. (hence the unit entry in the first position), between weak and strong importance when compared with the U.S.S.R. (hence the value 4 in the second position), of absolute importance when compared with China (hence the value 9 in the third position). We have values between strong and demonstrated importance when compared with France and the U.K. (hence a 6 in the next two positions), strong importance when compared with Japan and Germany (hence a 5 in the following two positions). For the entries in the first column we have the reciprocals of the numbers in the first row indicating the inverse relation of relative strength of the wealth of the other countries when compared with the U.S. and so on for the remaining values in the second row and second column and so forth.

Enter	Press	Output	Comment
	RST		
	R/S		
		(0)–Program displays	Program waits for matrix size to be entered from keyboard
7	R/S		Enter matrix size
		(12)–Program displays	Location of next value "x"
4	R/S		Enter value "x" for location displayed
		(13)–Program displays	
9	R/S		
		⋮	
		(67)–Program displays	
2	R/S		Note: Only the values enclosed in the triangle need be entered.
		(6)	Matrix complete
	(E)		Execute calculations, store and print values
		(7)	Execution completed and, if using printer, register values listed

If the printer is used, the following would be printed before displaying "7":

Value	Register	Comments
7.607030156	07	λ_{max}
.1011716927	08	CI
.0766452218	09	CR
.4168850758	10	Priority weight for row 1
1.	11	
4.	12	
9.	13	Row 1 values
6.	14	
6.	15	
5.	16	
5.	17	
0.	18	
3.287041983	19	Row λ for row 1
.2313379918	20	Priority weight for row 2
0.25	21	
1.	22	
7.	23	
5.	24	Row 2 values
5.	25	
3.	26	
4.	27	
0.	28	
1.779886814	29	Row λ for row 2
.0198181834	30	
.1111111111	31	
.1428571429	32	
1.	33	
0.2	34	
0.2	35	
0.14	36	
0.2	37	
0.	38	
.1578458455	39	
.0533237723	40	
.166666667	41	
0.2	42	
5.	43	
1.	44	
1.	45	
0.33	46	
0.33	47	
0.	48	
.3958396032	49	
.0533237723	50	
.166666667	51	
0.2	52	
5.	53	
1.	54	
1.	55	
0.33	56	
0.33	57	
0.	58	
.3958396032	59	
.1288822704	60	
0.2	61	
.3333333333	62	
7.142857143	63	
3.03030303	64	

3.03030303	65
1.	66
2.	67
0.	68
.9469626476	69
0.096428934	70
0.2	71
0.25	72
5.	73
3.03030303	74
3.03030303	75
0.5	76
1.	77
0.	78
.7243468766	79
0.	80
0.58	81
0.9	82
1.12	83
1.24	84
1.32	85
9.1061-68	86
-9.7057201 54	87
5.442295-51	88
-4.2034334-49	89

Table CR values

"Data values" of program code in program locations 240–271

FORTRAN COMPUTER PROGRAM

There are special instructions for using the analytic hierarchy program to compute eigenvector and consistency ratios. Please note that the first three steps are installation dependent. Check your own implementation.

1. Type LOGIN Project No./Program No. For example, if your project number (common for the course) and program number are 111301 and 335417, respectively, you should type: "LOGIN 111301/335417" and hit "RETURN."
2. The computer will prompt: "PASSWORD." Type your password. Your password will not get printed so that it may remain confidential.
3. To execute the analytic hierarchy program, type: "EXEC SAATY FOR [111400, 352101]" and hit "RETURN."
4. The computer will prompt: "ENTER THE # OF FACTORS IN 2ND HIERARCHY LEVEL. 3 COLUMNS OR SPACES ARE RESERVED FOR THIS NUMBER. IF YOU HAVE TO ENTER, SAY 4, IT SHOULD BE ENTERED AS 'SPACE' 'SPACE' 4." After you have entered the number of factors in the second level, the computer will check back to confirm if it is correct. If incorrect, type "9" and hit "RETURN"; otherwise just hit "RETURN."
5. To enter the numerical judgments, the computer will prompt: "ENTER THE UPPER TRIANGULAR PART OF THE MATRIX WITHOUT THE

UNIT ELEMENTS ON THE MAIN DIAGONAL. 3 COLUMNS OR SPACES ARE RESERVED FOR EACH ELEMENT. FRACTIONAL ELEMENTS LIKE 1/3 SHOULD BE ENTERED AS −3. THE ELEMENTS IN A ROW SHOULD BE ENTERED ON THE SAME LINE." The computer will accept the elements of the matrix rowwise. After you have entered all the elements in the upper triangular matrix the computer will print out the complete matrix, the weights corresponding to each factor, LAMBDA (MAX) and consistency index (CI).

6. The computer will now prompt for the number of factors in LEVEL 3 of your hierarchy and which of these are related to FACTOR 1 of LEVEL 2 and so on. The procedure outlined above may be followed for both complete and incomplete hierarchies. This program also computes the composite priorities for the last level and the consistency ratio of the whole hierarchy.

7. When finished, type K/F to log off.

```
C
C      INTERACTIVE PRIORITY HIERARCHY PROGRAM
C
       DIMENSION A(60),B(60,60),NZ(60),Y(60),RCT(10)
       COMMON CI,RCT
       DATA RCT/.0,.0,.58,.90,1.12,1.24,1.32,1.41,1.45,1.49/
C
C      2ND LEVEL
C
       WRITE(6,100)
100    FORMAT('  IF YOU WANT TO PROCESS SINGLE (UNRELATED) MATRICES',
      * ',  TYPE "S"; IF MORE INVOLVED, HIT "RETURN".'$)
       ACCEPT 101,ISEPR
101    FORMAT(A1)
       WRITE(6,102)
102    FORMAT('  IF YOUR HIERACHY IS PERFECT (COMPLETE), TYPE "P"; ',
      *'IF NOT, HIT "RETURN".'$)
       ACCEPT 101,IPERF
       TYPE 1001
1001   FORMAT('  ***NOTE: 1. WHEN YOU ARE ENTERING ANY NUMBER, PLEASE RE'
      *,'MEMBER THAT THERE ARE 3 COLUMNS OR SPACES RESERVED FOR EACH',
      *' NUMBER.'/11X,'2. IF YOU HAVE TO ENTER ONE NUMBER, SAY 7, IT ',
      *'SHOULD BE ENTERED AS "^^7" WHERE A "^" STANDS FOR A BLANK.'/
      *11X,'3. IF YOU HAVE TO ENTER A SERIES OF NUMBERS; SAY ',
      *'3,6,2; IT SHOULD BE ENTERED AS "^^3^^6^^2".'/
      *11X,'4. IN ENTERING THE UPPER TRIANGULAR PART OF ',
      *'THE MATRIX, FRACTIONAL ELEMENT LIKE 1/3 SHOULD BE ENTERED AS '/14
      *X,'"^-3"; THE ELEMENTS IN A ROW SHOULD ENTERED ON THE SAME LINE.',
      *' UNITY ELEMENTS IN THE MAIN DIAGONAL ARE UNNECESSARY.')
       LEVL=2
1000   TYPE 1002
1002   FORMAT(2X,'ENTER THE # OF FACTORS IN 2ND HIERARCHY LEVEL'$)
       ACCEPT *,NA
1004   FORMAT(I3)
       TYPE 1006,NA
```

```
1006    FORMAT(2X,I3,'? IF WRONG, ENTER "9", OTHERWISE HIT "RE',
        *'TURN".'$)
        ACCEPT 1008,YN
1008    FORMAT(F1.0)
        IF (YN .GT. 5) GO TO 1000
        CALL MTXIN(A,NA)
        IF(ISEPR.EQ.'S')GOTO 1000
C       TRC=TOTAL RANDOM CONSISTENCY FOR THIS HIERARCHY
C       TC=TOTAL CONSISTENCY OF THIS HIERARCHY
C       RCT()=RANDOM CONSISTENCY TABLE
C
C    THE FOLLOWING LEVEL
C
3000    LEVL=LEVL+1
        LEVL1=LEVL-1
        CALL ZERO(B(1,1),B(60,60))
1009    TYPE 1010,LEVL
1010    FORMAT(' ENTER THE # OF FACTORS IN LEVEL',I3,
        *'. IF YOU WANT TO STOP HERE, ENTER "0".'$)
        ACCEPT *,NB
1012    FORMAT(I3)
        TYPE 1013,NB
1013    FORMAT(3X,I3,'? IF WRONG:"9", ELSE:"RETURN".'$)
        ACCEPT 1008,YN
        IF (YN .GT. 5) GOTO 1009
        IF (NB .LE. 0)GO TO 1080
C
        DO 3050 NF=1,NA
        CALL ZERO(NZ(1),NZ(60))
        IF(IPERF.NE.'P')GOTO 3007
        DO 3005 I=1,NB
3005    NZ(I)=I
        NC=NB
        GOTO 3012
3007    TYPE 3009,LEVL,NF,LEVL1
3009    FORMAT(' ENTER ALL # OF FACTORS IN LEVEL',I3,' RELATED TO ELEMENT'
        *,I3,' OF LEVEL',I3,', ON THE SAME LINE BY ASCENDING ORDER:'$)
        ACCEPT 3011,NZ
3011    FORMAT(60I3)
C   EXAM LAST ONE
        DO 3013 I=1,60
        IF(NZ(I))3013,3015,3013
3013    CONTINUE
3015    NC=I-1
        TYPE 3017,(NZ(I),I=1,NC)
3017    FORMAT(3X,60I3)
        TYPE 3016
3016    FORMAT('  IF NOT CORRECT-"9", ELSE-"RETURN".'$)
        ACCEPT 1008,YN
        IF(YN.GT.5)GOTO 3007
3012    IF(IPERF.EQ.'P')WRITE(6,3099)LEVL,NF
3099    FORMAT(' LEVEL:',I3,'   MATRIX:',I3)
        IF(NC.NE.1)GOTO 3018
C       NC=1,ONLY 1 ELEMENT CONNECTED
        B(NZ(1),NF)=1.
        GOTO 3050
3018    CALL MTXIN(Y,NC)
        TC=TC+A(NF)*CI
        TRC=TRC+A(NF)*RCT(NC)
C ONLY RELATED ELEMENTS HAVE WEIGHTED VALUES
        DO 3019 I=1,NC
3019    B(NZ(I),NF)=Y(I)
3050    CONTINUE
        TYPE 3051,LEVL,LEVL1
3051    FORMAT(6X,'** LEVEL',I4,' WITH RESPECT TO LEVEL',I4)
        TYPE 1024,(A(I),I=1,NA)
```

```
1024   FORMAT(' WEIGHT:',(10F10.6))
       DO 1028 I=1,NB
       TYPE 1026,(I,(B(I,J),J=1,NA))
1026   FORMAT(I8,(10F10.6))
1028   CONTINUE
C      COMPOSITE
       DO 3053 I=1,NA
       DO 3053 J=1,NB
3053   B(J,I)=B(J,I)*A(I)
1060   DO 1066 I=1,NB
       S=0.
       DO 1064 J=1,NA
1064   S=S+B(I,J)
1066   A(I)=S
       TYPE 3054,LEVL,(A(I),I=1,NB)
3054   FORMAT(6X,'** COMPOSITE PRIORITIES FOR LEVEL',I4/(10F10.6))
       NA=NB
       GOTO 3000
C      CONSISTENCY OF THE HIERARCHY
1080   CH=TC/TRC
       TYPE 1082,CH
1082   FORMAT('  CONSISTENCY RATIO  OF THE HIERARCHY (C.R.H.) =',F7.4)
       STOP
       END
C***********************************************************************
       SUBROUTINE MTXIN(W,NFCTR)
       DIMENSION C(60,60),W(60),CW(60),W2(60),RCT(10)
       COMMON CI,RCT
2006   TYPE 2100
2100   FORMAT(2X,'ENTER THE UPPER TRIANGULAR PART OF THE MATRIX.')
2008   FORMAT(F1.0)
       NFCTR1=NFCTR-1
       DO 2110 I=1,NFCTR1
2102   TYPE 2103,I
2103   FORMAT(4X,'ROW',I3,':'$)
       I1=I+1
       ACCEPT 2104,(C(I,J),J=I1,NFCTR)
2104   FORMAT(20F3.0)
       TYPE 2105,(C(I,J),J=I1,NFCTR)
2105   FORMAT(3X,20F3.0)
       TYPE 2101
2101   FORMAT('  IF NOT CORRECT-"9", ELSE-"RETURN".'$)
       ACCEPT 2008,YN
       IF(YN.GT. 6 )GOTO 2102
       DO 2110 J=I1,NFCTR
       IF(C(I,J))2106,2108,2108
2106   C(I,J)=-(1.0/C(I,J))
2108   C(J,I)=1.0/C(I,J)
2110   CONTINUE
       DO 2114 I=1,NFCTR
2114   C(I,I)=2.
C
C  FIND INITIAL W
C
       TS=0.
       DO 2124 I=1,NFCTR
       S=0.
       DO 2122 J=1,NFCTR
2122   S=S+C(I,J)
       W2(I)=S
2124   TS=TS+S
       DO 2126  I=1,NFCTR
2126   W2(I)=W2(I)/TS
C
C   CW=W
```

```
C
      K=0
2127  TS=0.
      K=K+1
      DO 2130 I=1,NFCTR
      S=0.
      DO 2128 J=1,NFCTR
2128  S=S+C(I,J)*W2(J)
      W(I)=S
2130  TS=TS+S
      D=0.
      DO 2138 I=1,NFCTR
      W(I)=W(I)/TS
2138  D=D+ABS(W(I)-W2(I))
      IF(K .GT. 10000) GO TO 2142
      IF (D .LT. 1.E-15) GOTO 2142
      DO 2137 I=1,60
2137  W2(I)=W(I)
      GOTO 2127
2142  DO 2140 I=1,NFCTR
      C(I,I)=1.
2140  TYPE 2141,(C(I,J),J=1,NFCTR)
2141  FORMAT(17F7.4)
C
C  CW/W=LAMDA(MAX)
C
      DO 2146 I=1,NFCTR
      S=0.
      DO 2144 J=1,NFCTR
2144  S=S+C(I,J)*W(J)
      CW(I)=S
2146  CONTINUE
      S=0.
      DO 2148 I=1,NFCTR
2148  S=S+CW(I)/W(I)
      YMAX=S/NFCTR
      CI=0.
      CR=0.
      IF(NFCTR.LE.1)GO TO 2149
      CI=(YMAX-NFCTR)/(NFCTR-1)
      IF(NFCTR.LE.2)GO TO 2149
      CR=CI/RCT(NFCTR)
2149  TYPE 2150,(W(I),I=1,NFCTR)
2150  FORMAT('   WEIGHTS=',(10F10.6))
      TYPE 2152,YMAX,CI,CR
2152  FORMAT('   LAMDA(MAX)=',F11.6,6X,'C.I.=',F11.6,6X,'C.R.=',F11.6)
      TYPE 2154
2154  FORMAT(' IF YOU WANT TO REDO THIS MATRIX,',
     * ' ENTER "9", ELSE "RETURN".'$)
      ACCEPT 2008,YN
      IF(YN.GE.5)GOTO 2006
      RETURN
      END
```

APL COMPUTER PROGRAM

This program consists of four subroutines: Generalized, Vec, Eig, and Compare. *Vec* is a dyadic function used to transform the input into a reciprocal matrix. *Eig* is a monadic function that provides the principal eigenvalue and eigenvector of a reciprocal matrix. *Compare* is a subroutine that combines Eig and Vec and allows the user to input the pairwise comparison judgments. A feature of this program is that only the upper triangular part of the reciprocal matrix of comparisons is introduced into the computer. The matrix is introduced column by column. For example, if the matrix is

$$
\begin{array}{ccccccc}
x & 1 & 2 & 1/3 & 4 & x \\
x & & 1 & 5 & 6 & x \\
x & & & 1 & 7 & x \\
x & & & & 1 & x \\
\end{array}
$$

then the vector introduced is

$$2 \quad 1/3 \quad 5 \quad 4 \quad 6 \quad 7$$

Reciprocals are introduced as negative numbers. Thus the vector that is really introduced is

$$2 \quad {}^-3 \quad 5 \quad 4 \quad 6 \quad 7$$

The main program is *generalized*. The steps of the program are:

1. Introduce the number of levels in the hierarchy.
2. Identify the level with the maximum number of elements, and introduce the number of elements.

More details of the program are given in the function named Describe.

```
        ∇DESCRIBE[□]∇
     ∇   DESCRIBE
[1]      'TO USE THIS PROGRAM THE USER MUST TYPE THE WORD GENERALIZED.'
[2]      'THIS SUBROUTINE WILL START BY ASKING HOW MANY LEVEL THE      '
[3]      'HIERARCHY HAS,   THEN IT WILL CONTINUE ASKING WHAT THE MAXIMUM'
[4]      'NUMBER OF ELEMENTS IN THE LEVELS IS,'
[5]      'RECIPROCALS MUST BE INTRODUCED AS NEGATIVE NUMBERS, I.E.,    '
[6]      'IF YOU WISH TO INTRODUCE THE VALUE .25, YOU WOULD HAVE TO TYPE'
[7]      '-4 WHICH IS OBTAINED BY DEPRESSING THE KEY UPPER CASE 2      '
[8]      'FOLLOWED BY THE NUMBER 4,   THE REST IS EASY, TRY IT,        '
[9]      '2X2 MATRICES DO NOT REQUIRE THE CONSTRUCTION OF A PAIRWISE'
[10]     'COMPARISON MATRIX,   REMEMBER THIS,'
[11]     'NOTE:'
[12]     'IF YOU WISH TO PROCESS INDIVIDUAL MATRICES WITHOUT REQUIRING '
[13]     'HIERARCHIC COMPOSITION USE THE SUBROUTINE SINGLE WHICH IN TURN'
[14]     'USES THE FUNCTIONS MATRIX AND EIGENVECTOR,   THESE TWO FUNCTIONS'
[15]     '(MATRIX AND EIGENVECTOR) ARE USED TO CONSTRUCT THE RECIPROCAL '
[16]     'MATRIX AND COMPUTE THE EIGENVECTOR, RESPECTIVELY,            '
     ∇


        ∇GENERALIZED[□]∇
     ∇   GENERALIZED;I;I;W;Q;K;UV;L;R;M;N;J;SUB;A;T;U;H1;H2;K1;B;SB
[1]      'HOW MANY LEVELS IN THE HIERARCHY?'
[2]      I←□
```

```
[3]    CI←(I)⍴0
[4]    CR←(I)⍴0
[5]    'MAXIMUM NUMBER OF ELEMENTS IN THE LEVELS?'
[6]    I←⎕
[7]    W←(I,I,I)⍴0
[8]    E←(I,I)⍴0
[9]    Q←2
[10]   K←⍳I
[11]   UV←K∘.=K
[12]   W[Q-1;;]←UV
[13]   L←2
[14]  L5:R←⍳0
[15]   'HOW MANY ELEMENTS IN LEVEL       ';L;'?'
[16]   M←⎕
[17]   →LOOP00×⍳L=2
[18]   'HOW MANY ELEMENTS IN LEVEL       ';L-1;'?'
[19]   N←⎕
[20]   →LOOP20
[21]  LOOP00:N←1
[22]  LOOP20:'ENTER THE NAMES OF THE ACTIVITIES'
[23]   INPUTNAMES
[24]   J←1
[25]  LOOP1:'WHICH ELEMENTS OF LEVEL      ';L;'    ARE SUBORDINATED'
[26]   'TO ELEMENT      ';J;'    OF LEVEL       ';L-1;'?'
[27]   SUB←,⎕
[28]   →LOOP2×⍳0=1↑SUB
[29]   'IS A COMPARISON MATRIX USED?'
[30]   A←⎕
[31]   →LOOP4×⍳2=⍴A
[32]   T←COMPARE
[33]   →LOOP5
[34]  LOOP4:'WHAT ARE THEIR IMPACTS ON ELEMENT      ';J;'?'
[35]   T←,⎕
[36]   T←T÷+/T
[37]  LOOP5:U←M⍴0
[38]   U[SUB]←T
[39]   R←R,U
[40]   →LOOP3
[41]  LOOP2:R←R,M⍴0
[42]  LOOP3:J←J+1
[43]   →LOOP1×⍳J≤N
[44]   Z←(,N,M)⍴R
[45]   Z←⍉Z
[46]   →LOOP10×⍳L=2
[47]   'IMPACTS OF LEVEL      ';L;'    ON LEVEL      ';L-1
[48]   ACT[L;;],(8 4 ⍕Z)
[49]  LOOP10:→L1×⍳(I=M)∧(I=N)
[50]   →L2×⍳(I=M)
[51]   →L3×⍳(I=N)
[52]   H1←((I-M),N)⍴0
[53]   H2←(I,I-N)⍴0
[54]   W[Q;;]←(Z,[1]H1),H2
[55]   →L4
[56]  L1:W[Q;;]←Z
[57]   →L4
[58]  L2:H2←(I,I-N)⍴0
[59]   W[Q;;]←Z,H2
[60]   →L4
[61]  L3:H1←((I-M),N)⍴0
[62]   W[Q;;]←Z,[1]H1
[63]   →L4
[64]  L4:W[Q;;]←W[Q;;]+.×W[Q-1;;]
[65]   'COMPOSITE PRIORITIES AT LEVEL      ';L
[66]   ACT[L;;],(8 4 ⍕((M,1)⍴(W[Q;;])[;M;1]))
[67]   CI[Q]←E[Q;]+.×W[Q-1;;1]
[68]   'DO YOU WANT TO ELIMINATE LOW PRIORITY ACTIVITIES?'
```

```
[69]    B←⍞
[70]    →LOOP6×⍳2=⍴B
[71]    'WHAT ACTIVITIES WOULD YOU LIKE TO ELIMINATE?'
[72]    SB←,⍞
[73]    K←1
[74]  LOOP7:W[Q;SB[K1];]←0
[75]    K1←K1+1
[76]    →LOOP7×⍳K1≤(⍴SB)
[77]    W[Q;;]←W[Q;;]÷(1↑(+/⍀W[Q;;]))
[78]    'COMPOSITE PRIORITIES AT LEVEL    ';L
[79]    ACT[L;;],(8 4 ⍕((M,1)⍴(W[Q;;])[⍳M;1]))
[80]  LOOP6:L←L+1
[81]    Q←Q+1
[82]    →L5×⍳L≤I
[83]    TCI←+/CI
[84]    TCR←+/CR
[85]    'HIERARCHICAL CONSISTENCY      '; 6 4 ⍕(TCI÷TCR)
     ▽


        ▽EIGEN
        ▽EIG[⎕]▽
     ▽   R←EIG A;B;F;D;C
[1]     B←A+(⍳F)∘.=⍳F←1↑⍴A
[2]     R←R÷+/(R←+/B)
[3]   L:F←R
[4]     R←R÷+/(R←B+.×R)
[5]     →L×⍳1.000000000E¯25<(+/|R-F
[6]     'LAMBDA '; 6 3 ⍕1↑(A+.×R)÷R
[7]     D←((1↑(A+.×R)÷R)-1↑⍴A)÷(1↑⍴A)-1
[8]     'CONSISTENCY '; 6 3 ⍕D
[9]     C←11⍴0 0 0.58 0.9 1.12 1.24 1.32 1.41 1.45 1.49 1.49
[10]    'CONSISTENCY RATIO '; 6 3 ⍕(D÷C[⍴R])
[11]    E[Q;J]←D
[12]    CR[Q]←C[M]
     ▽


        ▽VEC[⎕]▽
     ▽   A←N VEC V;I;J;K
[1]     →((2×⍴V)=N×N-1)/L2
[2]     'REAL LENGTH ';(N×N-1)÷2
[3]     T←COMPARE
[4]   L2:A←(N,N)⍴0
[5]     A[1;1]←1
[6]     K←0
[7]     I←1
[8]     V←((V>0)×V)-(V<0)÷V
[9]   L1:A[⍳J;I]←1÷A[I;⍳J]←V[K+⍳J+I-1]
[10]    K←K+J
[11]    A[I;I]←1
[12]    →(N≥I←I+1)/L1
[13]    A←⍉A
[14]    8 3 ⍕A
     ▽


        ▽COMPARE[⎕]
     ▽   S←COMPARE;V;R
[1]     'ENTER THE UPPER TRIANGULAR PART OF THE MATRIX'
[2]     V←⍞
[3]     R←0.5×1+(1+8×⍴V)*0.5
[4]     S←EIG R VEC V
     ▽
```

```
        ∇SINGLE[☐]∇
    ∇   S←SINGLE;V;R
[1]      'ENTER THE UPPER TRIANGULAR PART OF THE MATRIX'
[2]      V←☐
[3]      R←0.5×1+(1+8×⍴V)*0.5
[4]      S←EIGENVECTOR R MATRIX V
    ∇


        ∇EIGENVECTOR[☐]∇
    ∇   R←EIGENVECTOR A;B;P;D;C
[1]      B←A+(⍳F)∘.=⍳F←1↑⍴A
[2]      R←R÷+/(R←+/B)
[3]    L:P←R
[4]      R←R÷+/(R←B+.×R)
[5]      →L×⍳1.000000000E¯25<+/|R-P
[6]      'LAMBDA ';6 3 ▼1↑(A+.×R)÷R
[7]      D←((1↑(A+.×R)÷R)-1↑⍴A)÷(1↑⍴A)-1
[8]      'CONSISTENCY ';6 3 ▼D
[9]      C←100⍴((0 0 0.58 0.9 1.12 1.24 1.32 1.41 1.45 1.49),(90⍴1.49))
[10]     'CONSISTENCY RATIO ';6 3 ▼(D÷C[⍴R])
    ∇


        ∇MATRIX[☐]∇
    ∇   A←N MATRIX V;I;J;K
[1]      A←(N,N)⍴0
[2]      A[1;1]←1
[3]      K←0
[4]      I←1
[5]      V←((V>0)×V)-(V<0)÷V
[6]    L1:A[⍳J;I]←1÷A[I;⍳J]←V[K+⍳J←I-1]
[7]      K←K+J
[8]      A[I;I]←1
[9]      →(N≥I←I+1)/L1
[10]     A←⍉A
[11]     8 3 ▼A
    ∇


        ∇INPUTNAMES[☐]∇
    ∇   INPUTNAMES;I1;SUB
[1]      ACT←(L,M,25)⍴' '
[2]      I1←1
[3]    L13:SUB←☐
[4]      ACT[L;I1;]←SUB,((25-(⍴SUB))⍴' ')
[5]      I1←I1+1
[6]      →L13×⍳I1≤M
    ∇
```

References

ALEXANDER, JOYCE, and T. L. SAATY. "The Forward and Backward Processes of Conflict Analysis." *Behavioral Science,* vol. 22, pp. 87–98, March 1977.

————. "Stability Analysis of the Forward-Backward Process." *Behavioral Science,* vol. 22, pp. 375–382, November 1977.

ANDERSON, N. H. "Information Integration Theory: A Brief Survey." In *Contemporary Developments in Mathematical Psychology,* ed. D. H. Krantz and others, vol. 2. San Francisco: Freeman, 1974.

ARROW, KENNETH J. *Social Choice and Individual Values.* New Haven: Yale University Press, 1970.

BATSCHELET, F. *Mathematics for Life Scientists.* New York: Springer-Verlag, 1973.

BAUER, LOUIS, H. B. KELLER, and E. L. REISS. "Multiple Eigenvalues Lead to Secondary Bifurcation." *SIAM Review,* vol. 17, no. 1, January 1975.

BAUMOL, W. *Business Behavior, Value and Growth.* New York: Macmillan, 1959.

BELL, R., and R. WAGNER. *Political Power.* New York: Free Press, 1969.

BELLMAN, R. E., and L. A. ZADEH. "Decision-Making in a Fuzzy Environment." *Management Science,* vol. 17, 1970.

BLUM, M. L., and J. C. NAYLOR. *Industrial Psychology—Its Theoretical and Social Foundations.* New York: Harper & Row, 1968.

BOGART, KENNETH P. "Preference Structures I: Distances Between Transitive Preference Relations." *Journal of Mathematical Sociology,* vol. 3, pp. 49–67, 1973.

BRONSON, GORDON. "The Hierarchical Organization of the Central Nervous System." In *International Politics and Foreign Policy: A Reader in Research and Theory,* ed. James A. Rosenau. Rev. ed. New York: Free Press, 1969.

BUCK, R. C., and D. L. HULL. "The Logical Structure of the Linnaean Hierarchy." *Systematic Zoology,* vol. 15, pp. 97–111, 1966.

CHIPMAN, J. "The Foundations of Utility." *Econometrica,* vol. 28, no. 2, 1960.

CHURCHMAN, C. WEST, and H. B. EISENBERG. "Deliberation and Judgment." In *Human Judgments and Optimality,* ed. M. W. Shelley II and G. L. Bryan. New York: Wiley, 1969.

CHURCHMAN, C. WEST, and PHILBURN RATOOSH (eds.). *Measurement—Definitions and Theories.* New York: Wiley, 1959.

CLIFF, N. "Complete Orders from Incomplete Data: Interactive Ordering and Tailored Testing." *Psychological Bulletin,* vol. 82, no. 2, pp. 289–302, 1975.

COGAN, E. J., and others. *Modern Mathematical Methods and Models,* vol. 2. Committee on the Undergraduate Program, Mathematical Association of America, 1959.

COOMBS, CLYDE H. *A Theory of Data.* New York: Wiley, 1964.

DAVID, H. A. *The Method of Paired Comparisons.* London: Charles Griffin & Company, 1969.

DOBSON, RICARDO, T. F. GOLOB, and R. L. GUSTAFSON. "Multidimensional Scaling of Consumer Preferences for a Public Transportation System: An Application of Two Approaches." In *Socio-Economic Planning Science,* vol. 8. New York: Pergamon Press, 1974.

DULMAGE, A. L., and N. S. MENDELSOHN. "Graphs and Matrices." In *Graph Theory and Theoretical Physics,* ed. Frank Harary. New York: Academic Press, 1967.

DYER, J. S. "An Empirical Investigation of a Man-Machine Interactive Approach to the Solution of the Multiple Criteria Problem." In *Multiple Criteria Decision Making.* Columbia: University of South Carolina Press, 1973.

ECKART, CARL, and GALE YOUNG. "The Approximation of One Matrix by Another of Lower Rank." *Psychometrika,* vol. 1, no. 3, pp. 211–217, September 1936.

ECKENRODE, R. T. "Weighting Multiple Criteria." *Management Science,* vol. 12, no. 3, pp. 180–192, November 1965.

EISLER, HANNES. "The Connection Between Magnitude and Discrimination Scales and Direct and Indirect Scaling Methods." *Psychometrika,* vol. 30, no. 3, pp. 271–289, September 1965.

ENCARNATION, J. "A Note on Lexicographical Preferences." *Econometrica,* vol. 32, no. 1–2, 1964.

FARQUHAR, PETER H. "A Survey of Multiattribute Utility Theory and Applications." *Studies in the Management Sciences.* Vol. 6. Amsterdam: North-Holland Publishing Company, 1977.

FECHNER, G. *Elements of Psychophysics,* vol. 2. Translated by Helmut E. Adler. New York: Holt, Rinehart and Winston, 1966.

FISHBURN, P. C. *Decision and Value Theory.* New York: Wiley, 1964.

————. "Independence in Utility Theory with Whole Product Set." *Operations Research,* vol. 13, pp. 28–45, 1965.

————. "Methods of Estimating Additive Utilities." *Management Science,* vol. 13, no. 7, pp. 435–453, 1967.

————. "Arrow's Impossibility Theorem: Concise Proof and Infinite Voters." *Journal of Economic Theory*, vol. 2, pp. 103–106, 1970.

————. *Utility Theory for Decision Making*. New York: Wiley, 1972.

FITZ, RAYMOND, and JOANNE TROHA. "Interpretive Structural Modeling and Urban Planning." University of Dayton, 1977.

FROBENIUS, G. "Über Matrizen aus nicht negativen Elementen." *Sitzber. Akad. Wiss. Berlin*, Phys. Math. Kl., pp. 456–477, 1912.

GAL, T., and J. NEDOMA. "Multiparametric Linear Programming." *Management Science*, vol. 18, no. 7, 1972.

GALE, DAVID. *The Theory of Linear Economic Models*. New York: McGraw-Hill, 1960.

GARDNER, MARTIN. "The Hierarchy of Infinites and the Problems It Spawns." *Scientific American*, no. 214, pp. 112–118, March 1966.

GEOFFRION, A. M., J. S. DYER, and A. FEINBERG. "An Interactive Approach for Multicriterion Optimization with an Application to the Operation of an Academic Department." *Management Science*, vol. 19, no. 4, 1972.

GILLETT, J. R. "The Football League Eigenvector." *Eureka*, October 1970.

GREEN, P., and F. CARMONE. *Multidimensional Scaling and Related Techniques in Marketing Analysis*. Boston: Allyn & Bacon, 1970.

GREEN, P., and V. RAO. "Conjoint Measurement for Quantifying Judgmental Data." *Journal of Marketing Research*, vol. 8, pp. 355–363, August 1971.

GREEN, P., and YORAM WIND. "New Way to Measure Consumers' Judgments." *Harvard Business Review*, July–August 1975.

GUILFORD, J. P. "The Method of Paired Comparisons as a Psychometric Method." *Psychological Review*, vol. 35, pp. 494–506, 1928.

GUTTMAN, LOUIS. "The Principal Components of Scalable Attitudes." In *Mathematical Thinking in the Social Sciences*, ed. P. F. Lazarsfeld. New York: Russell & Russell, 1969.

HAMMOND, K. R., and D. A. SUMMERS. "Cognitive Dependence on Linear and Nonlinear Cues." *Psychological Review*, vol. 72, no. 3, pp. 215–224, 1965.

HARRIS, E. E. "Wholeness and Hierarchy." In *Foundations of Metaphysics in Science*. New York: Humanities Press, 1965.

HERBST, P. G. *Alternatives to Hierarchies*. Leiden: H. E. Stenfert Kroese, 1976.

HILL, J. DOUGLAS, and JOHN N. WARFIELD. "Unified Program Planning." *IEEE Transactions on Systems, Man, and Cybernetics*, vol. SMC-2, no. 5, pp. 610–621, November 1972.

HIRSCH, G. "Logical Foundation, Analysis and Development of Multicriterion Methods." Ph.D. dissertation, University of Pennsylvania, 1976.

HOTELLING, H. "Analysis of a Complex of Statistical Variables into Principal Components." *Journal of Educational Psychology*, vol. 24, pp. 417–441, 498–520, 1933.

HUBER, GEORGE P. "Multi-Attribute Utility Models: A Review of Field and Field-Like Studies." *Management Science*, vol. 20, no. 10, June 1974.

INTRILIGATOR, MICHAEL D. "A Probabilistic Model of Social Choice." *Review of Economic Studies,* vol. 40, pp. 553–560, October 1973.

JOHNSON, CHARLES R., THEODORE WANG, and WILLIAM BEINE. "A Note on Right-Left Asymmetry in an Eigenvector Ranking Scheme." *Journal of Mathematical Psychology,* January 1979.

JOHNSON, RICHARD M. "On a Theorem Stated by Eckart and Young." *Psychometrika,* vol. 28, no. 3, pp. 259–263, September 1963.

JOHNSON, STEPHEN C. "Hierarchical Clustering Schemes." *Psychometrika,* vol. 32, no. 3, pp. 241–254, September 1967.

JULIEN, PIERRE-ANDRE, P. LAMONDE, and D. LATOUCHE. *La Méthode des Scenarios.* University of Quebec and Ministère d'Etat Sciences et Technologie, 1974.

KAHNEMAN, DANIEL, and AMOS TVERSKY. "Subjective Probability: A Judgment of Representativeness." *Cognitive Psychology,* vol. 3, pp. 430–454, 1972.

KEENEY, RALPH L. "Decision Analysis with Multiple Objectives: The Mexico City Airport." *Bell Journal of Economics and Management Science,* Spring 1973.

KEENEY, RALPH L., and CRAIG W. KIRKWOOD. "Group Decision Making Using Cardinal Social Welfare Functions." *Management Science,* vol. 22, no. 4, December 1975.

KEENEY, RALPH L., and H. RAIFFA. *Decisions with Multiple Objectives: Preference and Value Tradeoffs.* New York: Wiley, 1976.

KELLER, J. B. "Miscellanea: Factorization of Matrices by Least-Squares." *Biometrika,* vol. 49, pp. 1–2, 1962.

KLEE, A. J. "The Role of Decision Models in the Evaluation of Competing Environmental Health Alternatives." *Management Science,* vol. 18, no. 2, pp. 53–67, October 1971.

KOESTLER, ARTHUR, and J. R. SMYTHIES (eds.). *Beyond Reductionism: New Perspectives in the Life of the Sciences.* New York: Macmillan, 1970.

KRANTZ, DAVID H., and others. *Foundations of Measurement,* vol. 1. New York: Academic Press, 1971.

————. "A Theory of Magnitude Estimation and Cross-Modality Matching." *Journal of Mathematical Psychology,* vol. 9, no. 2, pp. 168–199. May 1972.

————. "Fundamental Measurement of Force and Newton's First and Second Laws of Motion." *Philosophy of Science,* vol. 40, no. 4, pp. 481–495, December 1973.

KRUSKAL, J. B. "Multidimensional Scaling by Optimizing Goodness of Fit to a Nonmetric Hypothesis." *Psychometrika,* vol. 29, no. 1, 1964.

————. "Nonmetric Multidimensional Scaling: A Numerical Method." *Psychometrika,* vol. 29, no. 2, 1964.

————. *How to Use MDSCAL, a Multidimensional Scaling Program.* Murray Hill, N.J.: Bell Telephone Lab., 1967.

KUNREUTHER, H., and PAUL SLOVIC. "Economics, Psychology, and Protective Behavior." *American Economic Review,* vol. 68, November 1978.

LINDGREN, B. W. *Elements of Decision Theory*. New York: Macmillan, 1971.

LINDSTONE, H. A., and MURRAY TUROFF. *The Delphi Method: Techniques*. Reading, Mass.: Addison-Wesley, 1975.

LOOTSMA, F. A. "Saaty's Priority Theory and the Nomination of a Senior Professor in Operations Research." Delft: University of Technology, 1978.

LUCE, R. D., and P. SUPPES. "Preference, Utility and Subjective Probability." In *Handbook of Mathematical Psychology*. Vol. 3. New York: Wiley, 1964.

MALONE, DAVID W. "An Introduction to the Application of Interpretive Structural Modeling." *Proceedings of the IEEE*, vol. 63, no. 3, pp. 397–404, 1975.

MANHEIM, MARVIN L. *Hierarchical Structure: A Model of Planning and Design Processes*. Cambridge: M.I.T. Press, 1966.

MARCUS, MARVIN, and HENRYK MINC. *A Survey of Matrix Theory and Matrix Inequalities*. Boston: Allyn & Bacon, 1964.

MARSHALL, C. W. *Applied Graph Theory*. New York: Wiley-Interscience, 1971.

MAY, KENNETH O. "Intransitivity, Utility, and the Aggregation of Preference Patterns." *Econometrica*, vol. 22, no. 1, January 1954.

McCRACKEN, R. F. "Multidimensional Scaling and the Measurement of Consumer Perception." Ph.D. dissertation, University of Pennsylvania, 1967.

McNEIL, D. R., and J. W. TUKEY. "Higher-Order Diagnosis of Two-Way Tables, Illustrated on Two Sets of Demographic Empirical Distributions." *Biometrics*, vol. 31, no. 2, June 1975.

MESAROVIC, M. D., and D. MACKO. "Scientific Theory of Hierarchical Systems." In *Hierarchical Structures*, ed. L. L. Whyte, A. G. Wilson, and D. Wilson. New York: American Elsevier, 1969.

MESAROVIC, M. D., D. MACKO, and Y. TAKAHARA. *Theory of Hierarchical Multilevel Systems*. New York: Academic Press, 1970.

MILLER, G. A. "The Magical Number Seven Plus or Minus Two: Some Limits on Our Capacity for Processing Information." *Psychological Review*, vol. 63, pp. 81–97, March 1956.

MINNICK, WAYNE C. *The Art of Persuasion*. Boston: Houghton Mifflin, 1957.

MORRIS, PETER C. "Weighting Inconsistent Judgments." In *Pi Mu Epsilon Journal*, 1979.

NIKAIDO, H. *Introduction to Sets and Mappings in Modern Economics*. Amsterdam: North-Holland/New York: American Elsevier, 1970.

PATEE, H. H. "The Problem of Biological Hierarchy." In *Towards a Theoretical Biology*, ed. C. H. Waddington, vol. 3. Edinburgh: Edinburgh University Press, 1969.

——— (ed.). *Hierarchy Theory: The Challenge of Complex Systems*. New York: George Braziller, 1973.

PINSKI, GABRIEL, and FRANCIS NARIN. "Citation Influence for Journal Aggregates of Scientific Publications: Theory, with Application to the Literature of Physics." In *Information Processing and Management*, vol. 12. New York: Pergamon Press, 1976.

Proceedings of the IEEE. Special Issue on Social Systems Engineering. Chapter 2: "Binary Matrices in System Modeling." March 1975.

RABINOVITCH, I. "The Dimension Theory of Semiorders and Interval Orders." Ph.D. dissertation, Dartmouth College, June 1973.

RIVETT, PATRICK. "Policy Selection by Structural Mapping." *Proceedings of the Royal Society (London)*, vol. 354, pp. 407–423, 1977.

ROSEN, ROBERT. "Hierarchical Organization in Automata Theoretic Models of Biological Systems." In *Hierarchy Theory: The Challenge of Complex Systems,* ed. H. Pattee. New York: Braziller, 1973.

ROSENBLATT, M. *Random Processes.* New York: Oxford University Press, 1962.

SAATY, THOMAS L. "An Eigenvalue Allocation Model for Prioritization and Planning." Energy Management and Policy Center, University of Pennsylvania, 1972.

————. "Measuring the Fuzziness of Sets." *Journal of Cybernetics,* vol. 4, no. 4, pp. 53–61, 1974.

————. "Hierarchies and Priorities—Eigenvalue Analysis." University of Pennsylvania, 1975.

————. "Hierarchies, Reciprocal Matrices, and Ratio Scales." *Modules in Applied Mathematics.* Cornell University, Mathematical Association of America, 1976.

————. "Interaction and Impacts in Hierarchical Systems." *Proceedings of the Workshop on Decision Information for Tactical Command and Control.* Houston: Rice University, 1976. Also Chapter 2 in *Decision Information,* Tsokos and Thrall, eds. Academic Press, 1979.

————. "Theory of Measurement of Impacts and Interactions in Systems." *Proceedings of the International Conference on Applied General Systems Research: Recent Developments and Trends.* Binghamton, New York, 1977.

————. "A Scaling Method for Priorities in Hierarchical Structures." *Journal of Mathematical Psychology,* vol. 15, no. 3, pp. 234–281, June 1977.

————. "Scenarios and Priorities in Transport Planning: Application to the Sudan." *Transportation Research,* vol. 11, no. 5, October 1977.

————. "The Sudan Transport Study." *Interfaces,* vol. 8, no. 1, pp. 37–57, 1977.

————. "Exploring the Interface Between Hierarchies, Multiple Objectives and Fuzzy Sets." *Fuzzy Sets and Systems,* January 1978.

————. "Modeling Unstructured Decision Problems: Theory of Analytical Hierarchies." *Mathematics and Computers in Simulation,* vol. 20, no. 3, pp. 147–157, September 1978.

————. "The U.S.–OPEC Energy Conflict: The Payoff Matrix by the Analytic Hierarchy Process." *International Journal of Game Theory,* 1979.

SAATY, THOMAS L., and MIGUEL H. BELTRAN. "Architectural Design by the Analytic Hierarchy Process." *Journal of the DMG,* April 1980.

SAATY, THOMAS L., and J. P. BENNETT. "A Theory of Analytical Hierarchies Applied to Political Candidacy." *Behavioral Science,* vol. 22, pp. 237–245, July 1977.

————. "Terrorism: Patterns for Negotiations; Three Case Studies Through Hierarchies and Holarchies." Study for the Arms Control and Disarmament Agency, 208 pp., 1977.

SAATY, THOMAS L., and M. W. KHOUJA. "A Measure of World Influence." *Journal of Peace Science*, Spring 1976.

SAATY, THOMAS L., and REYNALDO S. MARIANO. "Rationing Energy to Industries: Priorities and Input-Output Dependence." *Energy Systems and Policy*, Winter 1979.

SAATY, THOMAS L., and PAUL C. ROGERS. "Higher Education in the United States (1985–2000): Scenario Construction Using a Hierarchical Framework with Eigenvector Weighting." *Socioeconomic Planning Sciences*, vol. 10, pp. 251–263, 1976.

SAATY, THOMAS L., R. ROGERS, and R. PELL. "Portfolio Selection Through Hierarchies." *Journal of Portfolio Management*, vol. 6, no. 3, 1980.

SAATY, THOMAS L., and LUIS VARGAS. "A Note on Estimating Technological Coefficients by Hierarchical Measurements." *Socioeconomic Planning Sciences*, 1980.

————. "Hierarchical Analysis of Behavior in Competition: Prediction in Chess." *Behavioral Science*, May 1980.

SANKARANARAYANAN, A. "On a Group Theoretical Connection Among the Physical Hierarchies." Research Communication 96, Douglas Advanced Research Laboratories, Huntington Beach, California.

SAVAGE, C. WADE. "Introspectionist and Behaviorist Interpretations of Ratio Scales of Perceptual Magnitudes." *Psychological Monographs: General and Applied*, vol. 80, no. 19, whole no. 627, 1966.

SCHOEMAKER, P.J.H., and C. C. WAID. "A Comparison of Several Methods for Constructing Additive Representations of Multi-Attribute Preferences." Philadelphia: Wharton Applied Research Center, 1978.

SCOTT, DANA. "Measurement Structures and Linear Inequalities." *Journal of Mathematical Psychology*, vol. 1, pp. 233–247, 1964.

SHEPARD, R. N. "The Analysis of Proximities: Multidimensional Scaling with an Unknown Distance Function." *Psychometrika*, vol. 27, 1962.

————. "Analysis of Proximities as a Technique for the Study of Information Processing in Man." *Human Factors*, no. 5, 1963.

————. "A Taxonomy of Some Principal Types of Data and of Multidimensional Methods for Their Analysis." *Multidimensional Scaling: Theory and Applications in the Behavioral Sciences*, vol. 1. New York: Seminar Press, 1972.

SHEPARD, R. N., A. KIMBALL ROMNEY, and SARA BETH NERLOVE (eds.). *Multidimensional Scaling: Theory and Applications in the Behavioral Sciences*, vol. 1. New York: Seminar Press, 1972.

SHINN, A. "An Application of Psychophysical Scaling to the Measurement of National Power." *Journal of Politics*, vol. 31, pp. 132–951, 1969.

SIMON, H. A. "The Architecture of Complexity." *Proceedings of the American Philosophical Society*, vol. 106, pp. 467–482, December 1962.

SIMON, H. A., and A. ANDO. "Aggregation of Variables in Dynamic Systems." *Econometrica*, vol. 29, no. 2, pp. 111–138, April 1961.

SLUCKIN, W. "Combining Criteria of Occupational Success." *Occupational Psychology*. Pt I: vol. 30, pp. 20–26, 1956; pt. II: vol. 30, pp. 57–67, 1956.

SRINIVASAN, V., and A. D. SHOCKER. "Linear Programming Techniques for Multidimensional Analysis of Preferences." *Psychometrika*, vol. 38, pp. 337–369, 1973.

STEVENS, S. S. "On the Psychophysical Law." *Psychological Reviews*, vol. 64, pp. 153–181, 1957.

————. "Measurement, Psychophysics, and Utility." In *Measurement: Definitions and Theories*, ed. C. W. Churchman and P. Ratoosh. New York: Wiley, 1959.

————. "To Honor Fechner and Repeal His Law." *Science*, vol. 13, 13 January 1961.

STEVENS, S. S., and E. GALANTER. "Ratio Scales and Category Scales for a Dozen Perceptual Continua." *Journal of Experimental Psychology*, vol. 54, pp. 377–411, 1964.

STEWART, G. W. "Error and Perturbation Bounds for Subspaces Associated with Certain Eigenvalue Problems." *SIAM Review*, vol. 15, no. 4, pp. 727–764, October 1973.

————. "Gershgorin Theory for the Generalized Eigenvalue Problem $Ax = \lambda Bx$." *Mathematics of Computation*, vol. 29, no. 130, pp. 600–606, April 1975.

STOESSINGER, J. *The Might of Nations*. New York: Random House, 1965.

SUPPES, P., and J. L. ZINNES. "Basic Measurement Theory." In *Handbook of Mathematical Psychology*, ed. R. D. Luce and others. Vol. 1. New York: Wiley, 1963.

SUTHERLAND, JOHN W. *Systems: Analysis, Administration, and Architecture*. New York: Van Nostrand Reinhold Company, 1975.

THURSTON, L. L. "A Law of Comparative Judgment." *Psychological Review*, vol. 34, pp. 273–286, 1927.

TORGERSON, WARREN S. *Theory and Methods of Scaling*. New York: Wiley, 1958.

TUCKER, LEDYARD R. "Determination of Parameters of a Functional Relation by Factor Analysis." *Psychometrika*, vol. 23, no. 1, pp. 19–23, March 1958.

TVERSKY, AMOS. "A General Theory of Polynomial Conjoint Measurement." *Journal of Mathematical Psychology*, vol. 4, pp. 1–20, 1967.

TVERSKY, AMOS, and D. KAHNEMAN. "Judgment Under Uncertainty: Heuristics and Biases." *Science*, vol. 185, pp. 1124–1131, September 1974.

VAN DER WAERDEN, B. L. "Hamilton's Discovery of Quaternions." *Mathematics Magazine*, vol. 48, no. 5, pp. 227–234, November 1976.

VARGAS, L. "Sensitivity Analysis of Reciprocal Matrices." Chap. 3 of Ph.D. dissertation, Wharton School, University of Pennsylvania, 1979.

WALLER, ROBERT J. "The Synthesis of Hierarchical Structures: Technique and Applications." *Decision Sciences*, vol. 7, no. 4, pp. 659–674, October 1976.

WARFIELD, JOHN N. "On Arranging Elements of a Hierarchy in Graphic Form." *IEEE Transactions on Systems, Man, and Cybernetics,* vol. SMC-3, no. 2, pp. 121–140, March 1973.

————. "Developing Subsystem Matrices in Structural Modeling." *IEEE Transactions on Systems, Man, and Cybernetics,* vol. SMC-4, no. 1, pp. 74–80, January 1974.

————. "Developing Interconnection Matrices in Structural Modeling." *IEEE Transactions on Systems, Man, and Cybernetics,* vol. SMC-4, no. 1, pp. 81–87, January 1974.

————. *Societal Systems: Planning, Policy and Complexity.* New York: Wiley, 1976.

WEI, T. H. "The Algebraic Foundations of Ranking Theory." Ph.D. dissertation, Cambridge University, 1952.

WEISS, PAUL A. *Hierarchically Organized Systems in Theory and Practice.* New York: Hafner Publishing Co., 1971.

WEYL, H. "Chemical Valence and the Hierarchy of Structures." *Philosophy of Mathematics and Natural Science.* Princeton: Princeton University Press, 1949.

WHYTE, L. L. "Organic Structural Hierarchies." In *Unity and Diversity in Systems,* ed. R. G. Jones and G. Brandl. New York: Braziller, 1969.

————. "The Structural Hierarchy in Organisms." *Unity and Diversity in Systems,* ed. R. G. Jones and G. Brandl. New York: Braziller, 1969.

WHYTE, L. L., A. G. WILSON, and D. WILSON (eds.). *Hierarchical Structures.* New York: American Elsevier, 1969.

WIGAND, ROLF T., and GEORGE A. BARNETT. "Multidimensional Scaling of Cultural Processes: The Case of Mexico, South Africa and the United States." *International and Intercultural Communication Annual,* vol. 3, pp. 140–172, 1976.

WILKINSON, J. H. *The Algebraic Eigenvalue Problem.* Oxford: Clarendon Press, 1965.

WILLIAMSON, R. E., and H. F. TROTTER. *Multivariable Mathematics.* Englewood Cliffs, N.J.: Prentice-Hall, 1974.

WILSON, A. G. "Hierarchical Structure in the Cosmos." In *Hierarchical Structures,* ed. L. L. Whyte, A. G. Wilson, and D. Wilson. New York: American Elsevier, 1969.

WOODALL, D. R. "A Criticism of the Football League Eigenvector." *Eureka,* October 1971.

YU, P. L. "A Class of Solutions for Group Decision Problems." Center for System Science, University of Rochester, 1972.

————. "Cone Convexity, Cone Extreme Points and Nondominated Solutions in Decision Problems with Multiobjectives." University of Rochester, 1972.

YU, P. L., and M. ZELENY. "The Set of All Nondominated Solutions in the Linear Case and a Multicriteria Simplex Method." University of Rochester, 1973.

ZELENY, M. "Linear Multiobjective Programming." Ph.D. dissertation, University of Rochester, 1972.

————. "On the Inadequacy of the Regression Paradigm Used in the Study of Human Judgment." *Theory and Decision,* vol. 7, pp. 57–65, 1976.

Index